American
art of
our
century

American art of our century

LLOYD GOODRICH Director, Whitney Museum of American Art

JOHN I. H. BAUR Associate Director, Whitney Museum of American Art

PUBLISHED FOR THE Whitney Museum of American Art

BY FREDERICK A. PRAEGER, PUBLISHER, NEW YORK

RESEARCH BY Rosalind Irvine Curator, Whitney Museum of American Art

ILLUSTRATIONS are of works in the collection of the Whitney Museum of American Art.

BOOKS THAT MATTER Published in the United States of America in 1961

by Frederick A. Praeger, Inc., Publisher, 64 University Place, New York 3, N.Y.

LIBRARY OF CONGRESS CATALOG CARD NUMBER: 61–15642

contents

part one: 1900–1939

BY LLOYD GOODRICH

part two: 1940–1960

BY JOHN I. H. BAUR

part two (*continued*)

part one

1900–1939

BY LLOYD GOODRICH

1 American art in 1900

In the art of the United States, the first decade of the twentieth century brought fundamental changes. These changes were more revolutionary than any in the preceding two and a half centuries of art in America.

Let us consider the state of American painting and sculpture in 1900. The nineteenth century had seen a great growth in creativity, sophistication, and relations with the art of other countries. From the comparative provincialism of the Hudson River school and the old genre and portrait schools, American art had grown toward maturity in the hands of the post-Civil War generation. Inness had founded a landscape tradition at once native and related to the Barbizon school; Homer and Eakins had given a new strength and depth to the picturing of the American scene; Ryder had transformed the old literal romanticism into an imaginative expression prophetic of much in modern art; La Farge had contributed a riper knowledge of the great art of the past; the expatriates Whistler, Cassatt, and Sargent had made substantial contributions to the international art world; Saint-Gaudens had achieved the fullest embodiment of traditional ideals; the pioneer impressionists Robinson, Weir, Twachtman, and Hassam had brought from France the first vital movement since that of the Barbizon school. In this evolution, two main forces had been at work: native creativity, sometimes limited and provincial, but making its fundamental contribution; and international influences, which had furnished the necessary leaven of knowledge and new ideas. In the impact of the second force, there had been a time lag of a generation before European movements reached these shores; even impressionism had come to us fifteen years or so after its birth abroad. With all the growth that had taken place in the last third of the nineteenth century, the art of the United States was still a side current in the main stream of world art.

At the turn of the century had come a pause in the development of American art. Its older leaders were either no longer living or well on in years. The art world was in the hands of a younger generation, most of whom had studied in the academic schools abroad, particularly the Ecole des Beaux-Arts. Compared to their predecessors, they were less adventurous and more inclined to accept tradition, more cosmopolitan and less interested in the American scene. After Paris or Rome or Munich, the United States in its everyday aspects must have seemed raw and ugly, difficult to assimilate into art.

Few of them had Homer's or Eakins' robust ability to extract artistic content out of the crude ore of American life. Avoiding the common actualities, they devoted themselves to the ideals and environment of the upper and middle classes. Their art centered around family and home, pleasant occupations and recreations, the idyllic in nature. Women played a leading role in it. Seldom had American artists concentrated so much on the feminine. With the idealism which was so deeply ingrained in the nineteenth-century American mind, they pictured woman as a creature finer and purer than the male, not only more beautiful physically but embodying man's ideals of spiritual beauty. She appeared in many guises: Thayer's grave maidens, Brush's Madonna-like mothers, Tarbell's housewives, Dewing's decorative ethereal beings, and the symbolical figures of Cox, Blashfield, and French. Yet with all its preoccupation with the feminine, a characteristic of this art was its comparative sexlessness—its emphasis on refinement and virginal qualities, its puritanical avoidance of sensuality. The flesh-and-blood realism of Eakins was still outside the pale.

The interest in the American scene which had inspired earlier nineteenth-century genre painting had disappeared. The common life of the United States and its people—the life of farm, factory, and office; the teeming cities; the work and play of the larger population—found little expression. There was no hint of social conflicts or problems, no satire, indeed, little humor of any kind. The city was seldom pictured, and then only its politer aspects—Fifth Avenue, not Fourteenth Street. The new world of the machine age, of skyscrapers and factories and great bridges, had few admirers among established artists. To judge by their work, the Industrial Revolution had never occurred.

A similar idealism governed landscape painting. Earlier landscapists such as Cole, Inness, Heade, and Homer had seen nature as a drama of contending forces, as a being whose moods ranged from the somber to the idyllic. The American pioneers of impressionism had replaced this older romantic poetry with a gentler lyricism. They had concentrated on visual effects of light and atmosphere, and on a higher, purer palette. Opening up a new world of luminosity and color, impressionism had coincided with American society's increasing physical freedom and love of outdoor sports and recreations. Within a few years the new viewpoint had attained the widest acceptance of any movement from abroad. But inevitably it had become academic. Like the figure painters, the landscapists limited their range. Where the Hudson River school and its successors, with all their provincialism, had explored the continent and celebrated its wild picturesqueness, the landscapists of the 1890's and 1900's confined themselves to the more settled East, ignoring the United States beyond the Alleghenies. The man-made features of the country found little place in their work. New England's trim white villages were permissible, but not the raw Midwest towns. The evidences of industrialism and urbanization that were changing the face of America—railroads, factories, auto highways—were shunned. It was an idyllic art, focusing on the smiling aspects of nature.

The dominant idealism of American art reflected the viewpoint of established culture. It was the expression of a society that was prosperous, peaceful, and seemingly secure—that had not yet seen the face of modern war, the great Depression of the 1930's, the tremendous political, social, and psychological upheavals of the twentieth century. In these years before the first World War, all seemed for the best in this best of worlds. To this society, the world of today would have seemed an incredible nightmare. The United States of our parents and grandparents was in many ways a fortunate society, and the art which mirrored it still has a nostalgic charm.

The traditionalist artists of this generation are now completely out of fashion. But among them were a number who deserve a better fate. Chase's fresh eye and skilled hand and his happy combination of keen observation and zest for life; Weir's subtle, intimate poetry and muted, silvery harmonies; Hassam's sunlit lyrics of seashore and summer resort; Tarbell's and Benson's pleasant scenes of sheltered domesticity; Thayer's grave young goddesses with their air of serene strength and nobility; Dewing's fragile women in their remote, hushed, surrealist world; Saint-Gaudens' vigorous monumentality, combining idealism with solid, characterful naturalism; Vedder's fusion of romantic imagination and classic stylization—the work of all these men had positive virtues, not only as expressions of the prevailing culture, but in more purely artistic terms. Freshness of vision, skill of hand, sound draftsmanship, refinement of color and tonal values, and sensuous pleasure in handling pigment —such qualities have perennial value, regardless of changes in taste. Now that we are far enough removed from this generation to see it in perspective, we are beginning to reappraise it.

In artistic terms, the chief limitation of this period was in its basic artistic philosophy, which was naturalism: Painting and sculpture were primarily the representation of visual reality. Differences between schools were largely between modes of representation—the impressionists with their concentration on outdoor light and atmosphere, the Sargent school with its emphasis on photographic verisimilitude and brilliant brushwork, and the decorative aestheticism of Whistler and his followers. The main concern of all these schools was with light and appearances, technical skill, and taste. Of the deeper elements of form and design they seemed unaware, even in the old masters whom they admired. They showed no realization that art could be more than skillful or tasteful representation, that the great art of all periods and countries, beneath its representational aspects, had been creation in form, color, and design—a visual language as pure as that of sound in music.

In Europe, innovation had not stopped with impressionism. Cézanne, rejecting impressionism's preoccupation with visual appearances, had concentrated on sculptural form and the role of color in building it; Seurat had transformed contemporary actualities into classic monumental design; Gauguin had rediscovered the purity of the primitive vision; Van Gogh had expressed intense personal emotion in the most direct physical terms; Bonnard had translated nature into subtle arabesques of color and tone; and Matisse was already discarding the naturalistic image in favor of pure design. These successive innovations had formed a step-by-step evolution toward an art which would be completely independent of naturalistic representation. The European stage was set for movements which within a decade were to revolutionize the art of our century. But of all these stirring developments, established American art remained oblivious. The last movement of which it was aware was impressionism.

The United States art world of 1900 was completely under academic control. Today, when artists have so many opportunities to exhibit, it is hard to realize the state of things then. Only a few dealers handled American art, and fewer still would take a chance on an unknown. Almost the only way to get one's work before the public was in the regular exhibitions of museums or artists' societies, dominated by conservative juries who excluded anything unorthodox, and awarded to their own kind the prizes so dear to the academic mind. Getting into one of these big shows was a major event in a young man's career; it meant the difference between artistic survival or failure. Museums were still concerned chiefly with the art of the past; their scant recognition of contemporary creation was limited to the safely conservative. There was no museum devoted entirely or even largely to American art. Collectors, with a few honorable exceptions, were interested only in the old masters. Under these conditions, it was practically impossible for a non-academic artist to exhibit or sell his work.

But this academic domain was about to be invaded by two revolutionary forces. The first was the movement headed by the group called "the Eight" —the realists Robert Henri, George Luks, William J. Glackens, John Sloan, and Everett Shinn, and their allies Arthur B. Davies, Maurice Prendergast, and Ernest Lawson. The Eight and other realists who joined them were to break the spell of academic idealism and bring a franker, more robust attitude toward contemporary life, and they were to challenge the academic control of the art world. The second force, the modern movement from Europe, was to effect a revolution in the basic concepts of the nature of art. Together they were to transform American art in every respect—subject matter, viewpoint, style, artistic language.

2 the Whitney Museum of American Art

The origins of the Whitney Museum of American Art go back to the first decade of our century and to the beginnings of the realist and modern movements. It was at this time that Gertrude Vanderbilt Whitney began her activities in the field of American art. Already embarked on her career as a sculptor, by 1907 Mrs. Whitney had taken a studio in Macdougal Alley in Greenwich Village, then the center of the new forces. Her breadth of mind and of sympathy allied her with the progressives from the first. She was an early friend of Arthur B. Davies and Robert Henri, leaders of the Eight; and when the group held its first exhibition, in 1908, she bought four of the seven pictures that were sold—canvases by Henri, Luks, Lawson, and Shinn, all of which are now in the Whitney Museum collection. She supported the Madison Gallery, which showed liberal artists and where a few exhibitors, including Walt Kuhn and Jerome Myers, hatched the plan for a big independent exhibition that ultimately grew into the Armory Show, and she contributed the decorations of the Armory.

She had held informal exhibitions in her studio, and in 1914 she converted the adjoining house at 8 West Eighth Street into a gallery called the Whitney Studio, which gave regular shows of her fellow artists, especially the young and less known. To assist her, she secured the services of Juliana Force, who was thenceforth associated with all her art activities. Temperamentally, Mrs. Whitney and Mrs. Force were entirely different, the former with an innate dignity and reserve that made it distasteful for her to engage in the hurly-burly of art controversies, the latter energetic and dynamic, a born doer and fighter. But they shared certain essential qualities—largeness of vision, generosity, a liking for people, a sense of humor, a respect for the creative artist, and a sympathetic understanding of his problems. For the rest of their lives, they worked together in complete harmony for the advancement of American art. Both of them enjoyed the company of artists, and among their friends in the early days, besides Henri and Davies, were Sloan, Glackens, Du Bois, Speicher, Tucker, Sheeler, and the critic Forbes Watson, all of whom helped to shape their policies.

One of Mrs. Whitney's chief interests was the encouragement of new talent. In the spring of 1915, she formed the Friends of the Young Artists, "to give young artists in this country the opportunity to show their work." "The annual exhibitions of the established societies are already overcrowded," she explained, "and the private galleries seldom accept the work of unknown men, so that by organizing such exhibitions . . . we bring before the public work which they otherwise would have no opportunity of seeing." At first, competitive shows were held, with cash prizes awarded by juries. But in February, 1917, Mrs. Whitney announced a change in policy: "There will be no jury of awards. There will be no prizes. But the money which has been offered as prizes will be spent by the prize givers themselves in purchasing works of art. . . . First, the general public will not be influenced in its judgment by the verdict of a jury; second, the young artist will be encouraged by the fact that some one actually wants to possess his work." This principle of "no juries, no prizes," which governed all future exhibitions on Eighth Street, was in the air of the time; the Society of Independent Artists, patterned on the Paris Indépendants, was being formed, with Glackens as its first president (succeeded next year and thereafter by Sloan) and with Mrs. Whitney as one of its ten guarantors.

The Friends of the Young Artists was the germ of all future institutions sponsored by Mrs. Whitney. Out of it grew the Whitney Studio Club, founded in the spring of 1918, with Mrs. Force as director, and with a clubhouse at 147 West Fourth Street. A social and exhibiting center for artists, the Club was far from the exclusive institution that the name suggests. The only requirement for admission was talent; any serious artist who was introduced by a member could join. The dues were five dollars a year, but no great effort was made to collect them. Among the earliest members were Prendergast, Sloan, Glackens, Hopper, Coleman, Du Bois, Stuart Davis, Halpert, Jo Davidson, Schnakenberg, and Bouché. The membership soon grew to several hundred, mostly young men and women, but also older independents. No attempt was made to impose a creed; many viewpoints were represented. Eventually, the Club included most of the leading artists outside the academic fold, and some within it. Mrs. Force's sociability, vitality, and wit created a gay, friendly atmosphere. There were always exhibitions going on, and every opening called for a party. To many a young artist the Club was a warm, festive place where he could exhibit his work and meet his fellow artists.

One-man shows were a leading feature, often several of them held simultaneously in separate galleries. Among the scores of artists who received such shows (frequently their first) at the Club, the Whitney Studio, or their successor, the Whitney Studio Galleries, were Sloan, Lawson, Glackens, Tucker, Du Bois, Sheeler, Hopper, Coleman, Miller, Dasburg, Davis, Stella, Bluemner, Boardman Robinson, Schnakenberg, Marsh, Katherine Schmidt, Mattson, Carl Walters, Nakian, John B. Flannagan, Charles Howard, Fiene, and Curry. In the 1920's, a large proportion of the rising generation of liberals and modernists had their first showing at the Club. Aware that an artist's most crucial problem is selling his work, the Club carried on a continuous campaign to persuade the public to buy the works of living artists, with slogans such as "What Is Home Without a Modern Picture?" No commissions were taken on sales. From almost every show, Mrs. Whitney purchased works for her own collection. Annual members' exhibitions were held from the first, growing in size and quality until they rivaled the big academic shows. From 1924 on, they were circulated to museums in other cities. By this time, the Club was the most active and influential center of liberal art in the country. Outgrowing its original quarters, it moved in 1923 to larger galleries on Eighth Street, next to the Whitney Studio.

In the meantime, the Whitney Studio had continued as a separate entity with special activities. In 1920/21, an Overseas Exhibition of American Painting was sent to Venice, London, Sheffield, and Paris, consisting of 115 works by thirty-two artists, all contemporaries except for Eakins, who was represented by six canvases. Of this exhibition, Mrs. Whitney wrote: "To me it has always seemed a good plan for artists working in America to show their work in Europe—the oftener the better." Reversing this international exchange, the Studio held several foreign shows, including twenty recent paintings by Picasso in 1923.

Aside from these public activities, Mrs. Whitney contributed in many other ways to the cause of liv-

Gertrude Vanderbilt Whitney, by Jo Davidson.
About 1917.

ing American art. As a director of the Society of Independent Artists for fifteen years, she made up a large part of its annual deficits. She subsidized *The Arts,* which under Forbes Watson's able editorship became the leading liberal art magazine of the 1920's, championing American art, particularly that of the younger generation. And many individual artists were helped to go abroad or simply to pay their bills, whenever possible by buying their pictures.

By 1928, the Whitney Studio Club, now numbering about four hundred with a waiting list of as many more, had reached an impasse. To enlarge further was impossible; to refuse talented applicants, equally so. And its main purposes had been achieved: Dealers and museums were more hospitable to new talent; the academic monopoly had been broken. In the fall of 1928, the Club announced: "The pioneering work for which the Club was organized has been done. . . . The liberal artists have won the battle which they fought so valiantly, and will celebrate the victory as other regiments fighting for liberty have done—by disbanding."

For two seasons, 1928/29 and 1929/30, the Club was replaced by the Whitney Studio Galleries, concentrating on one-man shows of young artists, with more accent on selectivity and beauty of presentation. But this proved only a halfway house; the dealers were making such efforts less necessary.

Mrs. Whitney had now come to the conclusion that the greatest need was for a museum of American art, "unhampered by official restrictions, but with the prestige which a museum invariably carries," as Mrs. Force later wrote. At this time, there was no museum devoted entirely to American art, with emphasis on the contemporary; the nearest to this were the Newark Museum, long active in American art and design, and the Phillips Memorial Gallery in Washington and the new Museum of Modern Art, both international in scope. The Addison Gallery of American Art, with interests both historical and contemporary, was in process of formation at this time.

The foundation of the Whitney Museum of American Art was publicly announced on January 6, 1930. Mrs. Force was appointed director, with a curatorial staff all of whom, significantly, were artists—Hermon More, curator (later second director of the museum), and Edmund Archer and Karl Free, assistant curators. The buildings at 8, 10, and 12 West Eighth Street were remodeled by the architectural firm of Noel & Miller. The interior, designed by Bruce Buttfield, had an intimacy and a beauty of color and materials quite unlike the cold impersonality of most museums of the time. Mrs. Whitney presented her collection of about five hundred works acquired through the years—probably the largest private collection of contemporary American art—and this was increased by purchasing about a hundred examples of artists not previously or not well represented. The museum opened to the public on November 18, 1931.

Although it was new as a museum, the Whitney's guiding principles had been formed by years of experience, and today they remain essentially the same. While never precisely formulated, they might be stated somewhat as follows: The contemporary art of a nation has a special importance for its people, aside from comparisons with the art of the past or of other nations. Of a museum's functions, the most vital is not merely to conserve the past but to play an active part in the creative processes of the present. Contemporary American art is extremely diverse, and this calls for a broad viewpoint, recognizing all creative tendencies from traditional to advanced. A museum should always be open to the new, the young, and the experimental. It should never forget that the artist is the prime mover in all artistic matters; it should support his freedom of expression and respect his individuality. "It would be presumptuous to point out the road upon which art should travel," Hermon More wrote in the museum's first catalogue. "We look to the artist to lead the way.... As a museum we conceive it to be our duty to see that he is not hampered in his progress by lack of sympathy and support. It is not our intention to found a 'school,' our chief concern is with the individual artist." He also decried any narrow nationalistic definition of "American." "In limiting the scope of this museum to American art," he wrote, "we place the emphasis primarily on 'art' and secondarily on 'American.'" In practice, foreign birth or citizenship has never been a consideration, but only the artist's length of residence, past or projected, in the United States. During World War II, distinguished Europeans living in America were welcomed, and a special exhibition was given them.

The museum's origins had been unusual. The Whitney Studio Club had been an artists' association conducted on extremely democratic lines. But a museum has broader functions: not only exhibiting art, but collecting, studying, and publicizing it —and always maintaining standards of quality. The Whitney Museum's endeavor has been to carry on these new activities while preserving essentially the same relations with artists as in the past.

For a museum of contemporary art, exhibitions are a basic function. An essential feature of the Whitney's program has been the series of large annual shows of works by living artists, each represented by a single example. These annuals have been governed by the principle of "no juries, no prizes" established for the Friends of the Young Artists. In most similar exhibitions, a large proportion of the artists submit their works to a jury drawn from outside. But the Whitney annuals are entirely by invitation, the museum selecting artists and works. This system is based on the belief that the judgment of a staff familiar with present-day art and always on the lookout for new artists is as impartial and reliable as that of changing outside juries; that the system makes it possible to secure important works by leading figures while at the same time recognizing new talents and tendencies; and that it enables the museum to keep a balance between different schools and preserve consistent policies from year to year. The museum does not claim that this is the best method for all institutions, but only that it is the best for it, taking into account its purposes and resources and the enormous volume of contemporary art exhibited in the New York art world. To keep in touch with new artists, there are viewings every month or so to which artists send works for the staff to see. In every annual, a considerable proportion of exhibitors have not previously been represented. Over the

The Whitney Museum of American Art, West Eighth Street, New York: Entrance.

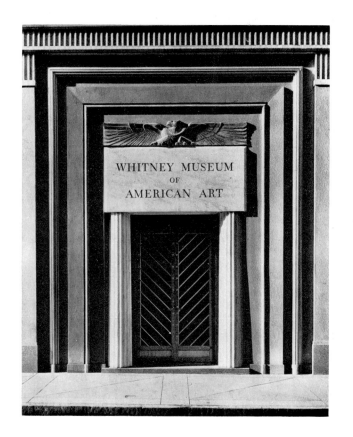

The Whitney Museum of American Art, West Fifty-fourth Street, New York: Façade.

years, nearly two thousand artists, from almost every state, have been included.

In its annuals, the museum has exemplified its belief in the diversity of contemporary American art by presenting a selection of what it considers the most interesting works by individuals of all schools. Since to err is human, it has preferred to err on the side of inclusiveness rather than exclusiveness. There has been no attempt to present "trends" as such, but since in any period certain trends will be dominant, an objective survey must inevitably reflect this. Through the years, successive trends—the American scene, regionalism, the social school, abstraction in all its forms—have been represented fully, though not exclusively, as their partisans would have preferred. In the 1930's, leftist critics chided the museum for being too art-for-art's-sake and insufficiently Marxist; a generation later, advanced critics deplored the inclusion of representational art, while conservatives complained about the proportion of abstract art.

The museum has never awarded prizes or medals, believing that in this age of diversity, to single out a few examples as the first, second, third, or fourth best is not only meaningless, but misleading to the public and unfair to the other exhibitors. Instead of giving prizes, the museum has set aside a fund for purchases. This policy of purchases instead of prizes, which the museum was one of the first to adopt, has had a wide influence. Most works in the annuals are for sale, and sales have increased every year. For many years, the museum charged no commissions on sales, but finding itself almost alone in this respect, it began in 1960 to collect a ten-percent commission, which is devoted to the purchase of works by living artists.

Besides the annuals, there have been many other types of exhibitions—of particular periods, subjects, or schools; private collections; regional shows; periodical "Young America" shows. One-man retrospectives have included many prominent living painters and sculptors. American art of the past has been covered by general surveys and by one-man shows of Feke, Earl, Homer, Ryder, Blakelock, Prendergast, and others. To show American art in many aspects and combinations has been the aim.

The exhibitions have been accompanied by full-scale catalogues based on original research, which have made substantial contributions to the literature on American art. Most of these exhibitions have been shown later in other museums throughout the country. The Whitney has also given New York showings to American exhibitions organized by other institutions.

The museum's permanent collection has grown steadily, and by the end of 1960 numbered 714 paintings; 235 watercolors, gouaches, and pastels; 237 drawings; and 185 pieces of sculpture—a total of 1,371 works. (These figures do not include works which after a number of years have been exchanged or withdrawn. The collection is reviewed periodically, but no work by a living artist is withdrawn except with his agreement. For eleven years, annual shows of prints were held and a sizable collection formed, but this department has not been active since 1943.) Believing that its pictures and sculpture should be seen as widely as possible, the museum has lent them to many exhibitions in this country and abroad, and has circulated special shows drawn from the collection. An average of over four hundred works are lent each year.

The collection was originally planned to cover the whole history of American art, and works of the past were acquired, including an outstanding group of primitives gathered by Mrs. Force, who was one of the earliest collectors of American folk art. But in 1949, the trustees decided that it was impossible to complete a historical collection equal to those of older institutions; all works produced prior to 1900 were sold and the proceeds used to increase the purchase fund for contemporary art. Since then, the museum has been devoted primarily to the twentieth century. Historical exhibitions are still held, but the collection is entirely of the present century, and purchases have been almost entirely of living artists. In early years, the museum did not make a practice of accepting gifts, but this policy was changed in 1948; since then there has been a steady increase in donations of both works of art and contributions to the purchase fund.

From its foundation, the museum sponsored research and publication in the American field, which was then the most neglected area of art history. In 1942, the museum, in cooperation with thirty museums and college art departments, established the American Art Research Council, to promote research and scholarship, to deal with problems of authenticity, and to record the works of leading artists, past and present. Its governing principle was that research in the contemporary field is as important as in the past, and calls for the same scholarly standards. The museum sponsored definitive books on Eakins and Homer by Lloyd Goodrich, and monographs on twentieth-century artists and themes by him and by John I. H. Baur. Over the years, its publication program on American art has been the most extensive of any institution.

In general projects on behalf of American art, the museum has played an active part. When, in the depths of the Depression, in 1933, the Federal government initiated the first governmental art program, the Public Works of Art Project, Mrs. Force was appointed chairman of the largest regional committee, and within twenty-four hours artists were on the Federal payroll producing works for public use. Eventually this region employed over nine hundred artists, a quarter of the national total. The Project's headquarters were at the museum, and the staff helped with administration. The PWAP established many of the policies followed by later governmental projects. In 1948, staff members helped to organize the Committee on Government and Art, the first body formed to deal with problems in this field, and the museum has acted as host to the National Council on the Arts and Government, representing all the arts. Exhibitions have been held in collaboration with governmental agencies, and the museum and its staff have helped to organize shows for circulation abroad by the Department of State, the United States Information Agency, and the American Federation of Arts.

In 1935, when the Society of American Painters, Sculptors and Gravers, which included many leading artists, adopted a policy of asking moderate rental fees for the use of members' works in exhibitions, Mrs. Force fought valiantly for the acceptance of the plan by her fellow museum directors, and although it was overwhelmingly rejected, the Whitney was one of the very few museums which paid rental during the year it was asked. More recently, staff members helped to organize the Joint Artists-Museums Committee, devoted to the mutual problems of these two basic elements in the art world.

The museum is maintained by the income from an endowment by Mrs. Whitney; it receives no funds from the city, has never charged admission, and has no regular membership except the Friends of the Whitney Museum. Its scope, determined by its resources, is clearly defined; it covers American painting, sculpture, and graphic art, but not architecture, design, prints, photography, or the motion picture. The size of its staff does not allow for full-scale departments of education or museum extension, or an art library open to the public. But to the museum and its staff, these limitations are more than compensated for by concentration on one of the most rewarding of all fields—contemporary creation. As a pioneer museum in its field, it has influenced older and larger institutions and has contributed to the phenomenal growth of public interest in American art over the past thirty years.

A basic fact about the Whitney is that, just as it grew out of an artists' association, it has continued to grow as a museum. As its activities increased, the Eighth Street building proved insufficient in exhibition space, and in 1939 four new galleries were added, almost doubling the capacity. But within a few years, the need for a new building became apparent, not only for more space but for more modern facilities and a location nearer the art center of New York. Eighth Street had warm associations with the past, but to fulfill its function the museum needed to be closer to the city's exhibition center. At this juncture, in 1949, the trustees of the Museum of Modern Art, aware of the Whitney's needs, offered to donate part of their land on West Fifty-fourth Street. This generous action, due largely to the initiative of John Hay Whitney, chairman of the board of the Museum of Modern Art, Nelson A. Rockefeller, president, and Stephen C. Clark, former chairman of the board, was all the more welcome because entirely voluntary and unexpected. It involved no institutional change; as Flora Whitney Miller, president of the Whitney

Museum, said: "Both museums wish to emphasize that this is not in any sense a merger, and that the two institutions will retain their independent existence. Both museums believe that in as broad and varied a field as contemporary American art, a variety of institutional viewpoints is healthy and necessary." The Whitney's field remained American art, that of the Museum of Modern Art the whole international field. Nor did it mean any lessening of the latter's active American program; in the words of John Hay Whitney: "The two institutions will continue their friendly competition in the field of American art."

Funds for the new building were generously donated by the Gertrude Vanderbilt Whitney Trust, a separate entity whose trustees are Mrs. Whitney's three children, Cornelius Vanderbilt Whitney, Flora Whitney Miller, and Barbara Whitney Headley. The architect was Auguste L. Noel, who had remodeled the Eighth Street structure. The decorative style of the interior, by Bruce Buttfield, retained the intimate character of the earlier museum. The exterior was designed in consultation with Philip C. Johnson, then director of the department of architecture and design of the Museum of Modern Art. The building, which opened to the public on October 26, 1954, provided not only greater exhibition space but better light, more flexible galleries (all partitions are movable), and improved storage facilities, which made the collection easily available to students and workers from other museums. The increased space made possible more exhibitions and more frequent showings of the collection; air-conditioning allowed the museum to be open in the summer, which had been impossible downtown; and the position in the heart of Manhattan enabled the museum to reach a much larger public. Attendance immediately increased between three- and four-fold, ranking the museum sixth among New York art museums—a growth especially gratifying since the other institutions cover wider historical and international fields.

In view of the quality and volume of creative production in the United States, the museum's great need was for more funds to purchase works by contemporary artists. In 1956, a group of leading

18

collectors and others interested in American art formed the Friends of the Whitney Museum of American Art, a nonprofit membership corporation devoted to furthering the welfare and progress of American art. The Friends' funds are used chiefly to purchase works for the museum's collection in collaboration with the museum, and some of the most important recent acquisitions have been made possible by their generosity. The Friends also carry on a number of other activities, such as staging periodical exhibitions and assisting with publications. The membership has grown steadily, and the formation of the Friends has marked an important step in the museum's history, helping greatly to broaden and strengthen the purpose for which the Whitney Museum was founded—that of bringing to the people of this and other countries the contribution to world culture made by the artists of the United States.

The museum's collection is now one of the largest public collections of twentieth-century American art. It is our hope that it represents in a fairly complete and balanced way the leading artists and schools of the period. In the following pages, using works from the collection, we will attempt to chart a course through the ever-changing movements and personalities in American art, from the first decade of the century to the present.

The Second-Floor Galleries.

3 the Eight and other city realists

In the opening decade of the new century, the academic domination of the American art world was challenged by a group of young realist painters—Henri, Luks, Glackens, Sloan, and Shinn. These five were close friends—all Philadelphians, all former students of the Pennsylvania Academy of the Fine Arts, and all except Henri ex-newspaper artists, at one time or another with the *Philadelphia Press*. This journalistic experience, by contrast with conventional art training, had given them a lively feeling for the contemporary world. Their leader was the oldest, Henri, vital, magnetic, a born teacher, filled with enthusiasm for both life and art, and with a gift for opening the eyes of others. Through his informal teaching, and still more by his personal friendship, he exerted a strong influence on his younger fellows. He encouraged them to graduate from newspaper work to painting; he confirmed their preference for the current scene; he introduced them to the great realists of the past, Velázquez, Rembrandt, and Hals, and their modern descendants, Goya, Courbet, Daumier, and Manet. A more immediate ancestor was Eakins, their Philadelphia predecessor in realism, whose viewpoint was handed down to them through his pupil Thomas Anshutz, under whom all five studied at the Pennsylvania Academy.

Rebelling against academic idealism, these young realists turned to the life around them, which meant the life of the city (at first Philadelphia, then New York, where they all settled). They loved the city as the nineteenth-century genre painters had the country. In their paintings, that vital, disorderly modern phenomenon the American city found artistic expression for the first time outside of popular illustration. They liked its night life, theaters, dance halls, saloons, prize fights, its excitement and glamour, its inexhaustible variety of human types and happenings. Preferring character to ideal beauty, they relished low as well as high life, the masses as much as the upper classes, the slums as much as Fifth Avenue (Luks and Sloan favoring the former, Glackens and Shinn the latter). They painted the urban scene with frankness and humor—a humor that for years had been sadly lack-

Arthur B. Davies. Crescendo. 1910. Oil. 18 x 40.

Maurice Prendergast. Central Park. 1901. Watercolor. 14⅛ x 21¾.

Robert Henri. Storm Tide. 1903. Oil. 26 x 32.

ing in our "fine" art, though not in our popular art. Their humor was good natured; it had an element of satire, but without the bitterness of the social school of the 1930's, a product of the Depression. The philosophy of some of them inclined toward radicalism, but this found no direct expression in their paintings—not even with Sloan, who was a socialist and the art editor of *The Masses,* for which he reserved his trenchant social commentary. The sense of evil and of human degradation revealed in a Toulouse-Lautrec or a Grosz was absent in their art. As to sex, there was a certain innocence in them; they painted the dance hall but not the bordello. While not idealizing the city, they saw it with a romanticism that overlooked its uglier aspects. Fundamentally, their art was an affirmative one. Within its limits, it had the firsthand contact with actualities, the authentic flavor, that has marked the best genre art of all periods.

Their style was based on direct observation. All were lively draftsmen: Glackens in his early illustrations and Sloan in his etchings produced some of the best graphic art of the period. They were in conscious revolt against impressionism, or rather against its academic American variety. Their emphasis on graphic quality was a protest against impressionist softness and vagueness. The darkness of their color, with its prevailing grays and browns, was a reaction from oversweetness and a return to the deliberately restricted gamut of Velázquez, Hals, Goya, and the pre-impressionist Manet. Compared to current European developments, their artistic language was far from advanced; it was their subjects and viewpoints that seemed radical to the orthodox art world. The shocked reaction of public, critics, and conservative artists was a symptom of America's artistic backwardness.

The Henri group believed strongly in artistic freedom—the artist's right to paint what and how he pleased and to get his work before the public. Henri and Sloan in particular were effective organizers and redoubtable fighters. Soon an able ally appeared in Arthur B. Davies. His own work stemmed from the nineteenth-century tradition of idyllic romanticism; he was a poet who pictured allegorical figures in landscapes of dreamlike

William J. Glackens.   Hammerstein's Roof Garden. c. 1901. Oil. 30 x 25.

John Sloan. The Picnic Grounds. 1906/07. Oil. 24 x 36.

Everett Shinn. Revue. 1908. Oil. 18 x 24.

beauty, and who combined a fresh lyrical vision with a technical skill beyond that of most academicians. But Davies was also a cultivated mind, aware of new developments abroad and dedicated to the principle of artistic independence. He brought into the group the pioneer modernist Maurice Prendergast; and later they were joined by Ernest Lawson, an impressionist more realistic than his academic colleagues, liking to paint the city and its outskirts.

In 1904, four of the Philadelphia realists, plus Davies and Prendergast (six of the future Eight), held an exhibition at the National Arts Club in New York that brought strong reactions pro and con. The critics, under headlines such as "Startling Works by Red-Hot American Painters," expressed outrage, bewilderment, or plain curiosity—responses like those which were to greet the first modernist shows. Four years later, in 1908, the five realists and their three allies formed a group called the Eight and staged an exhibition at the Macbeth Gallery in New York that aroused much wider interest. The public flocked to see it. Some critics were hostile (a few violently so), but the general tone was open minded and frequently favorable. (Later accounts have exaggerated the critical opposition; the often-repeated phrases "apostles of ugliness," "the revolutionary gang," and "the black gang" were used by academic artists, not by the critics. "The Ashcan School," which has become the accepted title for the Eight, did not become current until the middle 1930's.) Prendergast was the most vehemently attacked; one reviewer called his work "an explosion in a paint factory." The Eight were an entirely informal body, and they never again exhibited as a group. But their show had an impact

John Sloan. Backyards, Greenwich Village. 1914. Oil. 26 x 32.

Jerome Myers. Summer Night, East Side Park. 1919. Oil.
25 x 30.

George Luks. Armistice Night. 1918. Oil. 37 x 68¾.

Anonymous gift.

George Bellows. Floating Ice. 1910. Oil. 45 x 63.

out of proportion to its size. It dramatized the growing opposition to academicism and awakened the
public and critics to the new forces. It and Alfred
Stieglitz' pioneer Matisse exhibition two months
later were landmarks in American art history.

For two decades, individual members of the
Eight (especially Henri, Sloan, and Davies) were in
the forefront of the fight for independent art. They
welcomed the modern movement, and in alliance
with its pioneers and other progressives, they played
essential parts in such events as the large "Exhibition of Independent Artists" in 1910, the Armory
Show of 1913, and the founding of the Society of
Independent Artists in 1917.

Henri and his fellow realists broke the spell of
academic idealism, and inaugurated a more vital
interest in the contemporary American scene. They
were soon joined by other painters of city life.
There was Jerome Myers, gentle poet of the slums,
the shabby world of the Lower East Side with its
crowded streets and its children dancing to the
hurdy-gurdy's tunes—an artist who saw his beloved
Manhattan with an idyllic vision. Henri as a teacher
encouraged realism; among his many students were
Glenn Coleman, whose portraits of mean streets
were less lyrical than Myers', more ironical and
poignantly melancholy; Edward Hopper, who as
early as 1908 was painting the city and small town

with essentially the same uncompromising realism as later, but whose full development and recognition had to wait until the 1920's; Guy Pène du Bois with his satirical, acid glimpses of the privileged classes; and the gifted, precocious George Bellows, one of the most remarkable natural painting talents of his generation, who pictured the multitudinous life of the city with a technical brilliance rivaling Sargent's. Bellows' early works were among his finest: *Floating Ice* shows his vitality, his fresh eye and skillful hand, and his ability to translate aspects of the visual world into sensuously living pigment and color.

The original members of the Eight later developed out of their early naturalism (in Davies' case, romanticism) and produced art which made use of post-impressionist developments. The realists abandoned the restricted palettes of their youth. Glackens left behind the silvery grays of *Hammerstein's Roof Garden* for a Renoir-like luxuriance of color. Sloan's *Backyards, Greenwich Village* used a brighter, purer palette, probably due to his first full-scale contact with modern art in the Armory Show of the year before. Luks and Shinn enlarged the range and clarity of their color. Davies after the Armory Show developed a highly personal poetic variation of cubism.

The early city realists were pioneers of one of the main trends in twentieth-century American art— a reawakened interest in the American scene. All subsequent art concerned with native subject matter stems from their innovations: the regionalists' rediscovery of the broader United States, the American scene school's revealing portrait of our land, and the social school's satirical comments on our social system. Through both their art and their fight for artistic freedom, they brought about changes from which all artists benefited.

In historical perspective, we can see that the most vital American art of the 1910's and 1920's grew out of two main roots: the realism of the Henri group, whose great contribution was in subject matter and viewpoint, in the artist's relation to his environment; and the modern movements, which produced a fundamental revolution in artistic language.

4 primitives

A feature of American art from its beginnings was the wide prevalence of folk art. In early times, there were few art schools, and most artists were largely self-taught. Many were artisans—carpenters, house painters, sign and carriage painters—who never graduated into professionalism. But they had certain qualities that more sophisticated artists had lost. The primitive artist cut straight to the heart

John Kane.
Panther Hollow.
1930–31. Oil. 20 x 29.

of things. Instinctively, without theorizing, he realized that art is not the photographic copying of nature but the creation of a pictorial equivalent for nature. He retained the craftsman's respect for the physical substance and structure of the work of art. His eye was an innocent one, concerned more with the object itself than its illusory appearances. He had an innate gift for simplification, for recording the essentials. And if he was gifted, he had an instinctive feeling for form and color and line, and the patterns they created. So his art, within definite limits, represented something sound and pure that had been lost in the complexities of culture.

Hence its appeal to the modern artist, who was himself rebelling against an overdeveloped naturalism. A characteristic of modernism was its return to the primitive—the art of primitive peoples, of modern folk artists, and of children. The discovery of American folk art in the 1920's was due largely to modern-minded artists and collectors who recognized in this neglected field certain values they themselves were aiming for. Another factor was the American's search for native character and a native tradition free from imitation of European models.

As professional training expanded in the United States, folk art diminished, until by the twentieth century the genuine folk painter had become a rarity. Among the few authentic figures in our period, Joseph Pickett and John Kane were outstanding. Pickett, a carpenter, began to paint late in life, probably between 1914 and 1918, and produced only three or four pictures. His purpose was to record the history of his native town, New Hope, Pennsylvania. It was near there, at Coryell's Ferry, that George Washington had his headquarters be-

Joseph Pickett.   Coryell's Ferry, 1776. (Probably 1914–18.) Oil. 37½ x 48¼.

Louis M. Eilshemius. Figures in Landscape. 1906. Oil. 22½ x 25¾.

Gift of Louise Nevelson.

fore crossing the Delaware. In *Coryell's Ferry, 1776,* Pickett shows the General on a hill at the upper right, gazing through a telescope. The forms are built up in heavy paint with gravel and ground shells added, so that they stand out in actual relief. The flowing lines of river and trees, curiously suggestive of Chinese painting, fill the composition with rhythmic movements, which are anchored by the four-square solidity of the houses. The self-taught painter has achieved strong, vital design.

John Kane, of Pittsburgh—miner, steel-mill laborer, construction worker, carpenter, and house painter—took up art in middle life, and kept on painting houses even after he had achieved modest recognition in the late 1920's. Almost all his pictures were of Pittsburgh, its three rivers between steep hills, its many bridges, its mills and railroads —a picturesque city ignored by sophisticated artists or painted with veils of romance hiding its actualities. Kane saw its real character and pictured it

candidly, solidly, with a strong sense of structure. "I helped to build Pittsburgh's mills and homes; why shouldn't I paint it?" he said.

Louis M. Eilshemius was a more complex personality, not a folk painter, but that rare phenomenon, a genuinely naïve artist. All his life he retained an adolescent's imagination and sensibility. A poet of nature and amorous idylls, he gave free rein to his innocent fancy in visions which were barely saved from absurdity by his instinctive artistry. He was essentially an impressionist, but far from an orthodox one. Responding spontaneously to the lyrical in nature, he captured tender, springlike delicacies that more knowing artists missed. With continual rejection by the official art world, his fantasies became more and more tragic and violent—nightmares of jealousy, murder, and death. Belated recognition came toward the end of his career; exhibited in the juryless Independents, he was hailed by Marcel Duchamp and other modernists.

5 pioneers of modernism: post-impressionism and expressionism

Maurice Prendergast. The Promenade. 1913. Oil. 30 x 34.

Bequest of Alexander M. Bing.

Closely following the realist revolt of 1908 came the first waves of a more fundamental revolution, the modern movements from Europe. Widely varied, they had in common the concept of art as creation in free imagery and in the physical language of form and color. Matisse and the other fauves, the "wild beasts," were using natural forms more and more freely, creating powerful rhythmic design, raising color to a new purity and intensity. In 1905, the fauves appeared in full strength at the Salon d'Automne. Three years later began a new revolution, cubism. In these years, Paris was the center of innovations, crowding one upon another, that were to change the course of Western art.

In these stirring events, a number of Americans participated. Their forerunner was Prendergast, who in France in the early 1890's had known the work of Cézanne and Bonnard and had evolved his highly personal expression of simple sensuous delight in the spectacle of the world. His style from about 1908 showed an increasing freedom that paralleled fauvism. His processional compositions of women and children outdoors were rhythmic patterns of enchanting color, with a muted richness like the hues of tapestries. Though his design was more decorative than three-dimensional, Prendergast was the first American of his time to conceive the work of art as an independent creation having its own harmony and order.

From the opening years of the century, a growing number of young Americans went abroad, mostly to Paris, and came in contact with the new movements. Maurer arrived in Paris in 1897, Karfiol in 1901, Halpert in 1902, Sterne in 1904, Marin and Weber in 1905, Russell and Bruce in 1905 or 1906, Walkowitz and Marguerite Zorach in 1906, Dove, Carles, Pach, Macdonald-Wright, and Demuth in 1907, Benton, Covert, and Schamberg in 1908, Sheeler and Dasburg in 1909, and William Zorach and Preston Dickinson in 1910.

Most of these artists were in their early or middle twenties, with little or no previous knowledge of modern art, and they encountered it first in the successive showings of the fauves in the Autumn Salons. Cézanne's works in these Salons impressed

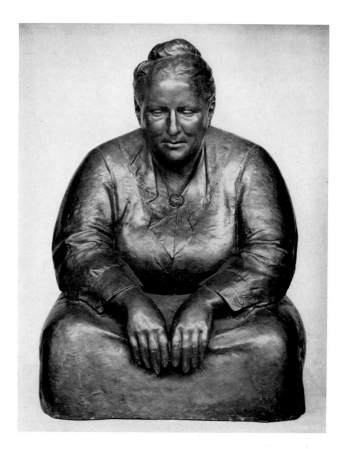

Jo Davidson. Gertrude Stein. 1920. Bronze. 31 high.

the Americans deeply. Eventually they met the Parisian leaders, who were of their own generation except Matisse. Modernism was puzzling at first, and they did not at once accept it. Matisse and the fauves exerted a stronger influence than Picasso and the cubists. Their own work abroad was seldom advanced, still tentative. By and large, they were followers, as was natural, rather than in the vanguard, and did not develop more advanced styles until after their return to America. But they were in closer touch with current trends than any preceding generation of Americans; and after their return, they launched the new movement earlier and on a broader scale than any previous movement in this country.

In their Parisian education, an important role was played by four American collectors, the Steins —Leo, Gertrude, and Michael, and the latter's wife, Sarah—the first extensive purchasers of Matisse and

Max Weber. Summer. 1911. Gouache. 24⅛ x 18½.

Picasso. Leo and Gertrude Stein's famous Saturday evening receptions, where one could look at their pictures and meet the painters, were frequented by almost every modern-minded American in Paris. It was the Michael Steins and a few others, including Max Weber and Patrick Henry Bruce, who in 1908 started the historic Matisse class, later joined by several other Americans.

The artists most closely associated with the Parisian movements reacted variously to them. Bernard Karfiol was akin less to the fauves than to the post-impressionists Cézanne and the later Renoir; he was a poetic painter of the nude and landscape, sensual and tender. Samuel Halpert was allied to the fauves,

especially early Derain, in his pronounced patterning, massive modeling, and heavy outlines. After Max Weber's return to America in 1908, his work, such as *Summer*, was also fauvist—idyllic compositions crowded with figures, luxuriant in form, rich rather than brilliant in color, and with a full-blooded sensuousness that made academic American art seem anemic. Alfred H. Maurer, a skillful and successful traditionalist when he settled in Paris, became converted to fauvism about 1907 and ranged from exuberant Matisse-like landscapes to sensitive, introspective figure painting sometimes approaching abstraction. After his final return to his native land in 1914, his art developed a strain of fantasy, haunting and disturbing, as in *Twin Heads*. Other Americans related to the fauves at one time or another were Bruce, Walkowitz, Carles, Demuth, and Marguerite and William Zorach.

A few American modernists evolved outside the Parisian orbit. Joseph Stella went first to Italy. Marsden Hartley became allied with the *Blaue Reiter* group in Munich. The German-born Oscar Bluemner, who returned to his native country in 1912 for a year or so, was akin to the German expressionists in his emphatic linear patterns and deep violent color and in the nightmare atmosphere of his nocturnes. Maurice Sterne, though one of the earliest to arrive in Paris, was interested equally in modern and older art, and in 1911 started on a four-year voyage to the East that included two years in Bali. A classicist and a strong draftsman, he pictured the dark passionate life of the tropics in an art which though representational was austerely concentrated on geometrical design, with affinities to the cubists and Duchamp.

The United States to which the young modernists began to return from Europe about 1908 was very different—a vast country whose material growth was far ahead of its artistic sophistication. In Paris, there had been two Salons open to them; in America all doors were closed. The only exception was Alfred Stieglitz' little gallery at 291 Fifth Avenue, which in 1908 began its pioneer exhibitions of modern art, including among many others the first American showings of Matisse, Picasso, Brancusi, and African Negro sculpture. But Stieglitz also believed strongly in the future of American art, and was the first to give one-man shows to Maurer, Marin, Hartley, Dove, Carles, Bluemner, Nadelman, and O'Keeffe.

For the larger public, however, the first introduction to European modernism came in the Armory Show of 1913. This began as one more of the independent American exhibitions such as the Eight had helped to stage, but under Davies' and Walt Kuhn's leadership, it grew into a big show of international modern art. The twenty-five artists (not museums or collectors) who organized it were liberals rather than modernists; they included all the Eight except Shinn. About three-quarters of the works were by Americans, mostly mild progressives. But the most stirring feature was the full representation of Cézanne, Gauguin, and Van Gogh, and the living men in Paris. The critics cried "mad-

Bernard Karfiol.   Boy Bathers. 1916. Oil. 28 x 36.

John Marin. Sunset. 1914. Watercolor. 16½ x 19¼.

Samuel Halpert. Brooklyn Bridge. 1913. Oil. 34 x 42.

Gift of Mr. and Mrs. Benjamin Halpert.

men" and "charlatans." The public was bewildered and angered—but it crowded to see the show. The Armory Show was the healthiest shock so far administered to American art. With it, modernism in full force burst upon our artists and public. Eight years after the Paris debut of fauvism and five years after that of cubism, the exhibition presented a full view of the current Parisian scene. No movement had ever been launched here in this way.

Though there were years of struggle ahead, for American modernism the Armory Show was a turning point. More galleries followed Stieglitz' lead; the Whitney Studio Club and the Society of Independent Artists were founded; more open-minded critics appeared; though most museums remained immovable, adventurous private collectors showed the way. By the middle 1920's, the modernists had more or less won their battle. Not that they were

Maurice Sterne. Bali Bazaar. 1913–14. Oil. 36½ x 39.

A. H. Maurer.   Twin Heads. c. 1930. Oil. 26⅜ x 18.

Gift of Mr. and Mrs. Hudson D. Walker (and exchange).

universally accepted, but only in the most reactionary circles were they still called lunatics. To the rising generation, modernism was an accomplished fact and a point of departure for new developments.

The modern movements as they developed in the United States were marked by fewer basic innovations than in Europe. The European modernists believed that the possibilities of representational art had been exhausted, and that the only path was a search for a new visual language. But American art had not yet reached this stage of evolution; until about 1908, our art was almost completely representational. The modernist revolution was the result of influences from abroad as much as of organic growth from within. Our art world was not yet the dynamic complex of new movements that made Paris the international center of experimentation.

The most frequent form which modernism took in America was expressionism. Expressionism is a broad word without clearly defined boundaries, but the only one to cover a major trend in modern art. It was first used to describe the German modern movements which, as opposed to impressionism,

Oscar Bluemner.
Old Canal Port. 1914.
Oil. 30¼ x 40¼.

Charles Burchfield.
Noontide in Late May. 1917.
Watercolor and gouache.
21⅜ x 17⅜.

aimed at the expression of subjective emotion. Fauvism and expressionism were the Gallic and Central European manifestations of the same general tendency; but the former was concerned more with aesthetic values, the latter with spiritual values. Eventually, the name was applied to the many varieties of contemporary art which are neither naturalistic nor abstract and whose common aim is to express emotion in imagery based on the real world but subjectively transformed. The expressionist embodies his experience of reality in imagery and design that are directly emotive. While representing the things of nature, he disregards their literal appearance, distorts them freely, trans-

lates them into pictorial symbols that tend toward abstraction. Expressionist style in general is marked by a strong reliance on color and by graphic freedom and richness of substance—a style that appeals directly through the senses to the emotions.

The American mind found expressionism particularly sympathetic. The aesthetic and formal have never appealed to Americans as much as emotional expression based on reality. Expressionism was a continuation of the long native tradition of romanticism, reinforced in our century by the appearance of many artists of Central European origin. Since the German expressionists were not well represented in the Armory Show or seen there-

John Marin.   Region of Brooklyn Bridge Fantasy. 1932. Watercolor. 18¾ x 22¼.

Marsden Hartley.   The Old Bars, Dogtown. 1936. Oil. 18 x 24.

after as much as the French modernists, it is evident that American expressionism was a parallel development rather than a result of influence.

Expressionism had no fixed creed, and it was as diverse as the artists who represented it. One of the most gifted was John Marin. A complete individualist, little influenced by five years in Europe from 1905 to 1910, his first real introduction to modern art came through Stieglitz after his return. He never practiced pure abstraction, though approaching it, but he used natural imagery with the greatest freedom, to express intense subjective emotion and to create dynamic pictorial design. His extreme sensitivity responded equally to the electric vitality of New York and the vibrant light and air of the Maine coast. An instinctive colorist, sometimes delicate, sometimes magnificently rich; a graphic master whose line was charged with life; an intuitive designer whose most spontaneous watercolors had a quality of inevitability—Marin was one of the purest creative artists of his generation.

A case of spontaneous expressionism without outside influences was the early work of Charles Burch-field. In his twenties, from 1916 to 1918, he painted a series of imaginative watercolors which set forth a personal nature poetry, endowing inanimate things with a life of their own, even visualizing sensations of heat and sound. Their imagery was as subjective as that of Van Gogh and the German expressionists; yet at this time he had seen no modern European art.

Marsden Hartley, aware and impressionable, passed through many phases after his German years; but essentially he was an expressionist, and in mature life he retired to the simplicities of his native Maine, and painted its seacoast and mountains in an elemental, massive style, powerful in design and color, yet with a visionary quality that recalled his early admiration of Albert Ryder.

Many other American artists can be numbered among the expressionists—Weber, Maurer, Carles, Walkowitz, Bluemner, Knaths, Rattner, Burlin, to name only a few. Expressionism brought to American art a new emotional freedom, warmer and more sensuous, franker in revealing personal emotion, and more direct and moving in its visual language.

6 pioneers of modernism: abstraction

In Paris, cubism had begun to evolve about 1908. By contrast with fauvism's expression of emotion through color and pattern, cubism was a search for new concepts of three-dimensional form. The object was analyzed into its geometric components, disintegrated, reassembled in new combinations, shown from different sides simultaneously. Subject matter was limited to the concrete and tangible, emotional content was avoided, color was subordinate and monochromatic. This early analytical phase lasted until about 1913, then flowered into the free, more chromatic inventions of synthetic cubism. In the meantime it had given birth to many other varieties of abstraction.

It had also produced its own revolts, such as Orphism, started by Robert Delaunay in 1912, which aimed at the utmost fullness of color and at pure abstraction, free from cubism's reminders of the object. Orphism in turn had a rival in Synchromism (meaning "with color"), launched in 1913 by two Americans in Paris, Morgan Russell and Stanton Macdonald-Wright. Both were intelligent theorists, and they had an articulate champion in the latter's brother Willard Huntington Wright, a brilliant if dogmatic critic who pronounced their movement the culmination of Western art. It is true that their theories went beyond Orphism in analyzing the relation of color to form; particularly the fact that the warm colors (red, orange, yellow) appear to advance toward the eye, while the cool ones (blue, violet, blue-green) retreat, so that color produces sensations of projection and recession that can be used to build form. Their clear statement of this principle was a definite contribution to modern aesthetics. After at first applying it to recognizable figures, the two Synchromists moved toward pure abstraction in 1913. That year they held exhibitions in Munich and Paris, and engaged in a merry war with the Orphists. But their actual paintings were much like their rivals'—compositions of multicolored prisms and whirling disks. Later they created more original and complex design, as in Macdonald-Wright's *Oriental* of 1918. A year or so later, however, both of them abandoned abstraction and returned to the figure. They had developed a method, but not a content. Yet their theories had influenced other Americans—Andrew Dasburg, and Thomas H. Benton, who was then striving to reconcile Renaissance form with Synchromist color.

Orphism had a disciple in the former fauvist Patrick Henry Bruce, who remained in Paris until the 1930's. After his Orphist phase, Bruce went his own way. His great concern was abstract structure. Uncompromising in their clarity, his paintings with their angular geometric shapes and pure color were thoughtfully designed and strongly constructed, with the relations between forms finely felt. From pure abstraction Bruce returned to semi-abstraction based on specific motifs, such as the still life on a table in *Painting*. But he remained consistent in his devotion to architectonics. Agonizing over his pictures, he painted few of them and destroyed most.

In the United States there had been little abstract art before the Armory Show. The show, with its full representation of the cubists, gave impetus to abstraction, and for the next decade a number of Americans practiced it—Weber, Dove, Walkowitz, Hartley, Dasburg, William Zorach, Konrad Cramer, Georgia O'Keeffe, and Man Ray. Most of these Americans were less concerned with strictly formal

Marsden Hartley.   Painting, Number 5. 1914–15. Oil. 39½ x 31¾.

Anonymous gift.

problems than the Europeans. Cubism had a few exponents, notably Dasburg, Weber, Zorach, and in modified form, Arthur B. Davies; but there was little orthodoxy among them. Even in Paris, analytical cubism had been the creation of a few artists over a few years. An experimental laboratory, it had been a phase (though a crucial one) of the broader evolution of abstraction. In America there was little such radical research. The most lucid American champion of cubism, in his writing and teaching as well as his painting, was Andrew Dasburg. After a period of pure abstraction, from about 1912 to 1916, his style became more or less representational, yet definitely cubistic. Concentrating severely on the geometric structure of natural objects and their translation into plastic design, he showed a concern for basic form unusual among American modernists. But though cubism had few followers, it was to exert a wide influence through its emphasis on three-dimensional form and its tendency toward abstraction.

In general, American abstract art inclined to be expressionist rather than formal. Max Weber, whose work from 1912 to 1916 revealed him as the most mature abstract painter of the time in this country, was also the most inventive exponent of cubism; but in his hands it became something quite different. His compositions based on New York were related to cubism in style, but their content— lyrical celebration of the modern city—was nearer to early Delaunay and the futurists. By contrast with analytical cubism's limited subject matter, they expressed sensations aroused by the whole spectacle of the city—they pictured light and movement, and took in elements of large space that cubism shunned. Of *Chinese Restaurant* Weber wrote: "On entering a Chinese restaurant from the darkness of the night outside, a maze and blaze of light seemed to split into fragments the interior and its contents. . . . The light so piercing and so luminous, the color so liquid and the life and movement so enchanting! To express this, kaleidoscopic means had to be chosen." Here was a chromatic fantasy far removed from the austerity of analytical cubism. In Weber's abstract work as a whole, a leading part was played by color, whose opulence recalled the

Arthur G. Dove.
Plant Forms. 1915.
Pastel. 17¼ x 23⅞.

Gift of Mr. and Mrs. Roy R. Neuberger.

44

Max Weber. Chinese Restaurant. 1915. Oil. 40 x 48.

artist's Russian origin; and the forms were less apt to be geometrical and rectilinear than free and curvilinear. Even his most cubistic works were fundamentally expressionist; his affinities were as much to Kandinsky's abstract expressionism as to cubism.

The same was true of another early abstractionist, Abraham Walkowitz, in his purely abstract linear arabesques, and his semi-abstract pictures based on New York, in which skyscrapers, crowded streets, and subterranean tunnels, seen as parts of a single great organism, were embodied in flowing linear patterns. Walkowitz is better known, however, for his expressionist idylls of men and women and children outdoors, embodying a simple love of humanity, and speaking in sensitive line and lyrical color.

These early manifestations of what has come to be called abstract expressionism (in many cases a more accurate term would be expressionist abstraction) occurred with little or no influence from its Central European counterpart, the abstract expressionism of the *Blaue Reiter* group. An exception was the case of Marsden Hartley, who in his three

Morgan Russell. Four Part Synchromy, Number 7.
1914–15. Oil. 15⅜ x 11½.

Gift of the artist in memory of Gertrude V. Whitney.

Abraham Walkowitz. New York. 1917. Watercolor,
ink, and pencil. 30⅝ x 21¾.

Gift of the artist in memory of Juliana Force.

years in Germany between 1912 and 1915 came in direct contact with the group and especially with Kandinsky's work. For Hartley it was a liberating influence, stimulating him to paint large bold compositions in powerful color, almost childlike in their directness and simplicity, but magnificent in decorative impact. Somewhat incongruously for an artist of Hartley's temperament, they incorporated symbols of current German militarism: flags, iron crosses, and the German national colors—red, white and black. Hartley was to go through further phases of abstraction before returning to representational expressionism about 1920.

More indigenous forms of abstraction were those of Arthur G. Dove and Georgia O'Keeffe. Dove's year and a half in France in 1907 and 1908 was mostly spent painting outdoors, away from Paris; and, as with Marin, it was after his return to Amer-

ica, and through Stieglitz, that he came in full contact with modernism and evolved his individual character. Dove's art was close to the earth; its motifs were derived from nature, its forms from those of trees, animals, clouds. His was a strongly personal style: free rhythmic forms, bold flat patterns, resonant earthy harmonies—an original expression, not of the schools, a product of emotion experienced. He was one of the first in this country to create pure abstractions; several small oils dating as early as 1910 were curiously parallel to Kandinsky's current work, though with no known influence. While always retaining his direct sources in nature, Dove remained consistent in his abstract or semi-abstract style.

For Georgia O'Keeffe abstraction was also a personal language growing out of nature. That enlightened teacher Arthur Wesley Dow (who had

Patrick Henry Bruce.   Painting. c. 1930. Oil. 35 x 45¾.

Anonymous gift.

Stanton Macdonald-Wright. "Oriental." Synchromy in Blue-Green. 1918. Oil. 36 x 50.

also taught Weber), with his principles of design based on Oriental art, had opened her eyes to the fallacy of academic naturalism; but her first independent creations (a series of drawings in 1915) were already marked by an original vision. While most of her work has been representational, from the beginning she also produced abstractions, some as pure as *Painting*. Both modes were the same in essence: in both the design was daring and effective, the balance of masses exactly planned, the style absolutely clear and precise. Yet always there was an element of enigma, a sense of dark depths behind the brilliant surface.

The first abstract movement in the United States lasted from about 1912 until about 1920. Most of its practitioners later returned to more representational styles, usually expressionist. Only a few —Dove, Stuart Davis, and younger men such as Calder, Noguchi, and Gorky—remained faithful to the abstract creed. This relatively short duration can be ascribed to several factors. In America abstract art was not, as in Europe, the product of long historical evolution. The American modernists did not feel, like many of their European colleagues, that representational art was finished, and that the only valid direction was toward abstraction. Our art world, having just been rudely awakened from its academic slumber, was not yet ready for so drastic a departure from tradition. Most American artists still felt the need for more direct relation with actualities. The novelty of abstraction, and the logic and pureness of its philosophy, had appealed particularly to youth; but many artists as they grew older were drawn back to representation, with all its wealth of associative values.

In the early 1920's came the inevitable reaction against advanced forms of modernism. In addition to the return to representation, there was a reawakened interest in the American scene, and a new concern with social content. For more than a decade—the 1920's and the early 1930's—advanced styles were much less in evidence here than abroad. Not until the middle 1930's did the second wave of abstraction, on which we are still riding, begin to gather force.

Georgia O'Keeffe. Abstraction. 1926. Oil. 30 x 18.

7 precisionists

In 1861 Gustave Courbet had urged his students to paint "railway stations, engine houses, mines and factories. These are the saints and miracles of the nineteenth century." But it was to be half a century later, and more than a century after the commencement of the Industrial Revolution, before the tremendous innovations of the machine age began to be used by modern artists—cubists, constructivists, and futurists. Such fundamental changes in the structure of society take time to be assimilated into art. In 1910 the Italian futurists still seemed revolutionary in proclaiming: "We must draw inspiration from the tangible miracles of contemporary life, from the iron network of speed encircling the earth. . . ." Reacting against cubism's limited subjects, the futurists glorified mechanization, dynamism, speed, and violence. Theirs was a highly conscious movement, delighting in manifestoes and public demonstrations. In 1912 they invaded Paris with an exhibition which was afterwards shown widely on the Continent. Invited to take part in the Armory Show, they insisted on separate galleries with their own box office—a demand which naturally was refused. Not until the San Francisco Exposition of 1915 was their work seen here as a group.

The United States of these years could be called a futurist country, building its skyscrapers and automobiles and pioneer planes, but its technology was considerably more advanced than its art. The dynamism of machine-age America had found little reflection in established art. Paradoxically, it had been most nearly expressed by French and Spanish cubism, Russian constructivism, and Italian futurism. Our most spectacular city, New York, had been pictured only by a few impressionists like Hassam, or by the romantic realists of the Eight, who had focused on its human aspects. But the American modernists who began to paint New York about 1912, Weber, Marin, Walkowitz, and Stella, were intoxicated by the city itself, a living organism—the upward thrust of skyscrapers, the sweep of great bridges, the kaleidoscope of night lights. They pictured these things not by literal representation but in the language of modernism. It was Weber in his cubistic compositions, Marin and Walkowitz in their expressionist watercolors, and Stella in his futurist fantasies, who first embodied in nonrepresentational form the essential energies of twentieth-century America.

Although one might expect futurism to appeal especially to Americans, it actually had only one out-and-out exponent in this country, Joseph Stella. Italian-born, living here since youth, he had already been fascinated by the steel mills of Pittsburgh before he returned to Italy in 1909. But it was in Paris in 1912 that he became involved in futurism and met its Italian leaders, probably during their exhibition. "When in 1912 I came back to New York," he wrote later, "I was thrilled to find America so rich with so many new motives to be translated into a new art. Steel and electricity had created a new world." Stella responded at once with a series of large futurist compositions, culminating in the five great panels of *New York Interpreted* (now in the Newark Museum), among the most remarkable imaginative visions of the modern city. *The Brooklyn Bridge: Variation on an Old Theme* is a later version of one of these panels. Of his first essay on this subject, in 1918, Stella wrote with characteristic flamboyance: "Upon the swarming darkness of the night, I rung all the bells of alarm with the blaze of electricity scattered in lightnings down the oblique cables, the dynamic pillars of my composition, and to render more pungent the mystery of the metallic apparition, through the green and the red glare of the signals I excavated here and there caves as subterranean passages to infernal recesses."

The United States of the machine age was pic-

Joseph Stella.
The Brooklyn Bridge:
Variation on an Old
Theme. 1939. Oil.
70 x 42.

tured in a quite different spirit, beginning about 1920, by certain painters who have been called precisionists: Demuth, Sheeler, Preston Dickinson, Niles Spencer, and others. These artists were concerned primarily with form and formal design, but their styles were generally representational, and they used the raw material of urban and industrialized America. In skyscrapers, factories, grain elevators, bridges, and machine-age structures of all kinds they found pure, clear-cut forms and a functional rightness; to them these monuments of our mechanized age had an unintended beauty. Some of them saw the same qualities in early American architecture. They were not interested in the human factor, like the Eight, or in the dynamism and romance of the modern world, like Stella; for them the city was a complex of forms. In the world they pictured, humanity with its turmoil and disorderliness played no direct part. Similarly, they favored the theme of still life—a controllable arrangement of forms.

While their style was representational, their fun-

damental purpose was to isolate the formal elements in external reality and translate them into design. Even their most realistic works were essentially formal. In this their art was related to abstraction. Design was conscious and planned; the forms inclined to the geometric and rectilinear; color was an attribute to form more than a direct means of expression; the vision was absolutely clear, precise, and sharp edged; the technique was smooth surfaced and highly finished. Impressionism's veiling of objects with atmosphere, and expressionism's subjective emotionalism, were equally avoided.

The precisionist style was derived to some extent from cubism. Though cubism had had few exponents in America, its influence had been wider than its practice. Its concentration on precise geometric form had affected painters who did not accept its degree of abstraction. Most of the precisionists admired cubism, and profited by its lessons. On the other hand, precisionism can be seen as the continuation of a historic tendency in American art: the precise realism of the Colonial limners, and of Copley, the Peales, Bingham, Heade, Harnett, and the *trompe-l'oeil* school. Oddly enough, cubism, by helping American painters discard impressionist vagueness, also helped them return to the clarity that had marked much American art of the past.

The relation to cubism was most evident in Charles Demuth's work of the 1920's. His earlier watercolors had revealed him as a master of the medium, sensitive and subtle, with mordant wit and a superb decorative gift. About 1919 he turned to architectural motifs, in tempera and then oil. Demuth was an artist of singular purity of purpose; his ruling passion was to create, out of the myriad forms of reality, plastic design embodying his classic sense of order. His creative imagination transformed everyday utilitarian objects, as in his portrait of a coal elevator in his native city of Lancaster, Pennsylvania, which with characteristic irony he titled *My Egypt*. As structure, eighteenth-century church steeples and twentieth-century factory chimneys interested him equally. His art was an inven-

Charles Demuth. Buildings, Lancaster. 1930. Oil. 24 x 20.

Anonymous gift.

Charles Demuth. My Egypt. 1927. Oil. 35¾ x 30.

Charles Sheeler. B[u]
County Barn. 1923.
Tempera and crayon.
19¼ x 25½.

Charles Sheeler. R
Rouge Plant. 1932. O
20 x 24⅛.

Lyonel Feininger. Gelmeroda, VIII. 1921. Oil. 39¼ x 31¼.

tive play with geometric forms of the utmost refinement. But with all its delicacy, it had an essential energy, in its dynamic lines of direction breaking up forms and creating an intricate web of diagonals. The fine balance of these contending forces gave his design a quality of inevitability. Beneath the exquisite surface, the structure was strong.

Somewhat similar to Demuth in a more limited range was the younger, short-lived Preston Dickin-son. An admirer of Oriental as well as modern art, he painted the industrialized scene, and still life, in a style that recalled the Japanese in its clearly defined linear patterns, the dusky richness of its harmonies, and its handsome decorativeness.

Of all the precisionists, Charles Sheeler has realized most completely the artistic possibilities of machine-age subjects: not only cities and structures, but the machine itself and its products. To him mechanical things have an aesthetic of their own, in their functional pureness and precision. He has found the same character in early American buildings, as in the geometric forms of the old Pennsylvania barns of Bucks County, in which he has noted "the strong relationship between the parts." Familiar from an early date with modern art, cubism in particular, he at one time approached abstraction, but never adopted it. After these cubistic essays he turned to a completely realistic vision, often of extreme photographic exactness, sharp in focus and with a crystalline clarity. (He is also a distinguished photographer, and his work in this field has fed his painting, and vice versa.) But even his paintings closest to visual reality are built on a structure of form and ordered design. The strong straight lines, the thrust and counterthrust of diagonals, the exactly considered relations of part to part, and the

Preston Dickinson. Industry. Before 1924. Oil. 30 x 24¼.

precise planning of three-dimensional space, produce concentrated design of a satisfying completeness. This command has increased through the years, as his period of straight realism (represented by *River Rouge Plant*) has been succeeded by a freer play with images and forms.

Niles Spencer's subject matter was similar to the other precisionists': architectural, industrial, or still life, without the human figure; and his style like theirs was clear and sharp edged. But he was even less concerned with objects as objects, seeing them more as massive, severely simplified forms. He differed also in his sensuous feeling for color and paint in themselves. His deep earthy color with its fine harmonic sense, and his rich pigment, were as integral to his artistic language as the forms they created. There was a certain deceptive quietness in his work, but his single-minded pursuit of essentials, of the relations between large, simple elements, resulted in strong design. In early years his style was relatively naturalistic, but as it developed, the planes became flattened out into patterns, increasingly bold and firmly constructed, until his later work was semi-abstract. His evolution illustrates the fact that precisionism, with its concentration on the geometry of forms, tended to see solid forms as assemblages of flat planes, and to convert these planes into two-dimensional patterns; so that the precisionist style passed over easily into formal abstraction.

In the meantime, native precisionism had been curiously paralleled by an expatriate American, Lyonel Feininger. Born and brought up in New York, at sixteen he had gone to Germany, where he was to remain until his sixties, returning to America for the last nineteen years of his long life. Feininger himself said that his love of ships, locomotives, machinery, and tall buildings had been acquired as a child and youth in Manhattan. In Germany he added the verticality of the Gothic. His style stemmed from early cubism, but his content was not so restricted; it embraced space and distance, light and darkness, subjective feeling and expressive color. His work was filled with romantic emotion, for the mystery of night, for solitude, for wide expanses of sky and sea with distant ships and lonely

Georgia O'Keeffe.   The White Flower. 1931. Oil. 30 x 36.

figures. The soaring lines of the church in *Gelmeroda* have the solemnity of organ music. Feininger's family background had been musical—he himself composed and played—and his art resembled music in expressing emotion through ordered design. With all its emotional content, it was architectonic, governed by an extremely refined sense of space and of forms existing in space. Though nearer abstraction than most of the American precisionists, he had remarkable affinities to them, especially to Demuth.

Georgia O'Keeffe is related to precisionism in her completely lucid style, and in certain of her subjects: the architectural aspects of New York, early America, and New Mexico. But she is little concerned with the machine age; her art is based on the things of nature. Among her most individual conceptions are her paintings of flowers, enlarged to fill the entire canvas. This magnification adds another dimension, transforms the single organism into a microcosm, a revelation of the beauty and mystery of natural structure.

8 sculpture, 1910-1939

In the first decade of our century, American sculpture was almost entirely conservative. Historically, this had always been true; our sculpture had never been as adventurous as our painting; for example, it had produced no parallel to impressionism. Its functions had been chiefly public: monuments and architectural decoration commissioned by official bodies. The classical tradition had hardened into an academic mold. Governed by an idealism that ignored the realities of the modern world, it expressed itself in outworn neoclassic symbols. Sculpture was conceived of as literal representation, a kind of three-dimensional photography.

There were a few exceptions to this formal idealism. The realism of the Eight had some counterparts in sculpture. Mahonri Young's laborers and prize fighters had a refreshing sense of reality. The life of the masses was pictured by Charles Haag and

Maurice Sterne. The Bomb Thrower. 1910/14. Bronze. 12 high.

Bequest of Mrs. Sam A. Lewisohn.

realization of form. Their most frequent subject was still the immemorial one of the human figure, especially the female figure. But they produced no icily perfect marble maidens. Their translation of natural form into sculptural form was free, disregarding literal proportions, using the figure as a motif for plastic creation. Their distortions, however, were not as violent as those of the fauve and expressionist painters.

The earliest and most powerful exponent of this freedom of form was Gaston Lachaise. Trained in the strict Beaux-Arts discipline, he came to America in 1906, at twenty-three. His first important work, and one of his finest, was *Standing Woman,* begun in 1912 and worked on for ten years. Lachaise's art was a hymn to the female and her sexual magnetism. His *Standing Woman* is commanding and triumphant: a magnificent body, broad hipped and full breasted. The gesture of the arms, at once imperious and welcoming, the buoyant balance of the superb figure poised on tiptoe, overflow with vitality and energy. The forms seem to expand from within, to be almost too abundant to be contained in their outer sheath. Rhythmic curves, ample yet subtle, run through the whole design. Great substance is combined with extreme refinement. One would think that sculptors through the centuries must have said all that could be said about the human body; but Lachaise's achievement triumphantly demonstrates the perennial vitality of the theme.

As Lachaise developed, his celebration of the power of sex was intensified. His freedom from normal proportions became startling. In the small late *Torso,* the elemental female forms—the swell of the hips, the contraction of the waist—have been exaggerated until the whole design has become a sexual symbol. Yet in some mysterious way a classic balance has been preserved.

A similar blend of classicism and freedom marked the work of Elie Nadelman. A unique figure in the Parisian art world before he came to America in 1914, he had anticipated cubism in some respects, but had preferred his personal version of the classic. His witty satires on society, with all their suavity and elegance, were highly original

plastic conceptions, governed by a severe purity of form.

Inventive play with the human figure has been used for both humorous and serious purposes by Hugo Robus, who since the early 1920's has worked in essentially the same style as today. His humor lies not merely in his subjects but in his forms, with their imaginative exaggerations and simplifications. Their smooth continuous flow makes his art primarily one of rhythmic movement. Line plays a role as essential as in drawing. That his style can be as expressive of tragedy as of humor, is proved by such a work as *Despair.*

William Zorach.   The Artist's Daughter. 1930/46. Georgia marble. 25½ high.

Lachaise and Robus were primarily modelers, creating works in clay or plaster to be cast in metal. But one of the features of the liberal trend in sculpture was a revival of direct carving in stone or wood. In the nineteenth century it had been rare for a sculptor to do his own carving; the standard practice was to model the piece and turn it over to a professional stone carver. In the early twentieth century, however, more sculptors began to carve their works themselves, from start to finish. Direct carving had several virtues; the piece was conceived from the beginning in its actual material, which played a part in determining the forms; and the sculptor had that intimate contact with its physical substance that is essential for any vital work of art.

Robert Laurent.   Kneeling Figure. 1935. Bronze. 23½ high.

John B. Flannagan.   Elephant. 1929–30. Bluestone. 15 long.

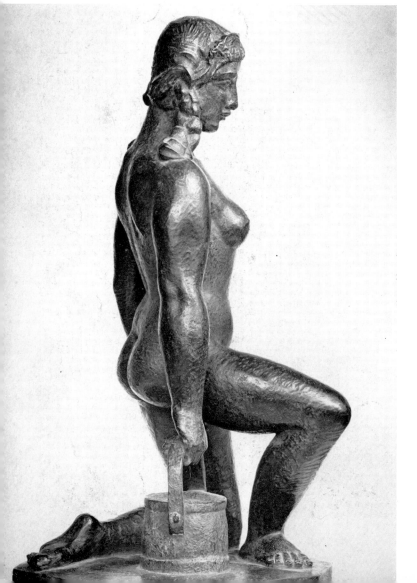

Direct carving tended toward simplicity, massiveness, and monumentality. Its increase was a manifestation of the general modern trend toward identity of the material and the forms made out of it; a trend which was also occurring in painting, and was to reach its extreme development in abstract expressionism.

To the academic sculptor, interested primarily in representation, the sensuous qualities of the material had been secondary: hence the preponderance of cold white marble. But the direct carvers loved the material for itself, using stones of a wide variety of colors and textures. Wood, previously considered too humble, began to be used as a major medium. There were new imported tropical woods: lignum vitae, ebony, sabicu, cocobolo—hard and heavy, beautiful in grain and color. Chaim Gross, one of the first to use them, said: "Their density offered a challenge that was far more stimulating than that of the softer woods."

A pioneer carver was William Zorach, who had started as a painter; converted to fauvism in Paris, he had later evolved an expressionist form of cubism. In 1917 he did his first carving, and five years later gave up painting. From the beginning his sculpture was less modernist than his painting. "I owe most to the great periods of primitive carving in the past," he has said, "not to the moderns or to the classical Greeks, but to the Africans, the Persians, the Mesopotamians, the archaic Greeks and of course to the Egyptians." The keynote of Zorach's art is a large simplicity, in content and style. His subjects are of elemental human meaning: the beauty and splendor of the body, and the love of man and woman and of mother and child. A deep, healthy sensuousness pervades his work. Its mood is one of repose, with no striving for violent movement or dramatic gesture. His style is monumental; the forms are massive and highly simplified, the rhythms ample and calm. His work is free from derivative stylization; it is concerned with fundamental forms, not with surface decoration. Zorach is also a skillful modeler, and a few of his major pieces are in metal, but to him direct carving "is greater than modeled sculpture, its problems are greater and its possibilities of creative expression are deeper."

Direct carving was Robert Laurent's method from youth. His early wood carvings, from 1911 on, showed some influence of Negro sculpture in their primitivism, but also an instinctive feeling for the material, a sureness of touch, and a strong sense of rhythm. In *The Flame,* living, ascending motion was captured in semi-abstract forms. Since the 1920's a favorite material has been alabaster, whose translucent delicacy has made it a perfect medium for the fineness of his carving, his flowing lines and subtle rhythms. Laurent has modeled as much as he has carved; his style in bronze, at first more realistic, was marked by combined energy and sensitiveness, as in his *Kneeling Figure.* In recent years his work has developed an increasing inventiveness of form, while preserving all its characteristic subtlety and skill.

José de Creeft learned direct carving by working in a Parisian shop where academic plasters were translated into marble. Spanish by birth, living in Paris for twenty-five years before coming to America in 1929, De Creeft remained singularly impervious to current fashions; his art looked back to older

Robert Laurent. The Flame. c. 1917. Wood. 18 high.

Gift of Bartlett Arkell.

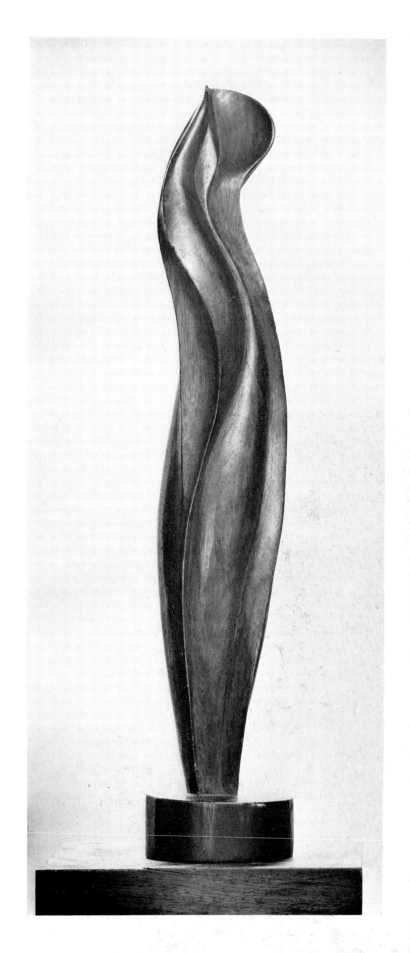

Hugo Robus. Despair. 1927. Bronze. 12 high.

Gaston Lachaise. Torso. 1930. Bronze. 11½ high.

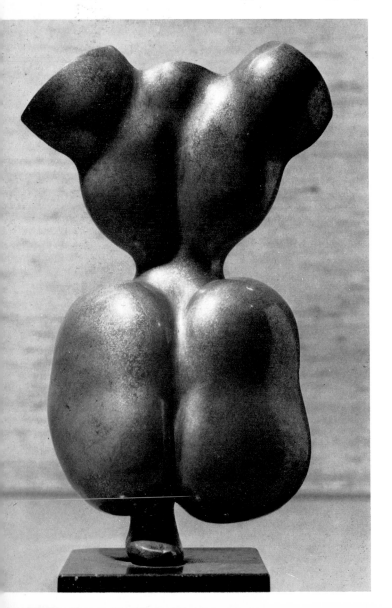

traditions, Oriental and pre-Columbian. His brooding figures with their massive limbs and broad primitive faces seem spirits of the earth, ancient, pagan, Mediterranean. An elemental poetry is embodied in stone carved with the utmost delicacy. *The Cloud* is all movement, not merely of the parts but of the whole; this cloud-woman is moving through space, blown by winds, changing shape—sensations achieved by the delicate balance of the forms and the exquisite fluidity of the carving.

John B. Flannagan was a simpler, ruder carver, forced by early poverty to use common field stone, but finding in it something elemental that expressed his mystical sense of the unity of all life, human and animal; in his own words, "a unity so complete it can see a figure of dignity even in the form of a goat." His art captured the essential life of creatures in the most direct, simplified forms. "My aim," he wrote, "is to produce sculpture with such ease, freedom, and simplicity that it hardly seems carved but rather to have endured so always."

Until the 1930's the prevailing concepts of American sculpture, even the most liberal, were still basically traditional. Sculpture was still representation of natural forms, usually the human figure, in traditional materials, and in design based on the central-

José de Creeft. The Cloud. 1939. Greenstone. 13½ high.

ized mass. The only outstanding exponent of advanced trends was Alexander Archipenko, early cubist sculptor and pioneer of such radical developments as the use of voids and concavities, light and motion, new materials and polychroming. Settling in America in 1923, he soon became an influential teacher. His graceful, rococo semi-abstract designs, based generally on the rhythms of the female figure, were almost the only advanced sculpture being produced in the United States in the 1920's. This situation contrasted sharply with that in Europe, where for more than two decades continuous innovations had been carried on by a succession of sculptors, from Brancusi to Moore.

But from the early 1930's a younger generation of Americans, including Calder, Noguchi, David Smith, Roszak, Lassaw, and De Rivera, began to work in advanced forms. By the end of the decade, the basic concepts of sculpture were in process of being revolutionized, not only in the trend toward abstraction, but in the very nature of sculptural form. Monumentality, solidity, and the centralized mass were being replaced by openness, extension, and fluidity. New materials were being used which called for radically new techniques: metals welded with a torch; plastics, glass, cement; machine-made products; natural objects—*objets trouvés*. Constructions relied on tensions and balances as in a bridge. Physical motion had been employed by Calder in his mobiles, whose gay, inventive shapes moved in the wind like the leaves of a tree. Instead of resting solidly on a pedestal, the new sculpture was as likely to be suspended—a parallel to the floating quality of the forms in much modern painting and, like the latter, an expression of our air-minded age. Sculptors such as Gabo and Lippold were carrying sculptural concepts a step further in their mobile abstract constructions of metal or plastic wires which caught the light—an art of light and motion rather than of solid forms. The 1940's and 1950's were to see revolutions in sculpture even more basic than in painting.

Alexander Archipenko.   Torso in Space. 1936. Metalized terra cotta. 50 long.

Gift of Mr. and Mrs. Peter A. Rübel.

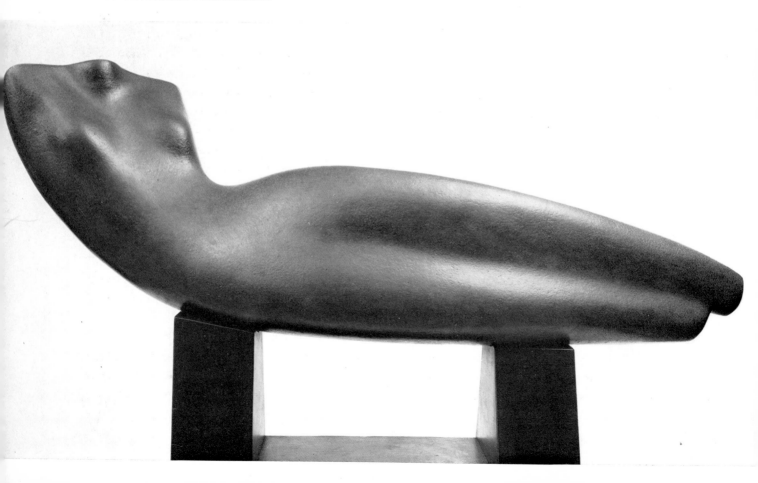

9 representational painting

In painting we have so far considered mostly the innovating tendencies, from the Eight's revolution in subject matter to the modernists' revolution in the language of art, which reached its furthest development in the abstractionists' rejection of representation. Nevertheless, representational painting continued—was indeed much more widely practiced than advanced styles in America until the late 1930's —and is still a major tendency today. But like all vital art in our century, it was affected by the new concepts. Academicians still clung to the nineteenth-century concept of naturalistic representation. But representational painting had another aspect, non-academic and creative. The creative representational painters shared in the formal discoveries of the time; they recognized that formal values were basic, that representation without them was valueless. But they believed that there need be no conflict between representation and formal elements. They were aware that the great art of the past had never been mere naturalism; that even in its most realistic tradition, that of Europe since the early Renaissance, realism had been united with design—three-dimensional design, in line and color, in round form and deep space, physical elements which speak as directly to the senses, and through the senses to the mind, as do sounds in music. Such design, they believed, could be achieved within a representational style, as it had

been through the centuries. They were basically traditionalist, but their tradition was not that of the academy; it was the tradition transmitted directly by great art.

One of the leading characteristics of American art since 1913 has been its diversity. In the swift successive movements of the period, some artists had been in the forefront, while others remained comparatively little influenced. Hence individuals and schools of many different viewpoints continued to exist simultaneously, all with their measure of validity. Some of the strongest figures of the time kept on working in styles uninfluenced by modernism, yet profiting from the discoveries of the century.

The painters included in this chapter were widely varied, but they had certain things in common. Although some were closer to modernism than others, they all painted in generally realistic styles, without the distortions of expressionism. Most (though not all) centered their art on the human figure. They were interested in the figure for itself, for its character, sensuous appeal, or qualities of form, rather than merely as part of an environment. In general, they were not concerned with storytelling, ideology, or subjective fantasy; their purpose was primarily aesthetic. The sensuous element was important to them, in varying ways and degrees. Compared to the precisionists, they were more painterly; while form was basic, color also played an essential role. With most of them, design was conscious and planned. Their painting methods were usually more complex than those of the impressionists and modernists; some of them went back to traditional techniques. In several directions they merged with other representational schools, such as the American scene or social painters; the divisions between them are necessarily arbitrary.

The realist members of the Eight continued to work in representational styles. While open-minded about modernism, they were not converted to it. Henri became a leading teacher, and his influence spread far beyond the original group—a liberating influence, encouraging the study of life instead of academic conventions. Some of his students, such as Hopper, Du Bois, Coleman, and Bellows, pursued the path of realism that he and his fellows had opened up. Others like Speicher turned to a more formal style; or like Kent, and Bellows in his later work, embarked on more romantic courses. All of these, and many more, had been stimulated by Henri to see and feel more freely.

The Eight's realistic trend was carried on by four of the original group—Henri, Luks, Shinn, and, for some years, Sloan. Luks developed a constantly bolder style, swift and summary, concentrating on the single impression. The individual person re-

Rockwell Kent. Shadows of Evening. 1921–23. Oil. 38 x 44.

George Luks.   Mrs. Gamley. 1930. Oil. 66 x 48.

mained the center of his art; he loved character wherever it could be found, the racier the better; and his genial humanism gave a warmth and glow to his commonest subjects. Conscious design was never his strong point, but he saw things largely and simply, and his zest for painting imparted a physical vitality to everything he did.

The genre tradition of the Eight had a younger exponent in Guy Pène du Bois. But his world was more sophisticated: that of the fashionable, of international pleasure-seekers. More a social satirist than any of the Eight, he had a merciless eye for the snob, the pretender, and the sensualist. His hard-boiled women were painted half in derision, half in fascination. Malice gave his style edge and intensity. His skillful simplification focused the spotlight on his victims, playing down background and details. Beneath his mordant characterization was a gift for linear rhythm, living form, and concentrated design.

Among the Eight, Lawson remained a consistent impressionist, but not an academic one—realistic in subjects, fresh in vision, rich in color and pigment. Glackens evolved from his early naturalism into an

Guy Pène du Bois. Woman with Cigarette. 1929. Oil. 36¼ x 28¾.

Ernest Lawson. High Bridge. 1934. Oil. 30 x 40.

Eugene Speicher.   Marianna. 1937. Oil. 45½ x 35½.

John Sloan. Nude and Nine Apples. 1937. Tempera and oil. 24 x 30.

Kenneth Hayes Miller. Shopper. 1928. Oil. 41 x 33.

Henry Schnakenberg. Conversation. 1930. Oil. 50¼ x 36.

impressionist art that celebrated the pleasures of summer, the human body, children, flowers—bathed in all-embracing light, and in an opulence of color rare in American painting. With the example of Renoir's late style, his forms grew ampler; but he never lost his innate graphic gift. In the hands of Glackens, Lawson, Allen Tucker, and a few other independents, impressionism continued to be a creative force in American painting.

Henri's vigorous naturalism was the background for Eugene Speicher's art, but instead of realistic genre he turned to realization of sensuous and for-

mal qualities as embodied in the figure, still life, and landscape. In this he was guided by a wide knowledge of older art, and in modern painting, of Cézanne and Renoir, with their synthesis of form and color, their creation of volume in terms of the utmost chromatic fullness. A naturally able painter, Speicher disciplined his gift in the service of conscious composition, controlled richness of palette, and brushwork which sacrificed display to the modeling of form. To the picturing of things pleasurable to the eye and the senses, he brought a characteristic largeness and repose.

Though not a Henri student, Leon Kroll has developed along generally parallel lines. Thoroughly trained in traditional schools, but early aware of the post-impressionists, he was one of the first to aim at uniting their organization of form with a representational style. The spirit of his work was idyllic and sensuous; his tranquil landscapes with their figures of bathing women combined a balanced completeness of subject with precise draftsmanship and absolute clarity of vision.

Rockwell Kent has long been a romantic figure in the American art world: explorer, traveler, writer, drawing his subjects from the far places of the earth —Alaska, Greenland, Cape Horn—nature at her wildest and most elemental, peopled with solitary figures of men and animals. These epic scenes he painted with a strong sense of pictorial drama, and in a bold, striking style, with massive, starkly simplified forms. While there was an element of theatricality, Kent must be credited with aspiring to subjects touched by few artists of our time. As with the later ambitious compositions of another ex-student of Henri, George Bellows, the greatness of the themes often exceeded the power of the artistic language in which they were expressed.

So far we have discussed artists associated with the Eight or with Henri's teaching, and we have noted the romantic elements which were mingled with their interest in form. A more austere concentration on formal factors was that of Kenneth Hayes Miller. A leading exponent of traditional values, Miller devoted his life to the study of design, particularly as achieved by the European masters of the sixteenth and seventeenth centuries. To him the foundation of enduring art was three-dimensional design. He aimed at the greatest substance; forms must be in the round, solid and weighty. At the same time, they must not lose their relation to the physical surface of the painting, which determined what he called the ground or picture plane—the pictorial space beyond which they must not project or recede. Design with him was fully pondered: the interrelations of all forms, their movements, the tensions they created, and the final order which dominated these conflicting forces.

Miller believed that there was no necessary antagonism between the forms of the real world and those of art; rather, an underlying harmony, for even though the artist transforms reality, all his concepts of form are based on it. In subject matter, he felt that the richest material, in both associative and plastic values, was that which was most familiar. For years his studio was on Fourteenth Street, which furnished many of his themes, as in *Shopper*, with its characteristic monumentality. He was a pioneer in the revival of traditional techniques. Impressionism and direct painting had all but destroyed the method

Isabel Bishop. Nude. 1934. Oil. 33 x 40.

of building form in underpainting, overpainting, and glazes, by which the old masters had achieved a combination of solidity, transparency, and depth impossible to secure by direct opaque painting. A teacher most of his life, Miller numbered among his students many younger representational painters, including several whose works will be discussed: Schnakenberg, Isabel Bishop, Brook, Kuniyoshi, Katherine Schmidt, and Marsh.

A parallel development took place in the work of John Sloan, who of all the Eight changed most fundamentally. When nearing sixty, in 1928, he com-pletely transformed his art. From characterful genre he turned to exploration of basic form, concentrating on the figure, especially the female nude. His women were far from the conventional type of model: sturdy, muscular, with no obvious sex appeal, and none of the usual languor; even the reclining figures, as in *Nude and Nine Apples,* seem full of energy, ready to spring up. Surface sensuousness was absent; flesh looked like polished metal. "Works of art are made of wood and bronze and oil paint, not flesh and blood," Sloan said. The figure was translated into relief sculpture, with the solidity and

Hermon More. Rocky Hillside. 1934. Oil. 32 x 42.

Walt Kuhn. The Blue Clown.
1931. Oil. 30 x 25.

tactile existence that Sloan believed were the essentials of form. In technique, he developed a method based, like Miller's, on study of the old masters: the forms underpainted, with color added in overpaintings. One feature was his use of line-work as the final stage, to complete the modeling, create textures, and achieve tangibility. These figure pieces of his last twenty years, which ran completely counter to prevailing trends, had a robust vitality and an idiosyncratic character that place them among the strongest plastic creations of the period. Sloan, like Miller, was an outstanding teacher, and their dual emphasis on form had a wide effect.

For Isabel Bishop the unity of form and movement has always been of central importance. Move-

Henry Varnum Poor.   Autumn Fruit. 1932. Oil. 18 x 26½.

Leon Kroll.   A Road Through Willows. 1933. Oil. 26 x 42.

Alexander Brook. The Sentinels. 1934. Oil. 32 x 48¼.

ment is of the essence of her art: not just the representation of actual motion, but the movement of the forms themselves. She has a strong sense of the continuity of forms; they are continuous throughout the picture plane, not separated by their edges but merged, so that they seem to be of one basic substance. Everything is felt in purely painterly terms. Her color is grayed and delicate, a vibrating web of tones in which the forms are woven. Her range of subjects is not wide; sometimes the nude, as in the painting illustrated, with its grasp of bodily structure; more often the world of Union Square: working girls, vagrants—ordinary people, seen objectively but with understanding. Always there is a sense of movement: the momentary captured, and given the lasting life of form.

Henry Schnakenberg has been an individualist from the first, independent equally of academicism and current fashions. He is interested in many aspects of the world, for their aesthetic possibilities: their offering of things pleasurable in themselves, and from which design can be created. His aim is less to express subjective emotion than to build images of reality which are satisfying for both their associations and forms. He is a solid constructor, not an improviser; and his style is characteristically lucid and free from mannerisms. He has never fallen into the rut of specialized subjects; each painting stands by itself.

Paralleling the evolution of figure painting, new tendencies appeared in landscape. Where the impressionists had been interested primarily in chang-

Yasuo Kuniyoshi. I'm Tired. 1938. Oil. 40¼ x 31.

Louis Bouché. Stamford Harbor. 1932. Oil. 29 x 36¼.

ing light and atmosphere and appearances, the younger generation was concerned with nature's permanent realities, with her enduring forms, and their translation into pictorial design. In this they went back of impressionism to older traditions: to Ruisdael, Claude Lorrain, and Poussin in the seventeenth century, or to Corot and Courbet in the nineteenth. This new landscape school was centered in the year-round artists' colony of Woodstock, New York, and included, among others, Henry Mattson, Arnold Blanch, Ernest Fiene, Katherine Schmidt, and Georgina Klitgaard. One of its leading figures has been Hermon More, whose landscapes are based on a realization of the solid structure of the earth: rocky hills, rugged and massive, clothed with rich green woods; valleys with tranquil streams. There is

a sense of the largeness and grandeur of nature's forms that recalls the classic tradition of landscape, while the depth of color and tone reveals an undertone of strong romantic emotion.

Henry Varnum Poor's art is a lyrical one, pervaded with feeling for the earth and the seasons, for growth and flooding light. His constant awareness of the world of nature enters even into his still lifes, such as *Autumn Fruit*. He has been a leading ceramist as well as painter, and his style has a quality that suggests modeling in pliant clay; the forms are living, flexible, and finely shaped. He draws with the brush, freshly and spontaneously. In all his work there is a sense of complete naturalness, of a personal vision expressing itself in personal forms.

One aspect of the revolution in American art of

Niles Spencer.   The Green Table. 1930. Oil. 50 x 40.

our century was a changed attitude toward sex. The academic idealization of women, carried over from the nineteenth century, had been undermined by the paganism of the modernists; but even they tended to sublimate sexual emotion, to make the body a generalized symbol of *joie de vivre*. But the younger generation of the 1920's had a more realistic attitude, more direct and sensual, and also more relaxed, giving freer rein to humor, gaiety, and animal spirits. Typical of this change was the cosmopolite Jules Pascin, poet of sensuality and the female body, a superb draftsman, with a line of the utmost sensibility. A wanderer, with friends in every world capital, he came to America in 1914 and remained six years, becoming a citizen. With his gift of personal magnetism, he acted as a catalytic agent—yeast for the bread of his fellow artists. Among his closest American friends were Kuhn, Bouché, Brook, and Kuniyoshi; and in their work of these years one often sees something of Pascin. All representational painters, they had in common a direct sensuousness in subjects, style, and technique. Physical sensation played a vital role in their art. Painting to them was a sensuous experience; they loved pigment and its manipulation, and their pictures communicate this pleasure. But differing from the modernists, they combined this sensuousness with completely recognizable imagery and three-dimensional form and space.

The oldest, Walt Kuhn, who had been co-organizer of the Armory Show, was familiar with the worlds of circus, burlesque, and musical comedy, and his portraits of clowns and acrobats displayed a temperamental affinity for these performers, like Picasso's for harlequins. His showgirls in their elaborate uniforms had a gaudy glamour, and also a pathos; they were seen with both irony and love. An artist of instinctive physical power, Kuhn recorded the sensations of the eye with startling immediacy. In his most successful works he achieved bold, simple volume, and daring color that matched his subjects.

A similar sensuous vitality, but more subtle, animates Alexander Brook's paintings. His subjects are everyday and seemingly casual, but never banal; they possess visual wit, a quality never as broad as humor or as mordant as satire, but pungent. His love of painting, rooted in the senses, is revealed in the nervous life of his brushwork, the rich substance of his pigment, and the depth and resonance of his color, with its fine use of grays and blacks. *The Sentinels* is a record of intense visual sensation: a drama of light and shadow, with a penetrating mood of silence and waiting.

Louis Bouché has a singularly fresh eye; his motifs are always original and unexpected, revealing the pleasure that familiar things can give when seen through a witty and sophisticated vision. His is an easy, unforced gift; painting to him is evidently as natural as breathing. The decorative element in his early works, such as *Stamford Harbor,* has been replaced by a more direct, realistic style, notable for clarity, skillful use of color to create volume and space, and a zest for visual experience that gives life to the whole.

Yasuo Kuniyoshi, born in Japan, came to the United States in his youth, and his entire career was identified with this country. His early work, with its fantasy and unconscious humor, was a unique blend of the Oriental and Occidental. After two long visits to France in the 1920's, his style drew closer to Western naturalism. His subjects in middle years were not wide in range, lacking the fantasy that was to reappear in later life. His girls in various stages of dishabille, with their voluptuous impassive faces and their air of languor and pensiveness, were embodiments of sexual magnetism. For Kuniyoshi painting was a deeply instinctive process. His handling was rich and varied, ranging from heavy impastos to delicate transparent glazes. An innate refinement appeared in everything he touched. There were no flat or dull passages; the whole surface was alive. The picture was felt throughout as a plastic organism. The subtle distortions, such as the tilting of the horizontal planes to give them maximum value, revealed an Oriental concept of perspective which was also characteristic of modern art. Kuniyoshi's sense of form and design were instinctive more than intellectual, Oriental and modern rather than Renaissance; but by an entirely different road he arrived at the plastic form and design which other artists had reached by more traditional approaches.

10 the American scene

George Bellows. Dempsey and Firpo. 1924. Oil. 51 x 63¼.

The Eight had accomplished a revolution by turning for subjects to contemporary American life —in particular, the New York scene. But the revolution did not stop there; it was to expand in many directions, until it encompassed the whole country, and aspects of life they had never touched.

Of all the younger artists who carried on the Eight's realistic tradition, the most brilliant was George Bellows. His natural gifts were phenomenal: an observing eye, fertile pictorial inventiveness, and a sense of drama that sometimes verged on melodrama. His early direct realism was in many ways his most genuine phase. Then came an ambition for more spectacular themes, and his conversion to dynamic symmetry; and his vigorous native gift became involved in theories foreign to his temperament—a conflict which had not been resolved when his great talent was cut short in his early forties. His *Dempsey and Firpo*, painted the year before his death, contrasted with the smashing impact of his youthful prize-fight pictures; reflecting his theoretical preoccupations, it was more studied in composition, with an almost ballet-like rhythm.

John Sloan found his drama in the everyday life of city streets. Continuing to paint genre until the late 1920's, he became interested less in human incidents, more in the whole spectacle of the city: the movement of crowds and traffic, the varying moods of season and hour, and the play of lights—the city's and nature's. *Sixth Avenue Elevated at Third Street* is made up of two main elements: above, the passing trains against an evening sky of vivid peacock blue; below, the busy street with its interplay of lights. His design had become more conscious and much more complex, his construction more solid, and his color richer. In his paintings of these years, all Sloan's feeling for New York, compounded of first-hand realism and romantic emotion, found its fullest expression.

Compared to Sloan's positivism, Glenn Coleman's viewpoint was tinged with pessimism; his city sometimes seemed a prison. Yet he was devoted to it: the character of individual streets and buildings, the contrasts of old and new, the architectural chaos that was—and is—New York. The utter honesty of his portrayal, without a trace of glamour, and the quiet undertone of poignant melancholy made his work a moving expression of one man's vision of the city.

Edward Hopper's realistic picturing of the American scene began as early as 1908, but did not achieve recognition until the 1920's. Where the Eight had focused on the human factor, with the city merely a background, Hopper concentrated on the city itself. Often he chose times when it seemed uninhabited; in *Early Sunday Morning* no one is about, the street is empty, the shops closed. The subject is completely uncompromising: a row of identical houses, seen from directly in front, so that the dominant lines are severely horizontal. Yet the design is rich and satisfying; the strong foreground line forming a base for the massive forms above, the horizontals broken by the verticals of hydrant and barber pole, and by the repeated patterns of doorways and windows. Like many of Hopper's compositions, this conveys the sensation that the forms do not stop at the edges, that these buildings continue for blocks on either side. The vastness, monotony, and loneliness of the modern city have seldom been more intensely expressed. But the final emotion is affirmative: clear morning sunlight, stillness, and a sense of solitude, penetrating yet serene. With all its objectivity, the picture is pervaded with that poetry of places, of man's cities and structures, which has been a theme for artists through the centuries, from Piranesi to Chirico.

Hopper's portraits of the American scene outside the city contrast with those of the impressionists, who shunned the evidences of man and his works. He likes the man-made features that give the contemporary landscape its character: the ruthless lines of railroad tracks, the functional forms of factories and bridges, and American architecture in its most native manifestations, especially the stark houses and churches of New England. Beneath its naturalism, his art is one of form. His design is highly conscious, and often reveals a strong geometrical structure. But unlike the precisionists, he is also concerned with sensations of solidity and weight, light and time of day, and the emotion inherent in the place and the hour.

For two decades, the awakened interest in the

John Sloan. Sixth Avenue Elevated at Third Street. 1928. Oil. 30 x 40.

American scene was confined to the East, and particularly New York. The United States west of the Alleghenies, explored in the mid-nineteenth century by many artists, had been ignored since then. But with the 1920's all this was to change. The pioneer of this change was Charles Burchfield, who, after his early fantasies, began about 1920 to paint the region where he has lived all his life—eastern Ohio and western New York. Dreary towns of houses with false fronts, grim industrial cities, monstrous mansions of the President Garfield era—all these were pictured with merciless realism and a sure grasp of the character of inanimate things. But beneath his realism Burchfield was still the romantic, now in revolt against the ugliness of his environment. Yet there

was much more than satire, there was a deep attachment that gave his portrayal an intensity of emotion, often tragic. As he matured, the satire became less evident and the affirmation stronger—a realization of the poetry of common things and places. In the drab dilapidation of a scene like *Old House by the Creek* he found a melancholy beauty. Always he remained alive to nature, which is present in streets as in fields; his city scenes were quickened by a lyrical awareness of season and weather. He had become a realistic poet of the familiar, of things typical of a large part of America; a sensitive artist who had the courage to remain in his own region, and out of its ugliness and beauty to create his art.

A complete individualist, Burchfield never

thought of himself as starting a movement. The opposite was true of the leaders of regionalism—Thomas H. Benton of Missouri, Grant Wood of Iowa, and John Steuart Curry of Kansas. Born and raised in these three neighboring states (Wood and Curry as farm boys), they all studied in Europe and were exposed to modernism, but rejected it, returning to their own states to paint the native scene. They were champions of the regionalist philosophy that there was a special virtue in an artist's identification with his own section—a virtue that was lost in cosmopolitanism. To them the Mississippi Valley was the heartland of America, and its people and folkways had a uniquely American character. This character was to be found in the country rather than in cities. They prized the old-time virtues of this rural mid-America—and, no less, its old-time sins. Themselves artists of considerable cosmopolitan experience, they were not blind to its provincial and humorous aspects, and their attitudes (Wood's and Benton's in particular) had a definite strain of satire. But it was not hostile satire; it was rather a liking for native idiosyncrasies, a blend of humor and affection. In all this there was an element of nostalgia; they were picturing a world that was a survival, and that was already giving way to the march of standardization.

Benton had lived three years in Paris, from

Glenn O. Coleman.   Downtown Street. 1926. Oil. 33 x 44.

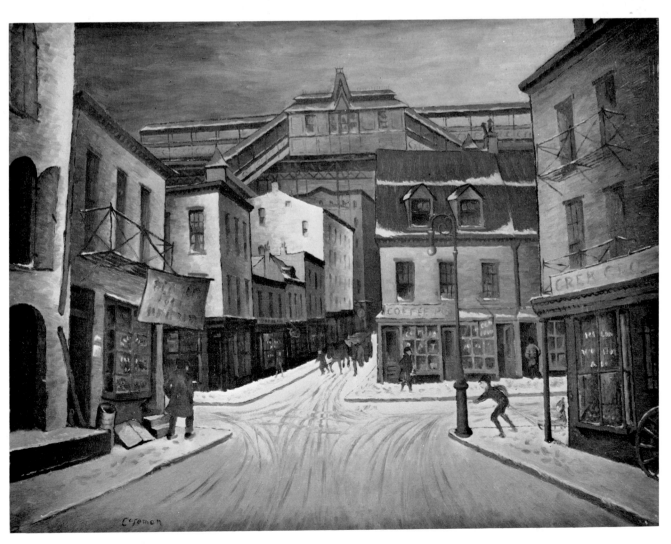

1908, and later had experimented with Synchromism, before he finally repudiated all modernism, and evolved theories of design based on Renaissance art. Then during ten years he spent summers roaming through the South and Midwest, on foot or by car, making thousands of drawings, which furnished raw material for his paintings from the late 1920's on—a panorama of the America he loved, the America of dirt farmers, hillbillies, cotton pickers, Mississippi steamboats, revival meetings. These and many more such subjects he has pictured with furious energy, gusto for native character, and flamboyant humor. His style is far from literal; a fantastic exaggeration transforms people, things, even the face of nature. Every object is concrete and tangible, and filled with energetic rhythms; every inch of the canvas is crowded with forms and movements. In

spite of overemphasis, his work has vitality and substance—qualities not too common, which should make it survive its present unfashionableness. Benton's gifts are particularly suited to mural painting, and he was a pioneer in breaking with academic neoclassicism and attacking native and contemporary themes. One of his earliest projects was *The Arts of Life in America,* commissioned by the Whitney Museum in 1932 for its Eighth Street building, and now in the New Britain Museum of American Art.

Though Grant Wood also spent some time in Paris, the turning point of his career was a visit to Munich in 1928, when he saw fifteenth- and sixteenth-century Flemish and German painting, whose highly finished realism fitted his temperament. After his return to Iowa his chief subject matter became the rural life of the state, with excur-

Edward Hopper. Early Sunday Morning. 1930. Oil. 35 x 60.

Edward Hopper. House on Pamet River.
1934. Watercolor. 19¾ x 24⅞.

Charles Burchfield. Ice Glare. 1933.
Watercolor. 30¾ x 24¾.

sions into American history. His viewpoint was a curious mixture of belief and nonbelief; one often feels a tongue-in-the-cheek attitude, and occasionally a complete skepticism about established mores; *Daughters of Revolution* was as devastating a satire as any leftist's. His *American Gothic* had an unsparing candor that has made it a classic of Americana. If he had given free rein to these realistic and satiric gifts, he might have been a more revealing interpreter of his region, instead of a rather self-conscious exponent of its virtues. This cautious viewpoint was matched by a deliberate stylization harking back to the precision and simplification of American folk art.

Compared to his two fellow regionalists, John Steuart Curry was a more natural and unforced art-

Thomas Hart Benton.   The Lord Is My Shepherd. 1926. Tempera. 33¼ x 27⅜.

ist, who without dogmatism or self-consciousness painted the rural life he knew well in his native state, and in Wisconsin, where his last ten years were spent. His early *Baptism in Kansas* may at first seem a satire, but this is more because of its subject than its spirit, which is serious: a familiar country ceremony recorded sympathetically and with a certain pathos. In his mature work his feeling for the life of nature, at once realistic and poetic, found full expression—the ample, generous Wisconsin earth, its fruits and animals, its distances and wide skies. His style showed a simple sensuousness of color, light, and handling that was lacking in his colleagues' work. His grasp of bodily structure and movement was reinforced by study of the Renaissance masters, but without stylization.

Regionalism was a highly conscious school, with Benton as its most articulate spokesman. On the negative side, it was hostile to modernism, especially abstraction; to both the School of Paris and that of New York; and, in general, to internationalism in art. During the 1930's it became a wide and active movement. This was a decade of expanding artistic frontiers within the United States, stimulated partly by the governmental art projects, whose stated theme was "The American Scene." But by the end of the decade, regionalism was declining. Its cultural isolationism ran counter to growing internationalism, and its artistic conservatism to the increasing tendency toward abstraction. In the next two decades, regional differences were submerged in the nationwide trend toward advanced art.

The limitations of regionalism are obvious enough. But partly because of its own intemperate propaganda, it has been too sweepingly condemned. It was surely no crime for artists to paint the world in which they had been born and brought up, which they knew well and loved—or even to paint it in a representational style. Viewed dispassionately, their work was an authentic record of important and neglected aspects of America. For the first time since the nineteenth century, the world of mid-America was pictured with vitality and humor. And in purely artistic terms, the best regionalist painting had qualities of substance and energy that may well make it more highly valued in the future.

Meanwhile, in New York a new generation of

John Steuart Curry. Baptism in Kansas. 1928. Oil. 40 x 50.

urban realists had appeared. Several were former students of Kenneth Hayes Miller: Reginald Marsh, Katherine Schmidt, Edward Laning, Isabel Bishop, and Charles Locke; others included Paul Cadmus and the Soyer brothers. These younger painters pictured city life with a realism more drastic than that of the Eight; they saw its seamy side, the tawdriness of much of its glamour, and its elements of poverty and misery. Their increased social awareness was due partly to the Depression, but their presentation was objective, without comment on the social order. While their attitude was more pessimistic and sometimes more satirical than the Eight's, their basic motivation was affirmative—love of the city in its myriad aspects. It was an attachment no less deep for being also critical.

Reginald Marsh's art was built almost entirely out of the multitudinous life of New York. Humanity was the center of interest. His range was wide, from café society to Bowery bums—the human animal in his infinite variety. He liked character, in people, places, and things. His viewpoint was unsentimental, humorous, seeing through false glamour, but fascinated by the endless spectacle of the city. The populace's pleasure-seeking activities attracted him: sex as publicly presented, the magnetic

Grant Wood. Dinner for Threshers. 1933. Pencil. 17¾ x 26¾. (Left section.)

power of the female body. In burlesque houses, on the beach at Coney Island, in the mad world of Luna Park, he found the human figure in all its vitality, beauty, and grotesqueness. His mastery of the body was based on constant observation and drawing, and on thorough study of anatomy. His absorption in the contemporary scene was equaled by his devotion to the masters of the High Renaissance and the seventeenth century. Like them, he conceived of painting as the design of sculptural form within the three-dimensional picture plane. In its rich profusion of forms and its continuous movement, his design was baroque rather than classic.

From the beginning of her career Katherine Schmidt concentrated on certain fundamentals: the creation of round forms in deep space, with complete clarity; every object clearly defined, its exact position in space and its relations to all other objects fully understood. Her motifs—still life, landscape, the figure—were selected largely for their possibilities as form; her viewpoint was objective, with no attempt to express subjective emotion directly. In the 1930's appeared a new note of social content: figures of ordinary men, shabby and humble. With no overt social message, there was a clear preoccupation with the lot of the forgotten man in those troubled years. The strong organization of

every element, the finely felt relations, the dominant sense of order, showed the same austere integrity; but there was a new fullness of form and a new tonal quality, with pervading silvery grays furnishing a ground in which all the forms were unified.

Raphael Soyer's world is that of humanity in the poorer sections of the city. Sometimes he peoples the drab streets with the derelicts of society, down-and-out men with their anxious, harried faces, their patient resignation. They are shown with complete objectivity; we know where the painter's sympathies lie, but there is no propaganda. In a more cheerful mood, the streets are thronged with working girls, pictured without flattery—thin, sometimes homely, a little hungry looking. Soyer's feeling for character is extremely sensitive and true, capturing all the subtleties of shape and contour that make the person an individual like no one else in the world. His women are seen with intimate understanding, tenderness, and a touch of humor. The magic of light absorbs him, and he uses it with unobtrusive skill to model forms, and to reveal what interests him most —the essential character of the individual human being.

In few other countries were artists so vitally concerned with their native environment as in the United States from 1905 to 1940. Conditions were

Grant Wood. Dinner for Threshers. 1933. Pencil. 17¾ x 26¾. (Right section.)

les Burchfield.   Old House by Creek. 1932–38. Oil. 34½ x 57.

The Subway is fast - *Certainly!*
But *the Open Air Elevated*
gets you there quickly, too
~ and with *more comfort*

Why not use the "L"?

EAST-18

Does the Sex Urge
Explain, Judge
...ter's Strange
...earance

Reginald Marsh.   Why Not Use the "L"? 1930. Egg tempera. 36 x 48.

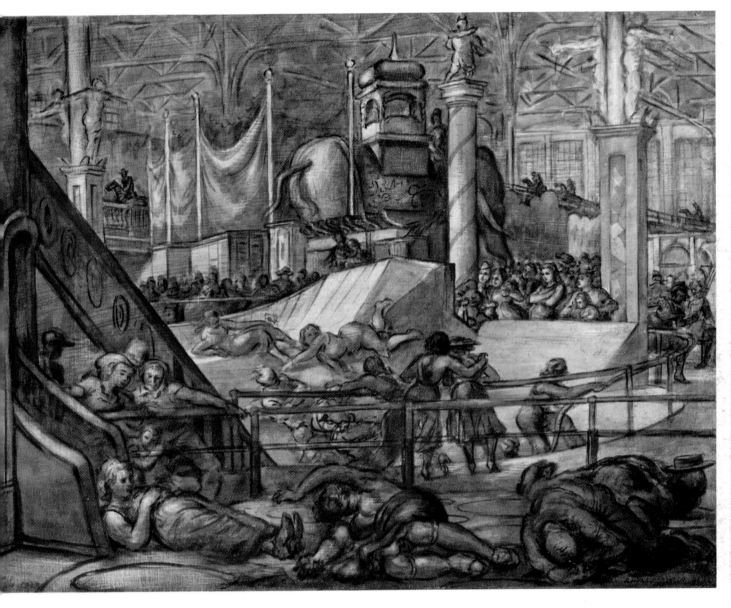

Reginald Marsh. Human Pool Tables. 1938. Egg tempera. 29¾ x 40.

Gift of Mrs. Reginald Marsh and William Benton.

different here from those in older nations: a huge expanding country, enormously vital and diversified, which had been untouched by preceding generations of artists. To the new generation it was an unexplored world, and yet their own—a world to be known, understood, and assimilated into art. This modern America in all its grandeur and disorder, its strength and grotesqueness, was now for the first time observed by artists, by men of visual sensibility, with eyes experienced in the ordered beauty of art. Here was a challenge that did not exist for European artists. Hence the American scene attracted some of our strongest painters, and called forth their full powers.

Quite aside from their artistic achievements, these painters (like the writers who were carrying on a parallel exploration of America) made a solid contribution to our understanding of our own country. They opened our eyes to everything that their predecessors had avoided. They dispelled the old idealistic vision of the United States, and showed us a series of images, more and more revealing, of our country and our people, our land and what we had made of it.

Katherine Schmidt. Broe and McDonald Listen In. 1937. Oil. 30 x 24.

Raphael Soyer. Office Girls. 1936. Oil. 26 x 24.

11 the social school

The twentieth-century artist's relation to the governing forces of society is quite different from his predecessors'. Until the French Revolution, art had a definite social function: to act as pictorial spokesman and historian for royalty, aristocracy, or the church. But the Revolution changed all this. Capitalism and the modern state offer the artist no such system of beliefs, nor such imagery, as did the spiritual and temporal powers of the past. The creative artists of our age have been individualists rather than institutionalists, libertarians rather than authoritarians, interested in human and democratic values more than in championing material power and wealth. For some, socialism in its early Utopian phases had a strong appeal.

The cataclysm of the first World War, and the revolutions and counterrevolutions that followed, shattered the seemingly secure world of before the war. They brought home to artists, as to everyone else, the fact that political and social matters directly affect all of us. The artist's previous unconcern with such questions gave way to a growing social awareness. Modern war, with its mechanization, its increasingly destructive weapons, and its involvement of whole populations, was no longer the heroic hand-to-hand combat celebrated by the old masters, and since World War I most artists have been strongly antimilitarist.

The Depression of the 1930's gave American artists a firsthand realization of the economic ills of society. Even in normal times, painters and sculptors (except a fortunate few) are underprivileged citizens, and in hard times, they are the first to suffer. Widespread hardship among artists in the early 1930's produced a growing trend toward the left. This was intensified by the rise of fascism abroad. Like their fellows in other democracies, American artists were aroused by the Nazis' suppression of artistic freedom and their racial persecutions. These threatening events caused many to look to communism as the hope of mankind, and blinded them to its own brand of repression.

All these developments stimulated efforts to organize for economic security and defense of cultural freedom. In 1933 the Artists' Union was formed, on a trade-union basis, reaching 1,700 members within two years. In the words of its vice-president, Stuart Davis, "the artist recognizes his alignment with those who have not—the workers." The newly established government art projects gave Union members a sense of their social function and needs—and something to fight. There ensued a period of mass meetings, protests, strikes, picketing, and riots such as the art world had never witnessed. In 1936 a broader organization was launched: the American Artists' Congress, "For Peace, Democracy and Cultural Progress," and against "War, Fascism and Reaction, destroyers of art and culture." The Popular Front was endorsed, the expansion of the government projects was demanded, and the regionalist and American scene schools were branded as chauvinist. Though the Congress included individuals of differing viewpoints, its hard core became increasingly Marxist. While fascism was excoriated, the Soviet Union was always supported, even after the Moscow trials and the 1939 treaty with Nazi Germany. But when the Congress upheld the Russian invasion of Finland in 1940, its more intelligent members resigned, and its influence evaporated.

In the trough of the Depression, in 1933, the Roosevelt Administration had started a series of Federal projects employing artists for public work in their own field. While only a minute part of a vast relief operation, the projects were nevertheless the most extensive artist-employment programs ever undertaken by a modern democracy. They broke the conservative monopoly on public art, gave liberals their first opportunities in this field, and replaced academic neoclassicism with a lively interest in American life and history. And they did this while remaining relatively free of either censorship or official propaganda. Many leading artists were enabled to survive as artists, and future leaders

Ben Shahn. The Passion
of Sacco and Vanzetti.
1931–32. Tempera.
84½ x 48.

Gift of Edith and Milton
Lowenthal in memory of
Juliana Force.

were given their first support. While the works produced sometimes suffered from the emergency nature of the program, they also included some of the best public art so far executed. With the end of the projects in the late 1930's, the academic monopoly was reinstated. But in their few years, the projects had done more for contemporary creation than any single agency in our history.

Before the 1930's, political and social comment had been confined to cartoons, and had not been expressed in the so-called fine arts, even in the work of socialists like Sloan. But with the Depression, and the deepening international crisis, appeared the first movement concerned primarily with social themes. Its doctrine was that art must have social content to be valid, and that the mere objective, sensuous, or formal representation of life was meaningless. In practice, social content meant criticism or protest. In orthodox social art, the United States was a land of starvation, injustice, lynchings, and labor massacres—a picture heavily weighted with Marxist clichés. In no other nation did artists say so frankly, loudly, and persistently what was wrong with their country. And many did so while on the Federal payroll—a unique example of democratic freedom of expression. Artistically, the chief external influence was fortunately not the academic naturalism of official Soviet art, but the freer, more vital style of the Mexican revolutionary painters Rivera, Siqueiros, and Orozco, all of whom executed murals in this country.

By the middle 1930's the social school was more dominant than even the rival nativist schools, especially in the large cities. Its influence, it is true, was due as much to propaganda as to its actual products. The Congress was based on economic and political

Isaac Soyer. Employment Agency. 1937. Oil. 34¼ x 45.

beliefs, not on artistic viewpoints; most works in its exhibitions were quite innocuous in subjects, even including some abstractions. Its national chairman, Stuart Davis, never painted an orthodox social picture. The number of primarily social artists was not large, and the majority of their works, as with any topical school, have not stood the test of time.

But the movement also included individual artists who treated social themes with imagination and power. Their veteran was William Gropper, long a radical cartoonist, whose strong convictions gave edge and intensity to his drawings. A more sophisticated artist than most cartoonists, he also presented his ideas in paintings that had the forceful imagery of his graphic work, and an added element of evocative symbolism.

Ben Shahn's art from the first was dedicated to social content, but with complete independence of viewpoint and style. Like liberals of all shades of opinion, he was deeply moved by the execution of the anarchists Sacco and Vanzetti during the Red hunts of the 1920's, after a trial under a biased judge and on questionable evidence. Because of wide protests, a three-man committee headed by President Lowell of Harvard had been appointed, and their adverse report sealed the two men's fate. Shahn commemorated this tragedy in a series of twenty-three gouaches. The large *Passion of Sacco and Vanzetti* combines three of the subjects: the victims, the Lowell committee piously paying its last respects, and the courthouse with a portrait of the judge. The generous, bitter indignation behind the picture makes it one of the most powerful modern indictments of injustice. Its impact is intensified by the absolute directness and clearness of the imagery, and by the strong design with its bold pattern of diagonals.

Philip Evergood's *Lily and the Sparrows* is less a social commentary than many of his pictures, but it has all his sympathy for poverty, and his fantasy. It was based on seeing a little girl in a tenement window, feeding birds; but this actuality has been transformed by the painter's personal alchemy into the haunting inner reality of a dream; the ghostlike face with its strange smile seems suspended in air.

Though the social movement, as a movement,

William Gropper. Farmers' Revolt. 1933. Ink. 16 x 19.

George Grosz. Couple. 1934. Watercolor. 25¼ x 17¾.

could not survive the world events of the late 1930's, it had a permanent influence on American art. It broadened subject matter to include issues vital to everyone; it brought moral convictions into painting and sculpture, and a new boldness of comment and satire; it introduced new elements of imagination and new forms of symbolism. Social content is still an essential ingredient of our art, and has its strong individual exponents. It is no longer the simple propaganda or protest of the 1930's, but an art which uses social material for imaginative ends. The tremendous issues of our troubled time—the remembered horror of the two greatest wars in history, the mounting tensions of our world, the fears for the survival of civilization—are reflected in the work of many artists, though often in disguised forms. They are expressed more or less directly in George Grosz's obsessive memories of the horrors of war, in Robert Gwathmey's sardonic comments on the South and the Negro, in Jack Levine's mordant portraits of our rulers. With other artists, social content has become material for fantasy and symbolism: Shahn's recent parables of the modern world, Evergood's strange visions, Peter Blume's richly inventive allegories. To these artists, the world in which they live, its hopes and fears, its broad human meanings, are essential material out of which to create art. Their work reveals an imaginative content deeper and more complex than that of a generation ago. The social movement, by enlarging the range of content and viewpoint, enriched the art of today.

Ben Shahn. Scotts Run, West Virginia. 1937. Tempera. 22¼ x 27⅞.

Philip Evergood. Lily and the Sparrows. 1939. Oil. 30 x 24.

12 fantasy

Parallel with the revolution in form effected by the modern movements occurred a revolution in imagery. Just as there was a liberation from naturalism in form and design, there was also a liberation from the naturalistic representation of actualities. The objective facts of the external world were transformed by the subjective fantasies of the inner world of the mind. We all know the inexhaustible profusion of imagery which rises to consciousness in dreams and half-waking states—a creative activity of the subconscious mind, without conscious volition. Such imagery, embodying our deepest desires and conflicts, has an affinity to art; as Nietzsche said, in his dreams every man is an artist. This hidden world, drawn on by much great art of the past, had been lost in nineteenth-century naturalism, and its rediscovery has been one of the fundamental achievements of our century.

In Europe the process began almost simultaneously with modernism, and was allied with modern psychology, particularly the exploration of the subconscious through psychoanalysis. Then in 1916 came Dada, product of the disillusion and despair of war and postwar years: an iconoclastic assault on all accepted values. Though primarily destructive, its antirationalism nevertheless sowed seeds for the future. Out of it grew surrealism, a serious, systematic movement using the subconscious as the fundamental source of art.

One root of Dada had originated about 1915 in New York, where Marcel Duchamp and Francis Picabia lived during the war, and where together with the American Man Ray they launched a proto-Dada movement. But Dada remained an exotic; the United States was not as shattered by the war as Europe, nor did we have the burden of a great artistic past to revolt against. Similarly, surrealism, founded in Paris in 1924, did not become acclimated here until several of its European leaders arrived in the late 1930's.

But long before that, spontaneous native manifestations of the trend toward free imagery had appeared. These Americans were not connected with the highly organized movements of Dada and surrealism; they were individuals, unconnected even with one another. They had neither Dada's destructive motivations nor surrealism's link with psychoanalysis; they were responding to the general spirit of the time. There was Eilshemius, with his naïve fantasies, first idyllic, then tragic. There were Charles Burchfield's watercolors of 1916 to 1918. There was Ivan Le Lorraine Albright, who by the middle 1920's was creating his compelling images of age and dissolution, with their intense macabre realism. There was Yasuo Kuniyoshi, whose work from 1921 on revealed an instinctive fantasy, basically Oriental in its fascination with all forms of organic life, down to the most minute—human beings and cows, snakes and birds, weeds and flowers—pictured in free, dreamlike associations, and with clear sexual symbolism.

Equally individualist, Edwin Dickinson presents the phenomenon of a highly skilled traditionalist whose subject matter is far removed from academic conventions: a visionary world of ambiguous figures and objects. He avoids verbal explanations, but of *The Fossil Hunters* he has said that it resulted from his interest in certain fossils he had himself found. This motif seems revealed in the whole concept: figures lying on rocks in trancelike sleep, beneath folds of drapery partly pulled back to disclose them, and enshrouded in darkness pierced by dim light as in a cave. The sense of immobility and silence, of a buried world, is intensified by the deep night colors. But under the subdued light the forms are completely clear, painted with sure command, sculptural largeness, and rich substance. Building his pictures slowly, Dickinson has produced only a few on the scale of *The Fossil Hunters*, which took a hundred and ninety-two sessions extending over two years.

Edwin Dickinson. The Fossil Hunters. 1926–28. Oil. 96½ x 73¾.

Yasuo Kuniyoshi.   Sleeping Beauty. 1924. Ink and pencil. 14 x 19¾.

Gift of Mrs. Edith Gregor Halpert.

Franklin C. Watkins.   Soliloquy. 1932. Oil. 25¼ x 30¼.

In the early work of Franklin Watkins, fantasy expressed itself in wild romantic themes filled with picturesque action, or, as in *Soliloquy,* in moods of Byronic introspection. But fantasy was also inherent in the forms themselves, with their flamboyant movements and skillful distortions, recalling his admiration for El Greco. Later this imaginative vein was combined with characterful portraiture, among the finest of our period—searching, sympathetic, yet completely without flattery.

In his evolution from early expressionism toward his present abstract style, Morris Kantor about 1930 passed through a phase of modified individual surrealism, using double images—one image superimposed over another, or rooms seen from both inside and outside. These devices were entirely personal, creating an evocative poetry, a haunting sense of mystery.

Though closer to surrealism than almost any other American-trained painter, Peter Blume has never belonged to the movement; his whole approach is conscious and rational. His paintings are elaborate allegories, logically conceived, complex in imagery, and executed with the precision and detail of the fifteenth-century Italian and Flemish masters he admires. While his vision is completely

Peter Blume.   Light of the World. 1932. Oil. 18 x 20¼.

Morris Kantor. Skyrocket. 1933. Oil. 28 x 24.

realistic, his combination of elements is fantastic—a distortion not of things themselves but of their relations to one another and to their setting. Yet these apparently incongruous figures and objects are seen on closer study to have clear underlying connections. *Light of the World* embodies the concept of the museum as a light. The lantern at which the actors are gazing is the lens of a lighthouse—to be exact, Highland Light on Cape Cod. As the artist said to James Thrall Soby, "You got the feeling of being inside a huge glittering eye radiating all the colors of the rainbow." Most of the other elements are objects actually in the Metropolitan Museum. The lantern is a flower whose stem is an obelisk, with leaves formed by specimens of architectural cornices. On the base stands the Museum's model of the apparatus used to erect "Cleopatra's Needle"

in Central Park; in the background is the Museum's model of Notre Dame. All these objects are incorporated into a pictorial structure that is unified and satisfying. Blume's paintings, conceived with infinite care, often take years to complete. But beneath their meticulousness is a vital energy that has become more pronounced with each work. He cares nothing about current fashions, and his naturalistic style and startling color make no concessions.

The freeing of imagery in our century has been a basic revolution. It has restored fantasy to the role it occupied in the great art of the past; it has opened up the storehouse of myth and legend, and the collective imagination of mankind; it has replaced the worn-out symbolism of neoclassicism with living symbols, revitalized by their relation to the actuality of the human mind.

3 the trend toward abstraction

Arthur G. Dove.   Ferry Boat Wreck. 1931. Oil. 18 x 30.

Gift of Mr. and Mrs. Roy R. Neuberger (and purchase).

The first American abstract movement had lasted only about a decade. From about 1920 until the early 1930's, little abstract art was produced in the United States. The dominant schools—regionalism, the American scene, the social painters—were not only representational but concerned almost entirely with native subject matter. But abstract art, like music, is an international language, without references to specific content or place. The cultural nationalism of the 1920's was hostile to it, as was the insistence on social content. Its few adherents were like members of an underground movement.

Of its pioneers, only Dove in this country and Bruce in France remained faithful. But a few of their fellow modernists turned toward abstraction about 1930. Alfred Maurer in his last few years experimented with geometric patterns. Another early fauve, Arthur B. Carles, who had evolved a decorative art of still life and flowers, transformed the same motifs into luxuriant fauvist abstractions. Carles loved full-blooded color and the sensuous pleasure of handling paint, and his exuberant chromatic compositions were rich in pigment and spontaneous brushwork.

Of a younger generation, Stuart Davis developed his strong individual art without early foreign experience. As a student of Henri he had seen the Armory Show—"the greatest single influence I have experienced in my work." After a post-impressionistic phase, he began in the 1920's to geometrize objects into massive forms suggesting Picasso and Léger. But Davis was always his own man—vital, positive, humorous, with a grasp of the tangible realities of the contemporary United States. His innate plastic sense matured by independent thinking and experiment. He has recorded that in 1927 "I nailed an electric fan, a rubber glove and an eggbeater to a table and used them as my exclusive subject matter for a year." The result was his "eggbeater series" of nonrepresentational geometric paintings. The actual objects were a starting point for a year's concentration on forms and colors, their design, and their relation to the flat plane of the canvas. What was remarkable was the sureness and completeness of the compositions. The series foretold his future direction—design founded on actualities. "Everything I have done since has been based on that eggbeater idea," he has said. When he went to Paris the next year he turned again to representation, as in *Place Pasdeloup,* but with a new sense of the unity of planes, colors, and calligraphy.

There were few other exponents of abstract art until the early 1930's. But then the tide began to turn. Nationalism was broadening into internationalism. In Europe, abstraction had never gone into eclipse. More than a generation had passed since it began, and it was now far more widely practiced and diversified, with its creeds more fully formulated. Its historical inevitability as an original expression of the twentieth century had been accepted. And it was now reaching the United States in ever-increasing volume, by way of exhibitions and publications. A younger generation was now ready for it.

All this was reinforced by the arrival of several prominent Europeans, mostly from Germany, where the Nazis were suppressing all modern art. Even before that, in 1931, Hans Hofmann, who for years had conducted a school in Munich, settled here and soon had new schools in New York and Provincetown, becoming one of the country's most influential teachers. The Bauhaus at Dessau had been the greatest European center for the teaching of advanced art and design. Its principles were rational and functional, encouraging clarity and precision, and the geometric style. After it was closed by the Nazis in 1933 many of its leading figures found their way to America. Josef Albers came that

year, to teach, and to continue his nonobjective painting. Feininger returned in 1937. László Moholy-Nagy had been a moving spirit of the Bauhaus—painter, constructivist, designer, theorist, and originator of radical new teaching methods. Arriving here in 1937, he established a transatlantic successor to the Bauhaus in Chicago; and in his own work created some of his most completely realized paintings and constructions, demonstrating his lucid concepts of design and his imaginative use of materials, old and new. Fritz Glarner, not of the Bauhaus but of the related tradition of De Stijl, came in 1936.

By early 1935 the resurgence of abstraction was apparent enough to lead the Whitney Museum to stage an exhibition of "Abstract Painting in America"—a term rather liberally interpreted to include the semi-abstract. Next year came the founding of the American Abstract Artists, with forty members. Almost all were pure abstractionists, rejecting representation and imagery, aiming at art which should exist in purely plastic terms—by the physical materials of which it was composed, their properties of shape, color, and texture, and the designs created out of these elements. These artists' belief in the creed of abstraction had an almost religious fervor—and their corresponding scorn of representational art. In opposition to the social school, they saw no necessity for social content, or indeed for any relation to society as a whole. Their attitude can be seen as also a reaction from the disturbed state of the world—but in the opposite direction. In pure plastic creation they were building an aesthetic order independent of outer chaos—one of the artist's immemorial functions.

Curiously enough in view of later developments, many of them (perhaps the majority) were working in geometric styles, consciously planned, precise, sharp edged, severely rectilinear or with geometric curves. The painters concentrated on the flat surface of the picture, avoiding attempts to create sensations of deep space or of form in the round. Their nearest approach to the third dimension was design in superimposed flat planes. A number were constructivists, using actual three-dimensional materials.

This prevalence of geometric style in the 1930's

Stuart Davis.   Place Pasdeloup. 1928. Oil. 36¼ x 28¾.

Stuart Davis. Egg Beater, Number 2. 1927. Oil. 29⅛ x 36.

can be ascribed to several factors. The style was logical, clear, direct. Its purity was unquestionable; any more three-dimensional quality, or more complex, irregular forms, would have brought suggestions of imagery. And the style was related to the modern world, and specifically to the machine age. The dominant nationalist and social schools had not been concerned with the aesthetics of the machine, as were the precisionists, the constructivists, and the Bauhaus. Geometric abstraction, though not using mechanical motifs, was in harmony with the functionalism, precision, and impersonality of the machine. In this it resembled the severity of

functional architecture. Except for its abstract language, it bore much the same relation to the modern United States that precisionism had.

The style cannot be attributed to any particular influence. There were the Bauhaus artists, and Hans Hofmann, whose expressionism had a geometric foundation; and there were general international influences, of which the strongest were cubism, constructivism, and De Stijl. But none of these entirely accounts for the prevalence and the characteristics of American geometric abstraction at this time. It was evidently the expression of one aspect of the American mind, as precisionism had been. In these years it seemed that a characteristically American variation of formal abstraction was in the making.

A leader of the tendency, and its chief spokesman, was George L. K. Morris, who had studied with Léger in 1930, and had evolved a strong, clear-cut style with more three-dimensional quality than most, thoughtful in design and solid in substance. Other early members of the school who have since remained consistent were Burgoyne Diller, Carl Holty, and Ilya Bolotowsky. I. Rice Pereira in 1937 began her rectangular compositions with their fine feeling for spatial relations. A number of others who have since gone on to other modes were then working geometrically: Balcomb Greene, John Ferren, Byron Browne, and Ad Reinhardt, whose inventive forms were more complex than his present austere style.

Simultaneously, an opposite abstract tendency was making its appearance—free-form abstraction. Its origins could be traced back to early Kandinsky and the *Blaue Reiter* group, with their expression of subjective emotion, emphasis on color, and freedom and variety of forms. Another source was the protean genius of Picasso, with his synthesis of imagery and abstract language. Surrealism also was

Arthur B. Carles.   Bouquet Abstraction. c. 1930. Oil. 31¾ x 36.

Arshile Gorky. The Artist and His Mother. 1926–29. Oil. 60 x 50.

Gift of Julien Levy for Maro and Natasha Gorky in memory of their father.

Arshile Gorky.   Painting. 1936–37. Oil. 38 x 48.

making its contribution. An element of fantastic imagery, often transformed beyond recognition, was being assimilated into abstraction, freeing it from sterile purism, diversifying and enriching it, not only in associative values but on the level of pure form.

The American pioneer of this tendency was Arshile Gorky. An ardent student of the masters, past and present, he went through successive modern influences, from Cézanne to Miro, but he was no mere imitator; his nature was instinctive and sensual, with a passion for colors and forms. His retrospective portrait of himself and his mother, based on childhood memories, was still representational, but with an undertone of fantasy in its trancelike mood. Its monumentality shows his admiration for Ingres and the neoclassic phases of Picasso, but the character of the forms—flowing, sinuous, yet sure and powerful—is essentially the same as in his abstract work of twenty years later. In the late 1920's he embarked on abstractions, at first cubistic, then increasingly free in form and rich in symbolism. In *Painting* the influence of Picasso's recent work was obvious, but as always with Gorky, external influences were transformed into plastic creation. Thenceforth his individuality was to reveal itself progressively, in sumptuous color, strong linear design, and prodigal inventiveness of form. Gorky's fusion of surrealist imagery and highly developed abstract design was prophetic of the advanced tendencies of the 1940's.

A few others were combining surrealism and abstraction—such as Gorky's friend Willem de Kooning, who was varying his figurative work by occasional abstractions. Abroad, Charles Howard, associated with the British surrealists, was creating precise abstract compositions strangely suggestive of organic life. Bradley Walker Tomlin about 1939 turned from decorative still life to cubistic patterns with illusive images superimposed, pervaded by a melancholy poetry, and painted with sensitive, fastidious artistry. This phase, lasting about five years, was to be succeeded by the bold pure abstract style which made Tomlin one of the chief figures of abstract expressionism in the 1940's.

As the 1930's ended, a few other future leaders of abstract expressionism were painting abstractly: Clyfford Still, extreme individualist, who had done so for some years; and Jackson Pollock and William Baziotes, still tentatively. But most of the others were working in styles more or less representational, and were not to develop their fully abstract language until the middle 1940's.

Thus the 1930's had opened up two main paths

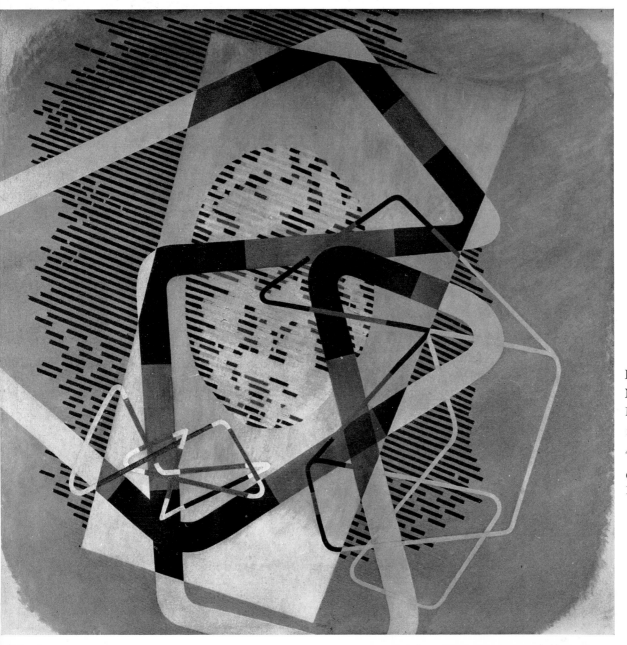

László Moholy-Nagy. Space Modulator. 1938–40. Oil. 47 x 47.

Gift of Mrs. Sibyl Moholy-Nagy.

George L. K. Morris. Nautical Composition. 1937/42. Oil. 51 x 35.

Bradley Walker Tomlin. Still Life. 1939. Oil. 34 x 46.

for abstract art: formal and free form. At the close of the decade, the future direction was not yet plain. The first path was being followed by many artists, with impressive results. Today it still includes many distinguished figures, and there are signs that it may assume a greater importance in the future. But the second path is the one that has been taken by a large majority of the *avant-garde* since 1940. Just as representational expressionism had been the main road for the first generation of modernists, abstract expressionism was to be for the generation of advanced artists who came to maturity in the 1940's. Like the older trend, its emotional expressiveness and freedom of form have responded to fundamental qualities in the American spirit.

part two

1940–1960

BY JOHN I. H. BAUR

4 romantic realism

What determines the creative life span of a style is one of the mysteries of art. Romantic realism, long a powerful movement in American painting, has unquestionably waned since 1940. It has never disappeared, and some of its finest examples are recent ones, but it is significant that most of the paintings reproduced here are by artists now dead or well past their middle years. Few younger painters have chosen to join them, and many older men who once belonged in their ranks have moved in other directions.

Perhaps one cause of this numerical decline has been the tendency of romantic realism to lose its true bearing. At its best, it is a form of realism modified to express a romantic attitude or meaning, but it has often escaped into what is just "good painting"—the sensuous manipulation of paint and painterly effects in a display of technical virtuosity. This preoccupation with method can be exciting and even creative in the youth of a movement, when its pioneers are forging a new vocabulary. But, once established, the vocabulary cannot be endlessly repeated for its own sake without deteriorating into mannerism; it must be used to say something. The only alternative is so to alter it that it again becomes a truly new method of expression, a new formal exploration. And this generally, but not always, leads the artist beyond the boundaries of the movement. The paintings illustrated by Karl Zerbe and Franklin Watkins might stand as examples here: The extraordinary textural treatment in the former,

the free distortions and arbitrary color in the latter, give these works their principal interest, though they also raise the question of whether they properly belong in this chapter.

The main line of romantic realism lies in an opposite direction. Nearly all the good romantic realists working today long ago established the structure of their vocabulary and are using it to express their deeper, more mature perceptions. They are linked not so much by their persistent devotion to realism in the face of opposing trends; they are more truly linked by the fact that they have something to say about the meaning of life, and that they speak their messages with conviction. Realism is important to them, for they deal with specific situations in the drama of man and nature, which only realism can adequately portray. But a realistic style per se is not their end and is therefore not sacrosanct. Several of them have become noticeably freer in technique as they have matured, using limited distortions where they need them and even semi-abstract passages, like the pattern of Burchfield's sky and branches or the floating design of Marsh's "El" structure. In other words, their formal means, though not altering radically, have continued to grow primarily in response to expressive needs.

What these artists have to say differs widely from man to man, but in general they fall into two groups: those who deal with subjective moods and those who are more concerned with the interpretation of events about them. Needless to say, these are arbitrary and overlapping categories, for the subjective moods of the first group are generally related to objective experiences, while the interpretation of objective events by the second group is necessarily a subjective activity. It is a matter of emphasis, and the same artist may, in different pictures, move toward one side or the other of the equation.

It is no accident, however, that the word "mood" occurs in the titles of two paintings reproduced (by Alexander Brook and Charles Burchfield), and it might equally well be applied to the canvases by Edward Hopper and Henry Mattson. Nowhere is the interrelation of nature and personal mood more plainly documented than in the passages in Charles Burchfield's journals that describe how *An April Mood* came to be painted. From these it is clear that the concept of a bleak landscape expressive of "the anger of God—a Good Friday mood" long preceded the discovery of an actual landscape which could serve as its vehicle. It was an actual landscape (near Boston, New York) which he painted, but the final picture took nine years to complete, largely because he worked on it only in the spring and only

Franklin C. Watkins. The Sideboard. 1941. Oil. 30½ x 36¼.

Karl Zerbe. Harlequin. 1943. Encaustic. 44 x 34.

Charles Burchfield.   An April Mood. 1946/55. Watercolor. 40 x 54.

Gift of Mr. and Mrs. Lawrence A. Fleischman (and purchase).

when the original mood again compelled him to do so. The heavy, almost expressionist distortions and the somber colors are a direct result of this concentration on a subjective theme.

Not all paintings of mood are so intimately tied to a specific place; Hopper and Mattson work today largely from memory, and their images are usually composite ones. Nevertheless, these images bear a strong stamp of actuality—Hopper's to an extraordinary degree. And just as Burchfield dealt with a particular season (indeed was unable to paint on his picture at any other time of year), so Mattson and Hopper have chosen specific times of day: a moonlit evening, exactly seven o'clock in the morning, a brilliant summer noon. This sense of objective reality is important, because the true magic of these artists is to reveal unexpected meanings in the shared and even commonplace sights about us. Hopper's painting is not only an evocation of light and heat and the uncompromising solidity of objects; it is also filled with a piercing loneliness, a hush, a sense of suspended and eternal time: what we have so

Henry Mattson.   Eventide. c. 1946. Oil. 27 x 36.

often seen takes on the aspect of a miracle. In a more overtly romantic spirit, Mattson opposes enduring rock and the vastness of sea in a drama that has always dwarfed and awed mankind and still manages to do so without becoming a cliché, because it is so humbly and so deeply felt. Equally romantic in another vein is the half-sensuous, half-poignant mood of Brook's frail model, painted with a caressing tenderness.

Perhaps the difference between these highly subjective pictures and those which seem to interpret more objective experiences can best be realized by comparing Brook's canvas with Moses Soyer's *Girl in Orange Sweater*. Both have posed a model half-length before a perfectly plain background and have painted her with equal tenderness. But Soyer has given us the portrait of an individual, with clearly delineated characteristics of her own, whereas Brook has deliberately obscured individuality to underline his personal response. The contrast is even greater with Edmund Archer's ruggedly objective portrayal of a basketball player. One must not, however, overemphasize these differences. Raphael Soyer's *The Brown Sweater* is a gallery of real people caught in characteristic poses and actions and at the same time an expression of the artist's love of these tenement dwellers—a love that fills all his work with a compassionate and gently melancholy mood. Reginald Marsh was plainly fascinated with the raffish types of the Bowery and painted them with a nearly impersonal keenness of observation. But he simultaneously transformed his squalid setting into an image of baroque mystery and splendor, while his people take on heroic proportions as they enact their cryptic dramas. This transformation has nothing to do with observation; it is achieved by masterly draftsmanship, by exaggerations of form and perspective, and by a deliberate manipulation of light and shade. It is both Marsh's personal vision and his alliance with the great romantic tradition of Callot and Piranesi.

In the work of all these artists, romantic realism has contributed richly to our painting of the last twenty years. But Marsh is no longer living, Watkins and Zerbe have moved in other directions, and most of the rest are well past mid-career. A few younger painters, such as Marvin Cherney and Ben Kamihira, are carrying forward the tradition, but whether it will continue to be a major element in our art remains uncertain.

OPPOSITE:
Edward Hopper. Seven A.M. 1948. Oil. 30 x 40.

BELOW:
Edward Hopper. Second-Story Sunlight. 1960. Oil. 40 x 50.

ABOVE:

Moses Soyer.   Girl in Orange Sweater. 1953. Oil.
30 x 24.

BELOW:

Alexander Brook.   Mood. 1947. Oil. 25 x 20.

Edmund Archer.   Howard Patterson of the "Harlem Yankees." 1940.
Oil. 34⅛ x 29⅛.

Reginald Marsh. White Tower Hamburger. 1945. Ink. 26¼ x 39¾.

Anonymous gift.

Raphael Soyer.   The Brown Sweater. 1952. Oil. 50 x 34.

Ben Kamihira.   The Couch. 1960. Oil. 63 x 79¼.

Sumner Foundation Purchase Award.

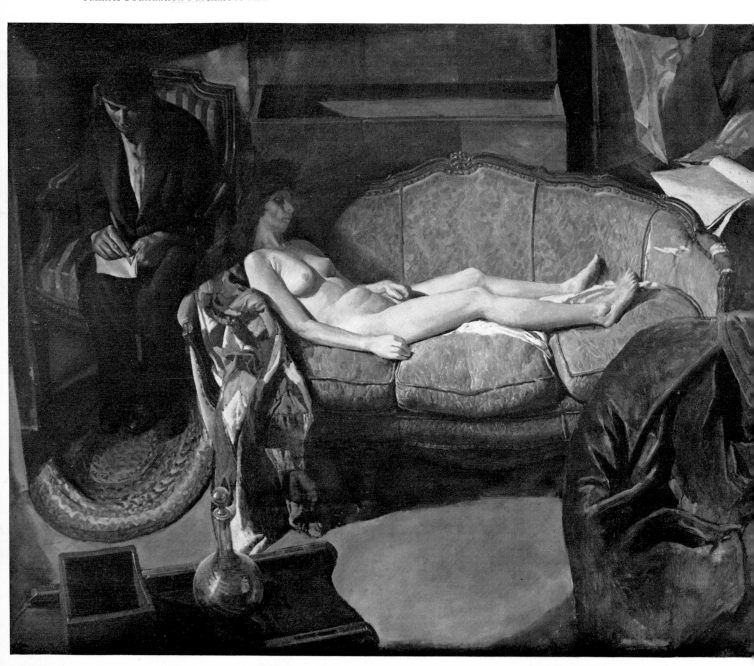

15 traditional sculpture

Traditionalism in sculpture has a double meaning, and because of this it has exerted a double force. In a formal sense, sculpture has a long tradition of dealing, either classically or romantically, with the human body or other living creatures. In a technical sense, sculpture has an equally long tradition of being either carved or modeled, a solid, three-dimensional object created by subtraction or addition, that is, by hewing away or building up form. The technical tradition has had a strong and lasting influence on the formal one and has proved both a limitation and a strength. Its limitations provoked the modernists' rebellion, but its strength has been a major factor in preserving the creative vigor of traditional sculpture through recent years.

The truth is that traditional techniques yield "sculptural" qualities which cannot be realized in any other way. The warm Botticini marble William Zorach uses in *The Future Generation,* the veined green serpentine of Koren Der Harootian's *Eagles of Ararat,* have an intrinsic beauty of their own which both artists have utilized in contrasting passages of rough and polished surfaces. The hewn look, the mark of chisel and point, the solidity, the sense of form emerging from the virgin stone, are all important parts of the aesthetic effect. Such works are rich in tactile values; they demand to be touched; they partake of the quality of precious objects. The hammered metal figures of José de Creeft and Saul Baizerman fall, technically speaking, about halfway between the restrictions of carving and the somewhat freer possibilities of modeling, and here, too, the materials and methods play important aesthetic roles. The dull fire of copper and the peculiarly luminous sheen of lead contribute much to the life of these pieces, while the hammered surfaces break and reflect light with an almost impressionist vivacity.

All these pieces are "realistic" in a sense, but the realism is strongly modified by the technical factors discussed above and, even more importantly, by the formal traditions with which the artists have allied themselves. Traditional sculpture is one of the few fields in which a genuine classicism still exists today. This has nothing to do with technique, for we find

William Zorach. The Future Generation. 1942–47. Botticini marble. 40 high.

it in the metal work of Baizerman just as strongly as in the carved work of Zorach. The marks of the classical approach are the flowing contours, the simple volumes harmoniously related, the poised and balanced compositions. They are the reflection of a rational attitude, creating an art not devoid of sensuousness, but measured, controlled, and tranquil. The difference between true classicism and the mannered imitation of Greek sculpture, which is the stock in trade of so many academic artists, lies in this inner spirit rather than in any formula of proportions.

The romantic approach is diametrically opposed. Contours are suppressed, planes blend into each other, asymmetry and motion replace static balance, light and shadow flash over the surface with an independent life of their own. Here, again, technique is not a controlling factor. Der Harootian's eagles sweep upward in a convoluted diagonal, but De Creeft's *Himalaya* is equally, if more subtly, asymmetrical. And the pitted stone, deeply undercut, of the first has its parallel in the active, mobile surface of the lead. The romantic spirit underlying these pieces is an elevation of feeling over mind, producing an art of drama rather than repose, of change and suggestion rather than final statement.

As long as sculptural qualities are valued—in the traditional technical sense of the term—it seems likely that artists will continue to express the two poles of man's nature by carving or building images of his form.

Koren Der Harootian.   Eagles of Ararat. 1955–56. Serpentine marble. 58 high.

José de Creeft.   Himalaya. 1942.
Beaten lead. 34½ high.

Dorothea Greenbaum. Drowned Girl. 1950.
Tennessee marble. 9 x 9½.

Saul Baizerman. Slumber. 1948. Hammered
copper. 40 long.

16 precise realism

Charles Sheeler.   Architectural Cadences. 1954. Oil. 25 x 35.

While romantic realism has waned since 1940, a new kind of extreme realism, hard surfaced and almost microscopic in detail, has grown steadily during the same years. Although it is not, perhaps, any more extreme than our *trompe-l'oeil* (or fool-the-eye) painting of the late nineteenth century, it truly deserves the term "new" because it is so different in feeling and character. It is not based on the pleasure of illusion for its own sake, it usually deals with a wider and more controversial range of subjects than still life, and it is primarily analytical rather than visual in character. It is more like a magnifying glass than a mirror.

Historically, the new realism had its source in two earlier movements. One of these, the painting of the precisionists, tended during the 1930's to lose some of its abstract qualities and to move toward a more detailed precision. Several of its founders, including Charles Sheeler and Niles Spencer, have painted into the present period, and although their work has always been more simplified in form and more abstract in design than that of the other realists, their influence has been felt in the architectural settings of younger painters like George Tooker and Robert Vickrey. It must be admitted that Sheeler himself, in late pictures like *Architectural Cadences*, virtually escapes from the realist camp altogether by his deliberate counterpoint of shadow and substance, which creates a floating, mirage-like image, poetic and insubstantial.

The other, and perhaps more influential, source of the new realism was the precise vein of American-scene painting inaugurated by Grant Wood in his *American Gothic* of 1930 (Art Institute of Chicago). And just as Wood alternately affirmed and denied that his picture was satirical, so, too, many of the later realists occupy a rather ambiguous position between objective statement and satirical intent. This is particularly true of Paul Cadmus, long a leading and controversial figure in the movement. To many, Cadmus' paintings, such as his *Fantasia on a Theme by Dr. S.,* seem to spring from a purely erotic fascination with certain sexual mores; to others, they are social satire of a brilliant and incisive kind. What-

Niles Spencer.   Apartment Tower. 1944. Oil. 32 x 24.

Gift of Mr. and Mrs. Alan H. Temple.

Paul Cadmus.   Fantasia on a Theme by Dr. S. 1946. Egg tempera. 13 x 13.

George Tooker.   The Subway. 1950. Egg tempera. 18⅛ x 36⅛.

Juliana Force Purchase.

ever one's interpretation, there can be no question about the artist's extraordinary technical facility, his skillful if sometimes eclectic sense of design (often reminiscent of early Renaissance art), and his uncanny ability to marshal keenly observed details to shocking effect.

Since 1940, a growing number of younger painters have explored somewhat the same field of social comment as Cadmus, though often with quite different emphasis and results. George Tooker is one of the ablest, both technically and in his imaginative use of realism. His haunted picture, *The Subway,* with its suggestion of multiple-mirrored perspective, is frighteningly real and, at the same time, pure hallucination. Henry Koerner, during the few years that he painted in this vein, also played freely with rearranged segments of reality, as in his *Vanity Fair,* which symbolizes man's social relations at various levels of civilization. Here the satirical implications seem more clearly defined, though they exist in the contrasting elements of the theme itself rather than in any caricatural handling. Like Cadmus, Koerner makes knowing use of historical formulas in perspective and design—usually Flemish or medieval.

The mechanism of the precisionists and the bru-

tality of Cadmus gave the new realism a tradition of hard objectivity not unlike that of the *Neue Sachlichkeit* movement in Germany. But it has also been transformed by other artists into a more romantic and poetic instrument, often charged with mystery or fantasy—a direction sometimes called magic realism. The difference in feeling is strikingly apparent if one compares Walter Murch's *Governor, II,* for instance, with the austerely functional turbines or locomotive drive-wheels Sheeler was painting in the late 1930's. Murch's machine is not only more freely rendered, with softly glowing highlights and edges that fade imperceptibly into the background; it has also taken on a mysterious character quite unrelated to its function. It looks like a living creature or a strange jumping jack animated by an unseen force —an effect heightened by the fact that the weights are not at rest against the crossbar, as they should be. The enigma is further compounded by the little ball, certainly no part of the governor, which reposes illogically on the lower gear. Where Sheeler was moved by the precision and impersonal power of the machine, Murch endowed it with imprecision (nothing is quite symmetrical) and with a cryptic personality of its own.

The same aura of mystery in commonplace ob-

Henry Koerner.   Vanity Fair. 1946. Oil. 36 x 42.

Walter Murch.   Governor, II. 1952. Oil. 40⅜ x 17¾.

Wildenstein Benefit Purchase Fund.

jects has been achieved by Carlyle Brown in his many still lifes, such as *The Red Cabinet*. Here, as in Murch's work, analytical realism has been tempered by a use of light and a quality of touch which combine to transform things. Brown has also shown an obsessive fascination with the shapes and textures of certain objects, particularly glasses and bottles, which he tends to repeat in such profusion that they lose their functional significance and exert a hypnotic effect, like a word said over and over. His painting itself is not unlike glass in its combination of fragility and strength; the evanescent lightness of his objects seems miraculously to withstand the violent pattern of shadows which cuts across them. Close to Brown in delicacy of handling is another young artist, Bernard Perlin, who has pushed realism of detail further than any artist since the pre-Raphaelites. The infinite patience and care with which every leaf and stem is painted in the background of *The Jacket* is an extraordinary technical achievement, but more significant is the way in which this mass of detail has been unified in a shifting pattern of light and dark and used as a luminous foil to the crumpled, shapeless coat. The poetic implications are many.

Finally, the new realism has, in the hands of several artists, been used for purely symbolic purposes, although the symbolism is often obscure. *The Rope* by Jared French and Robert Vickrey's *The Labyrinth,* completely unlike in other respects, both have the air of being enigmatic comments on the human condition. French was closely associated with Cadmus in the founding of the extreme realist movement and has dealt with a similar range of themes, but he has tended to do so on a more symbolic level, avoiding Cadmus' wealth of topical and explicit detail and sometimes approaching surrealism in the hallucinatory nature of his images. He also differs from Cadmus in the hieratic simplification of his figures, which remotely suggest the frozen action of Greek vase painting. Vickrey is a younger artist, not uninfluenced by abstract art in

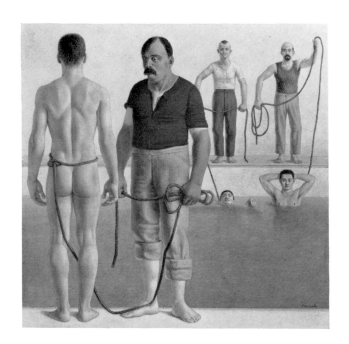

Jared French.   The Rope. 1954. Egg tempera. 13½ x 14¼.

Charles F. Williams Fund.

Bernard Perlin.   The Jacket. 1951.
Casein tempera. 28¼ x 19¾.

Wildenstein Benefit Purchase Fund.

many of his designs and obsessed with certain themes which he has repeated in numerous variations—the nun, the wall, and the poster. While he disclaims any literary intent in these pictures, the juxtaposition of cloistered figures and enclosing walls with great vistas of menacing space inevitably suggests symbolic connotations.

A much more precise symbolism fills the work Stephen Greene did during the late 1940's, particularly in the series devoted to crippled figures, of which *The Burial* is one. Deeply preoccupied with the moral and emotional nature of man, seeing him in the tragic light of the Old Testament, Greene was, in his own words, "concerned with man's final isolation, man suffering not so much for others but for himself and his own sense of incompleteness." The maimed body became the symbol of the maimed spirit, painted with the sparse simplicity he had learned from fifteenth-century German and Italian art.

The boundaries of the new realism are wide to encompass artists as diverse as these, not to mention such others as Ivan Albright and Andrew Wyeth. Their common ground is a notable lack of interest in illusionism for its own sake but a need to express themselves in the most precise imagery.

Robert Vickrey. The Labyrinth. 1951. Casein. 32 x 48.

Juliana Force Purchase.

145

Carlyle Brown. The Red Cabinet. 1954. Oil. 50¾ x 36¾.

Stephen Greene. The Burial. 1947. Oil. 42 x 55.

17 fantasy and surrealism

Surrealism, born in Paris in 1924, was defined by its founder, André Breton, as "pure psychic automatism, by which it is intended to express, verbally, in writing or by other means, the real process of thought. It is thought's dictation, all exercise of reason and every aesthetic or moral preoccupation being absent." It is apparent that surrealism is less a style than it is a program and a method. Its program is a serious search for the material of art in the subconscious mind, in dreams and hallucinations, in the irrational and atavistic layers of being. Its method is the most spontaneous possible transference of the images uncovered to canvas without consideration of form or design (automatism). Surrealism is an artistic parallel to Freud's researches, though on an intuitive rather than analytical level.

Surrealism did not reach America until the early 1930's, and its orthodox followers on this side of the Atlantic have never been numerous. Nevertheless, its influence here has been pervasive, not only on the painters of fantasy discussed in this chapter, but also on many realists and expressionists, who have made use of its irrational juxtapositions, and on the founders of our abstract-expressionist movement, who adopted its theory of automatism. Surrealism has, in short, been an important fructifying force in our mid-century art without ever becoming a very widespread movement in itself.

In Paris, the expatriate American Man Ray was an early adherent to surrealism, while in this country, Joseph Cornell and Federico Castellón were among its first followers. Castellón's *The Dark Fig-ure,* done in 1938, is an orthodox example of the "realist" phase of the movement, already exploited by Salvador Dali (who arrived in America the same year). Despite its dismemberments and its gruesome distortions of shape, proportion, and texture, Castellón's picture deals with recognizable things and figures, painted with the utmost faithfulness—a method which heightens the sense of vivid hallucination. Its irrationality need hardly be pointed out; it is of the same order that the Comte de Lautréamont (patron saint of the surrealists) had in mind when he wrote "beautiful as the chance encounter of a sewing machine and an umbrella on a dissecting table."

The movement gained impetus with the outbreak of World War II, which brought a number of European surrealists to America for asylum: Yves Tanguy, Kurt Seligmann, and Matta in 1939, Max Ernst in 1941. Of these, the first two made their homes here since, and contributed their very different and personal interpretations of surrealism to American art. Seligmann's painting is rooted in an extraordinary fusion of present and past, the spontaneous fantasy of the moment enriched by his memories of fantastic elements in earlier art, particularly the baroque. Of *The Balcony, I* he wrote: "The impulse to this painting was given when visitors gathered on the terrace of my studio in Sugar Loaf. Seen from below, the upper part of their bodies appeared as silhouettes against the sky, reminding me of the various 'balcony scenes' of the masters of the past, of certain statues on churches in

Federico Castellón.
The Dark Figure.
1938. Oil. 17 x 26⅛.

Kurt Seligmann.   The Balcony, I. 1949–50. Oil. 33 x 48.

Yves Tanguy.   Fear. 1949. Oil. 60 x 40.

Kay Sage.   No Passing. 1954. Oil. 51¼ x 38.

Louis Guglielmi.   Terror in Brooklyn. 1941. Oil. 34 x 30.

Italy, especially of San Michele in Lucca." Like baroque sculpture, his compositions have a theatrical quality, although the grand gesture seems often tempered by irony. The fantasy is that of a superb prestidigitator rather than of an obsessed mind.

Tanguy was more truly the surrealist in the unpremeditated nature of his imagery. He told James Thrall Soby (*Yves Tanguy,* Museum of Modern Art, 1955): "I found that if I planned a picture beforehand, it never surprised me, and surprises are my pleasure in painting." His forms grow out of each other in an evolving series of variations and mutations, which often build composite structures of extraordinary complexity. And what strange forms they are: sometimes vegetal, sometimes lapidary or metallic, almost but not quite like things seen, existing in a space that is almost but not quite like a known landscape, alternately obeying and defying the laws of gravity and equilibrium. The nightmare quality of these paintings, like *Fear,* springs largely from this hairbreadth dislocation of normal associations and visual logic. Tanguy's wife, Kay Sage, is also a true surrealist, though entirely unlike her husband. In *No Passing,* as in most of her paintings, she has constructed a fantastic world almost exclusively out of architectural elements, which have an alarmingly insecure look, like painted flats on an immense stage. Nearly always there is a dizzying perspective of luminous space, fading into a gray and dreamlike blankness.

Although few of our artists have embraced the whole surrealist approach, many of them have adapted its devices to their own ends, and these ends have been as diverse as social comment and private fantasy. Louis Guglielmi's *Terror in Brooklyn* is not an irrational picture in the surrealist sense; it is a highly conscious statement about the cruel impersonality of the city. But its effect comes from interweaving realism and fantasy as if they were one: the glass-imprisoned figures in the prosaic city street, Krug's Diner, and the strange bouquet above it. Like Sage, Guglielmi has exaggerated the depth of the perspective; at the same time he has given it a subtle touch of unreality by making the background a partial mirror-image of the foreground. In somewhat the same spirit, Peter Blume has commented on the violent religious faith of the Mexi-

Peter Blume.   Man of Sorrows. 1951. Tempera. 28 x 24.

153

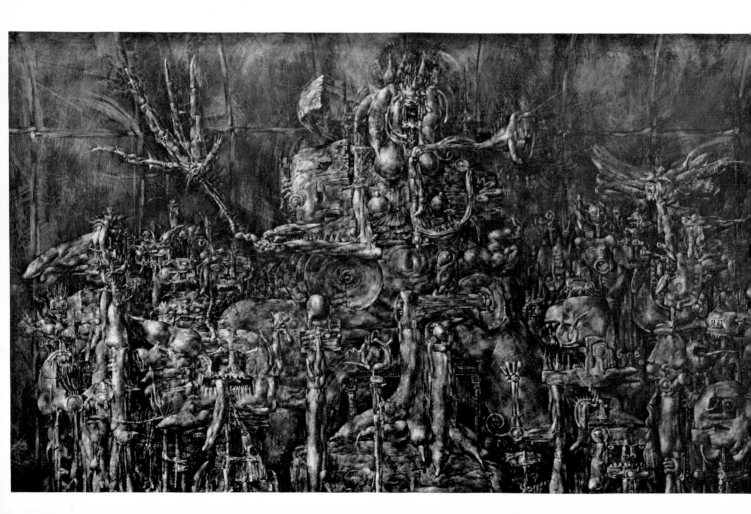

Theodore Roszak. Study for "The Furies." 1950. Ink. 25 x 38¾.

Morris Graves. Bird in the Spirit. c. 1940–41. Gouache. 21½ x 42.

Gift of the Friends of the Whitney Museum of American Art.

Gerald McLaughlin. The Empress. 1956. Oil. 48 x 92.

can Indians by an ambiguous mixture of the fantastic and the real. *Man of Sorrows* is, in his own words, not only Jesus but also his "polychrome statue and the living Mexican Indian himself under his burden."

It is harder to define the relation to surrealism of those other artists who have pursued their own private visions in realms far removed from common experience. Sometimes, as in Theodore Roszak's *Study for "The Furies"* or Gerald McLaughlin's *The Empress,* there is a strong surrealist flavor in the violent dismemberment of figures, the shocking juxtaposition of unrelated parts, and the hybridization of natural forms. But neither of these artists courts the dominant guidance of the subconscious (though they doubtless use it); rather, they are deliberately creating symbols for our time, symbols of destruction on the one hand and of mindless materialism on the other. Perhaps the works of Morris Graves, which look less surrealist on the surface than those of Roszak and McLaughlin, are

actually closer to the surrealist spirit of compulsive introspection. Graves, despite a certain debt to Mark Tobey's "white writing" technique and a shared fascination with Zen Buddhism, has always been an isolated painter concerned with the spiritual crises of his own most inward nature. The symbols that he has found for these—the wounded birds, the empty chalices, the springing pine tops—do not have the air of consciously devised symbols but of images which have forced their way upward from hidden recesses of the mind. Each theme he has painted over and over in endless variation until it has been replaced by another image equally demanding. While the results, mystical and poetic, are vastly different from those of surrealism with its predominantly sensual aura, both kinds of art seem to spring from not too dissimilar sources.

Today, orthodox surrealism seems very nearly dead as a movement, but the currents of fantasy and of spontaneity which it released in our art still flow strongly in many diverse channels.

Morris Graves.
Flight of Plover.
1955. Oil.
36 x 48.

Gift of Mr. and Mrs. Roy R. Neuberger.

3 social comment

The concern of many artists with man as a social being, discussed in an earlier chapter, has persisted strongly in recent years, but the emphasis has changed. The violent emotions of the 1920's and 1930's have abated a little, and in their place a more philosophical attitude toward man's foibles and a more compassionate understanding of his motives and weaknesses seem to have arisen. Perhaps this is simply a mark of the growing maturity of the pioneers in the movement, who are still its leading figures, but it may also be a reflection of our more prosperous times, compared with the Depression years, and of perceptible advances toward social and racial justice.

Whatever the causes, it is difficult to find today pictures which equal the savage indignation of Ben Shahn's Sacco and Vanzetti series or of certain early canvases by Jack Levine. Nor are there many echoes now of the despair in Isaac Soyer's *Employment Agency* or the bitterness in Philip Evergood's *Lily and the Sparrows*. Instead, the dominant attitude has shifted to one of sympathy and a warm humanity, often tinged with humor. Thus when Levine paints *Gangster Funeral*, it can scarcely be interpreted as an indictment of criminals or the conditions which produce them, but rather as an ironical and affectionate picture of a twentieth-century folk hero and his admirers, including mistress, wife, politician, and cop. Shahn's *Conversations* strikes a less sardonic note, but one of equal humor and affection, while the paintings reproduced by Robert Gwathmey, Joe Lasker, Jacob Lawrence, and Anton Refregier are all quiet tributes to the courage and dignity of their humble subjects. Various kinds of suffering and oppression may be implied in these canvases, but the villains themselves are absent, and one cannot escape the feeling that the true theme is our common humanity.

Another current approach to social comment, which was rarely found in the earlier paintings on specific issues, is through symbolism. Symbolism has its dangers; it can be imprecise and thereby lose its incisiveness. But this has been overcome in various ways. Evergood discovered a remarkably effective

Ben Shahn. Conversations. 1958. Watercolor.
39¼ x 27.

Gift of the Friends of the Whitney Museum of American Art.

one when he retold a biblical story in modern terms. The symbols in *The New Lazarus* are, as the artist says, "harsh and direct but they had to be in order to truly portray the cruelty and insupportable aggressions of which man has proved himself capable." Thus we have the lynched Negro and the bloody soldiers as contemporary parallels to Christ's suffering, while the see-nothing, hear-nothing, say-nothing symbols of a callous mankind are as indifferent to the figure on the cross as to the others. In contrast, there are the innocence of the children and the hope of new life and truth represented by Lazarus with his supporting women and angels. The old and the new, legend and immediate reality, are woven together, even in such details as the combination of modern dress with the iconography of Grünewald's famous crucifixion—including the flayed lamb.

Not all social symbolism is so precise. Shahn's *Everyman* is certainly more than a decorative arabesque; the straining figure at the bottom, supporting the odd pair above (rich man and charlatan?), has implications which can be interpreted in several ways. Similarly, George Grosz's *Peace, II* can be read as a purely factual painting of a lone survivor emerging from a bombed building. But to Grosz the ruin was the ravaged womb of the world and the "babymonster" in its center all of warped and hopeless mankind. "I call it a symbolical painting," he said, "the only form in which reality can be expressed in our period." Still more plainly symbolical is his *Waving the Flag*, which portrays one of the insect-derived "stickmen" invented by the artist in a whole series of wartime pictures as a distillation of mindless fanaticism. Quite aside from the question of symbolism, it is apparent that, of all these artists, Grosz alone showed little hope for humanity and small acceptance of its weaknesses. Nevertheless, he too traversed a path that led from the savage and specifically social satire of his early German cartoons to his last more philosophical, if deeply pessimistic, attitude.

Just as the general approach of our painters to social comment has changed with the passage of time, so also have their subjects. This is inevitable since social comment, by its nature, is a barometer of the issues which concern man at a given moment,

Jack Levine. Gangster Funeral. 1952–53. Oil. 63 x 72.

Robert Gwathmey.   Sowing. 1949. Oil. 36 x 40.

Jacob Lawrence. War Series: Another Patrol. 1946.
Shipping Out. 1947. Egg tempera. 20 x 16 each.

Gift of Mr. and Mrs. Roy R. Neuberger.

Joe Lasker.   Naples. 1952. Oil. 34¾ x 51.

Anton Refregier.   The Staircase. 1949. Tempera.
45 x 28¼.

and these seldom remain constant. In the earlier period the dominant themes were unemployment, working conditions, the idle rich, and the miscarriage of justice in a labor trial—all intimately connected with the Depression. In the later pictures reproduced here (with the possible exception of Shahn's *Everyman*), such themes have virtually disappeared, and a new range of subjects has replaced them. World War II, though not as prevalent a theme as its cataclysmic nature would seem to warrant, was the inspiration of works by Lawrence, Grosz, and Evergood. There have been many speculations as to why modern war has proved an intractable subject for painters, the most convincing being its vast and impersonal scope. As we have seen, Grosz and Evergood partially avoided the problem by adopting a symbolic treatment. Lawrence alone of this group attempted to convey the many-faceted impact of war on the common soldier by means of a related series of paintings which document not only its horrors but also its boredom, discomforts and spiritual aridity. Another topical subject, race relations, is hinted at, though only obliquely, in Gwathmey's *Sowing*, which, in his own words, is more a picture of a "typical farm activity."

The truth is that most of the paintings which today may be considered as social comment tend to deal with the nature of man and of his relations to other men rather than with specific economic problems. Often the illumination is cast by the artist's treatment of the most commonplace events—the poignancy of Refregier's wide-eyed children playing on a staircase or the clumsy earnestness of

Philip Evergood.   The New Lazarus. 1927–54. Oil. 48 x 83¼.

Gift of Joseph H. Hirshhorn.

OPPOSITE:

Ben Shahn.   Everyman. 1954. Tempera. 7

Shahn's conversationalists. Sometimes the note is satirical, as in the pictures by Levine and Dehn. Or again the artist may concern himself with the essential loneliness of man in even his most gregarious moments; Mitchell Siporin says his intent, in *Dancers by the Clock,* "is poetic paradox, a juxtaposition of gaiety and gloom, one jostling the other." These are not subjects that make newspaper headlines, but they are an integral part of man's life as a social being.

Stylistically, social-comment painting continues to be predominantly expressionist in character, as it was in the earlier period. But here, too, certain changes are apparent. The line dividing expressionism from caricature is thin. In the early and bitter days of protest and reform, the line was crossed more frequently than now. Shahn's acid lampoon of the righteous New England judges in the Sacco and Vanzetti case, Grosz's obvious caricature of a decadent couple, even Peggy Bacon's gentler ridicule, are cases in point. Caricature of this kind is a black-and-white proposition, all good or all evil, and it accorded well with the ideological battles of those years. Today the distortions, which are the hallmark of expressionism, tend to be subtler and are generally aimed at a more profound analysis of human character, with its multiple shadings and paradoxes of virtue and frailty. The contrast is nowhere more apparent than in a comparison of Levine's early and late work. The cops, gangsters, and politicians who inhabit *The Feast of Pure Reason* of 1937 (Museum of Modern Art) are savagely caricatured "types"; they reappear in *Gangster Funeral* of 1952–53 as believable members of the human race, looking uncannily like people we remember. They are not more realistically painted, but the distortions spring from understanding rather than hate. They are used to plumb character rather than to create it in the image of the artist's indignation. To varying degrees a similar evolution may be traced in the work of Shahn, Evergood, and others represented here. It is a development which seems to correspond, on the stylistic plane, with the growing maturity of these artists and the altered climate of our times.

Social-comment painting remains an important current in our art and is not likely to disappear as long as there are artists who are concerned with "the

George Grosz.   Waving the Flag. 1947–48. Watercolor.
25 x 18.

Adolf Dehn.   Jimmy Savo and Rope. 1944. Gouache. 14⅜ x 21⅜.

George Grosz.   Peace, II. 1946. Oil. 47 x 33¼.

proper study of mankind." It is based essentially on a moral premise: that art is not an end in itself but a means which the artist is morally obligated to use in the service of his fellow men. The use to which he puts it may change from the limited objective of specific social reforms to the more general one of creating an understanding of man's nature in his relations with others. But the underlying philosophy is the same—a generally liberal and humanitarian philosophy which finds life and art inseparable.

Mitchell Siporin. Dancers by the Clock. 1949. Oil. 40½ x 60⅛.

19 expressionism: painting

Of all the modern—as distinguished from traditional—movements, expressionism has been the most enduring. Futurism, Dada, surrealism have flourished and virtually disappeared; abstract art has waxed and waned in alternate cycles. But ever since the Armory Show we have had a vigorous group of expressionists, and their number has grown rather than diminished in the years since 1940. With many younger artists still developing their personal kinds of expressionism, there is no sign of the movement's ebbing. It remains a major current in our contemporary art.

This is particularly true if one includes within expressionism's flexible boundaries the abstract-expressionist trend of the 1950's, which has been widespread both here and abroad. But because the latter trend breaks so decisively with imagery, it will be discussed in the chapter devoted to free forms of abstraction, while the present discussion will concern itself only with expressionist works in a representational vein—paintings which deal with the recognizable world, though they distort it in varying ways and to various degrees in order to convey more vividly a mood or an emotion. Even with this limitation, expressionism embraces such different kinds of art that one may question whether it can justly be called a movement at all. Certainly there is little sense of solidarity or of a shared program among its leading figures. They seem rather to be painters impelled by inner necessity to express their romantic concept of life through a personal vision which has grown, in each case, from the artist's own nature. Their only common ground is the fact that they use marked distortions of visual reality and that these are aimed at the elevation of feeling over intellect as an ultimate value in the search for truth.

The traditional devices of expressionism, as it developed in earlier German sources, were an emphatic organization of thrusting, angular shapes and strong, often arbitrary colors, both resolved in a balance of strenuous oppositions. Many of our older artists owe something to this tradition. Their works are battlefields on which charged emotions are translated into forms and hues which clash and subside in vigorous rhythms. The late paintings of Marsden Hartley and the series Ernest Fiene based on the theme of a wrecked ship are symphonies of this energetic kind. Hartley, particularly, with his heavy outlines and stark designs in strong reds and blues, seems closest to German expressionism. In contrast, Abraham Rattner owes more to French tradition, to the stained-glass color of Rouault or French cathedrals, and to the anatomical dislocations of Picasso.

Ernest Fiene.   Variations on a Theme: "The Wreck, Number 2." 1948. Oil. 34 x 44.

Abraham Rattner.   Song of Esther. 1958. Oil. 60 x 48.

Gift of the Friends of the Whitney Museum of American Art.

John Marin.　Sea Piece. 1951. Oil. 22 x 28.

Gift of the Friends of the Whitney Museum of American Art.

Other artists of the older generation, though not uninfluenced by European sources, moved somewhat further from them. Two different ways in which they diverged are apparent in the very dissimilar styles which John Marin and Lyonel Feininger evolved late in life. Marin's development out of Cézanne was one of distillation—a constant search for a briefer, more intense way of drawing rock, wave, boat, cloud, until he perfected a series of energetic and nearly abstract symbols which he set to clashing vehemently. Feininger, starting with an already distilled, crystalline style (owing much to cubism and futurism), developed toward a more romantic freedom, toward ragged silhouettes and a deliberate indistinctness of form. In the end it was a sense of life's mystery that Feininger captured, a sense of its vitality that Marin found. In both cases their styles became the complete reflection of their temperaments and their aims.

Several younger artists, such as William Kienbusch and Herbert Katzman, have adapted the traditional methods of expressionism to a more abstract presentation by carrying Marin's process of distillation a degree further. At the same time a group of California painters—among them David Park, Elmer Bischoff, and Richard Diebenkorn—have come from abstract art back to a figurative style which is, at times, even more strongly reminiscent of German expressionism, although still marked by a kind of spontaneous handling and emphasis on medium—qualities which persist from these artists' abstract-expressionist beginnings. In the paintings of all these men, the mood varies greatly: from the pantheism of Kienbusch to the sensuality of Katzman's nudes, from the brutality of Park's rigid figures to the lyrical richness of Bischoff's landscapes. Yet they have in common an intensity of feeling which is the true characteristic of expressionism. "The artist requires strong dictates. . . . He must be driven by his own caring . . . his enthusiasms, infatuations, obsessions," Bischoff wrote. And this is the feeling, in essence, that makes Kienbusch's *Red Vine, Autumn, Dogtown* for him "a sort of ecstatic, savage, happy, secret landscape," rather than simply a beautiful one.

Lyonel Feininger. Manhattan Skyscrapers. 1942.
Ink. 21⅜ x 15¼.

Not uncommonly, our expressionists deal with profound issues of the spirit. Rico Lebrun's *Wood of the Holy Cross* and Max Weber's *Adoration of the Moon* are both religious pictures, one somber, the other ecstatic. Even when the theme is not ostensibly religious, spiritual values are often affirmed with an anguished intensity that twists this kind of art into distortions which are likely to be organic rather than angular (or formal), as if they were wrung from their creators and grew with an internal logic of their own. The tortured flesh of Leonard Baskin's brooding figures and the putrescent corpses which long obsessed Hyman Bloom may seem images of pure horror, but they are part of a quest for an understanding of suffering and death. While they are excursions into the shadows of life, they are not always tragic in their implications. Bloom's corpses turn oddly into bouquets of brilliant color suggesting an unsuspected beauty in decay, a transformation rather than a loss. Yasuo Kuniyoshi, at the end of his life, used color symbolically in somewhat the same way, though to a different end. Oppressed by the war and the rising tide of human suffering, he nevertheless clothed his paintings with a carnival brightness in ironic contrast to the somber mood that underlies them. The

er **Bischoff.**   Seated Figure in Garden. 1958. Oil. 48 x 57.

id Park.   Four Men. 1958. Oil. 57 x 92.

of an anonymous foundation.

Herbert Katzman. Two Nudes Before Japanese Screen. 1952. Oil. 76 x 43.

Juliana Force Purchase.

William Kienbusch.   Red Vine, Autumn, Dogtown. 1956. Oil. 41 x 56½.

Gift of the Friends of the Whitney Museum of American Art.

implication of tragedy encased in a brittle shell of gaiety is made more explicit by his frequent use of masked figures, clowns, and jugglers.

But expressionism is not always so anguished. Paintings are often born from the simplest events and experiences, which may strike some chord of response in the artist or perhaps only suggest formal possibilities worth exploring; generally a combination of both factors is involved. Karl Knaths' *Duck Flight* is, in his own words, "a composition of ordinary things at hand upon which I try to impose an art form, so that it becomes something to delight through beauty, as far as I can accomplish it." Grace Hartigan was amused and fascinated by the bridal mannequins in cheap clothing stores on the Lower East Side. From memory and photographs she painted their blank faces and elegant attitudes in a way that preserves the absurdity yet creates its own beauty of slow and ample rhythms. One insight into the way visual experience and emotion can be translated into forms which embody them and yet have their independent aesthetic being is provided by Lee Gatch in his description of *Jumping Joy.*

"*Jumping Joy*" was inspired," the artist writes, "by my young daughter's delight in that supreme and almost universal joy of all children—a two-minute jumping feast before bedtime; up and down, contracting into a ball, a flying circle teetering in mid-air, a whirling contour hard to fix, which

Rico Lebrun. Wood of the Holy Cross. 1948. Oil and casein. 80 x 30.

I tried to express by means of a double and overlapping circle. The contracting figure within the circles creates a cubic galaxy of shapes, a formal counterpoint to the great circle without. The geometric objects composing the room function as counterpoint to the blue sphere, at the same time interlocking with it and related to the shapes it contains. The smoking lamp is a symbol of the vibrations and disturbed currents of air set in motion by so much happy violence."

Out of such impulses and reactions, as well as a knowledge of art, personal style is born. Sometimes, as in Gatch's case or Abraham Rattner's *Song of Esther,* it is an enigmatic style, not easily read, approaching abstraction. That enigma can be used deliberately to create fantasy and a sense of poetic unreality has been demonstrated by Loren MacIver, whose panorama of Venice assumes the look of a mirage through its wavering horizon line, its iridescent, boatless sail, and its strangeness of proportions. John Heliker, too, has transformed familiar landscapes into visionary ones, fragmented in form and patched by light until they quiver with a poetic intensity of their own. Some of the same inner radiance shines through the deceptively flat and simple patterns to which Milton Avery reduces the world. While these designs have an abstract formal beauty, they do not, alone, account for the lyrical quality of his art. Other and even subtler elements are involved—the tenderness of edges, the deliberate awkwardness of the drawing, the suffused color. "I wandered the streets enchanted," Avery wrote of his

Max Weber.
Adoration of the
Moon. 1944. Oil.
48 x 32.

Leonard Baskin. Tormented Man. 1956. Ink.
39½ x 26½.

Living Arts Foundation Fund.

life in Paris when he painted *The Seine*. And it is this mood of enchantment that he has evoked with each stroke of the brush.

It is apparent, from even so partial a survey, that expressionism is one of our most flexible movements, and this may well explain why it continues, after so many years, to be a vital force in our art. It imposes no dogma—as futurism or surrealism did, for instance. Instead, it requires only that the artist trust his emotions and render these into art by whatever transformations of nature he can devise. There is no sign yet that the nearly infinite variations possible have been exhausted.

Hyman Bloom. The
Anatomist. 1953. Oil.
70½ x 40½.

Yasuo Kuniyoshi. Deliverance. 1947. Oil. 40 x 30.

Yasuo Kuniyoshi.   Juggler. 1952. Ink. 22 x 28.

Grace Hartigan. Grand Street Brides. 1954. Oil. 72 x 102½.

Anonymous gift.

Karl Knaths.   Duck Flight. 1948. Oil. 40 x 30.

Lee Gatch.
Jumping Joy. 1952.
Oil. 31½ x 31½.

Gift of Mr. and Mrs.
Roy R. Neuberger.

John Heliker.   From Cranberry Isle. 1956. Oil. 30 x 40¼.

Gift of the Friends of the Whitney Museum of American Art.

Loren MacIver. Venice. 1949. Oil. 59 x 93.

rett Spruce. Brushy Hillside. 1957.
24 x 30.

Philip Evergood. Virginia in the Grotto. 1960. Oil. 50 x 30.

Living Arts Foundation Fund.

ton Avery. The Seine. 1953. Oil.
50.

189

20 expressionism: sculpture

Expressionist sculpture, like expressionist painting, is charged with strong emotional tensions which it communicates by distortions of natural form and proportion. Expressionism, strangely enough, has attracted many fewer sculptors than painters in recent American art, but among them are several of our most powerful artists outside the abstract trend and a group of younger men, who are contributing notably to the movement.

Paradoxically, two of our leading expressionist sculptors, Jacques Lipchitz and Bernard Reder, are rooted in the classical tradition of French art. In Paris, where both reached artistic maturity, Reder was carving monumental stone figures somewhat akin to those of Maillol while Lipchitz was translating cubism into equally classical three-dimensional forms. In America both have moved in more romantic directions. Lipchitz has built an art of extreme emotional intensity, using massive rhythms, anguished gestures, and primitive dislocations of anatomy. The tortured convolutions of the design in *Sacrifice, II* and the nearly audible cry of the bird as the knife pierces its breast are pure expressionism—a catharsis of violence. Reder's development has been different. Nourished by an apparently inexhaustible reservoir of fantasy inherited from his Hasidic Jewish background, his imagination has created a private mythology peopled by Amazons and bulls, flowering cats and beautiful women with strange musical instruments. His style is baroque, creating a constant play of light and shadow, erupting with fanciful distortions. Yet in spite of the distance that both artists have traveled from their beginnings, it may be that their extraordinary plastic freedom has been made possible only by the formal discipline of those early years. Certainly it can be felt beneath their most complex inventions—a sense of rhythm, of balance, an ingrained memory of the traditional sculptural concept of the containment of forms within the block. They have never entirely abandoned classicism, although they have transformed its tranquillity to emotional fervor.

Jacques Lipchitz. Sacrifice, II. 1948/52. Bronze. 49¼ high.

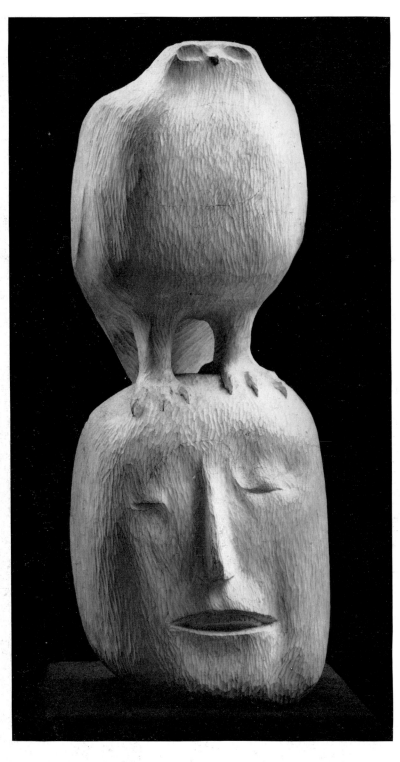

Leonard Baskin. Oppressed Man. 1960. Painted pine. 31 high.

An even older tradition, the monolithic sculpture of Egypt, has had a strong formative effect on the young artist Leonard Baskin, whose brooding figures have the compact and static frontality and the hewn look of a ritual art. But Baskin's macabre imagination seems obsessed with death and the defilement by man of his own flesh. His images are subtly distorted, as if by the reflection of an imperfect mirror, and this departure from a canon of impersonal perfection makes them the more horrifying.

Most of our contemporary expressionists owe less than these men to classical models and more to the romantic northern tradition, which, in sculpture, extends from Riemenschneider to Lehmbruck and Barlach. Such influences have plainly been felt by Doris Caesar, Chaim Gross, and Nathaniel Kaz, although they have been integrated into very different personal styles. Surely the elongation of Caesar's *Torso* owes something to Lehmbruck, but it owes more to her own awareness of the moving awkwardness of a woman's body that has been stamped with the imprint of life. Moreover, the gouged and pitted surface, the twisting movements of light and shadow, and the tenseness of the modeling are the individual means of a sculptor who evokes in nearly all her work the inward quality of a woman's experience. Kaz is more dramatic, less introspective. Like many expressionists, he is concerned with the stresses of opposites, in both a formal and a spiritual sense. *Cyrano* is the paradox of a poet in the body of a buffoon, "typifying conflicts such as square or round, good or evil, rough or smooth, light or dark, love or hate." Chaim Gross endows expressionism with a lighter aspect than it usually wears. Although he works with strong tensions of balance and romantic distortions, he does so with a gaiety and a vitality which seem the pure reflection of his own uncomplicated nature.

Bernard Reder. Adam and Eve. 1957. Bronze. 43½ high.

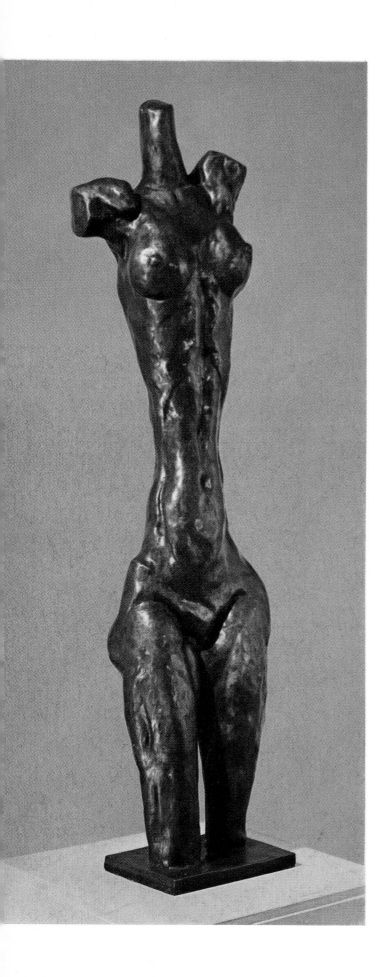

Doris Caesar. Torso. 1953. Bronze. 58 high.

All of these sculptors owe much, as we have seen, to tradition, whether classical or romantic. Their techniques, too, are the traditional ones of carving and modeling. David Smith, on the contrary, was one of the first in this country to break with these stylistic and technical concepts and to create a new kind of image, moving freely through space, by a new method, the welding torch. The revolution in which he played so important a part will be discussed more fully in the chapter on abstract sculpture, but there is nothing in the technique itself, or in the freedom of imagery it permits, that is necessarily abstract, as his own *Cockfight—Variation* demonstrates. The harsh violence of this piece and the appropriateness of its embodiment in cut, bent, and welded steel constitute a singularly native kind of expressionism with few links to Europe or to the past.

Smith himself has moved in a more abstract direction, but several younger sculptors, such as William King, Tom Hardy, and Ludwig Durchanek, have recently been using similar methods of construction to build figurative pieces which are generally expressionist in character. One can hardly say that their experiments so far constitute a significant widening of the movement, but expressionist sculpture remains a persistent current in our art.

Nathaniel Kaz.   Cyrano. 1950. Bronze. 34¼ high.
Wildenstein Benefit Purchase Fund.

David Smith.   Cockfight—Variation. 1945. Steel.
34 high.

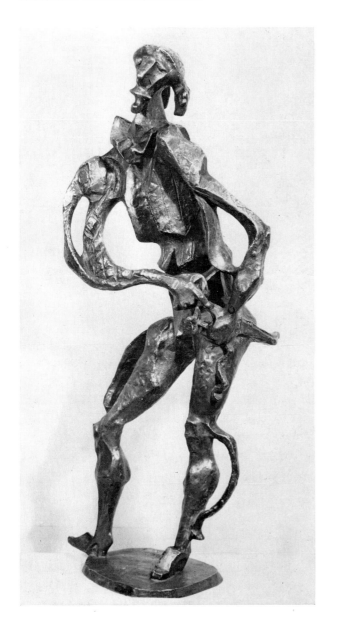

Chaim Gross. Sisters. 1946. Italian pink marble. 41 high.

21 semi-abstraction

There can be no doubt that abstract art has been a dominant movement in this country for the past twenty years, or that, of its many varieties, the kind known as abstract expressionism has been the most influential. This movement will be discussed more fully in the next chapter, but two of its pioneers—Arshile Gorky and Hans Hofmann—belong in these pages, as well as one of its leading figures, Willem de Kooning, who has never bound himself to a purely abstract form of expression. Indeed abstraction has become so much a part of the modern artist's vocabulary that many of our painters make use of its techniques and devices even when they are dealing with a concrete imagery.

Although the dividing line between invented forms and forms derived from nature has become increasingly shadowy, there is, nevertheless, a real difference, which goes deeper than the mere look of the picture. Total abstraction speaks a language which is either purely aesthetic or purely introspective. The moment that imagery enters, associations are established which relate the artist's experience to the forces of nature and to the experiences of other men. The danger, from the abstract artist's point of view, is that such associations may dilute the qualities he seeks—whether they are formal beauty or the intensity of self-examination. It was Gorky's difficult achievement to find a precarious point of balance between these elements. In nature he found patterns of procreation, growth, and decay, and these set up complex memory associations which he permitted to mix freely in pictures quite consciously designed aesthetically. *The Betrothal, II,* his biographer Ethel Schwabacher points out, is concerned with the interpretation of a sexual cycle, as the shape and union of forms suggests, but it also seems to have acquired some of its character from the early Renaissance painting by Paolo Uccello *The Battle of San Romano,* a print of which hung on Gorky's wall. Beyond these probably subconscious associations, *The Betrothal, II* is a painting in which sharp line and blotted, amorphous shapes work together in a counterpoint that is both delicate and full of vitality.

At about the same time that Gorky was developing his mature style (in the early 1940's), Hofmann began to move away from the limits of subject matter in a manner that was to add a new dimension to abstract expressionism. Hofmann's contribution might, with a little exaggeration, be called muscular. His art has a spontaneous, explosive quality, which comes from exuberance rather than introspection, and which led him to a slashing brushwork, a spattering of paint, and occasionally to the exploitation of accidental effects. While these devices were put to very different uses by other "action painters," Hofmann himself has always maintained a direct and joyful relation with the sensuous world, as he did in *Magenta and Blue,* of which he says, "Nature was my starting point; a full-scale palette my inspiration."

It is perhaps not too wide of the mark to see in Willem de Kooning's work the union of Hofmann's energy (though more savage than exuberant) and Gorky's self-probing. Like Hofmann, he has made of paint and its application a primary means of expression; the brush strokes have a ferocity of their own, and even when they describe an image, as in *Woman and Bicycle,* they go far to determine its character. (He told Peter Selz that his women had large breasts more because his arm moved naturally in ample curves than for any psychological reasons.) Nevertheless, the psychological content of this frightening apparition is undeniable. And if it is partly humorous in intention, as he has indicated, and a lampoon on the cult of the pretty girl in American life, it also seems drawn from a deeply personal reservoir of feeling.

William Baziotes is another artist who has sometimes been associated with abstract expressionism, but the connection seems tenuous except for the fact that he apparently permits his images to grow on the canvas without being fully conscious of where they will lead him or what other images they will attract to themselves—a method not unlike Gorky's. *The Beach,* for instance, grew in part from a trip to Florida where he was repelled by the heat, the dryness, the fossils on the shore. These are all suggested in the strange shapes of the foreground, while behind them is the shadowy outline of the rolling hills in his native Pennsylvania, where he retreated after his depressing Florida experience. Jon Schueler's very romantic landscapes of Scotland, like *Snow Cloud and Blue Sky,* may also owe a small debt to abstract expressionism, although in his case it is limited to the bold technical handling of paint and has nothing to do with the spirit of the work, for Schueler is a lineal descendant of Turner and is directly concerned with the glories and the poetry of nature.

Much of our semi-abstract painting today has even less connection with the abstract-expressionist movement and is sometimes actively opposed to it. Balcomb Greene is a leading figure in the revolt against a purely introspective and abstract approach, although he started his career as a geometrical abstractionist. Since 1943, however, landscape and the human figure have slowly found their way back into his work. That they have done so rather ambiguously may be due in part to his search for a means to express the wholeness of life—the inseparability of flesh and spirit, of light and matter—a search that has led him to a kind of interpenetration of forms that seems more abstract than it is.

Other artists have found still other reasons for using a combination of abstraction and imagery in their work. An effective symbolism almost always involves such a method because it requires an object with associations as symbol, yet must raise it out of its pedestrian, daily context to make it symbolically potent. Thus Charles Schucker says, "What concerns me is the human condition, man's constant effort to keep his equilibrium in a universe awesome in its potentiality and scope. . . . *The Bridge* is symbolic of the effort to span this infinity." And he paints it in an essentially abstract way, unanchored to the banks of reality. Similarly, George Mueller has created, in *The Study,* a brooding room which, by the severity of the design and its somber colors, creates a kind of metaphysical atmosphere. To him it might be "inhabited by one

em de Kooning.
nan and Bicycle.
–53. Oil.
x 49.

Arshile Gorky.   The Betrothal, II. 1947. Oil. 50¾ x 38.

William Baziotes.   The Beach. 1955. Oil. 36 x 48.

given to severe introspection, a philosopher, a physicist" and seems to symbolize an ascetic skepticism.

Historically, semi-abstraction is the oldest of all art forms and one of the most persistent. It stretches from cave man to cubist (the latter, of course, strongly influenced by primitive art). Today the expressive possibilities of its past manifestations continue to fascinate artists; in addition to its more contemporary guises, we find Robert Goodnough experimenting with a new kind of cubist organization and Joseph Glasco spontaneously adopting a direct and childlike imagery, which he himself has called an almost completely primitive form of expression. In the broadest sense semi-abstraction is not a style or trend at all, but simply a mid-point at which many styles have met visual reality and bent it to their own purposes.

Hans Hofmann.   Magenta and Blue. 1950. Oil. 48 x 58.

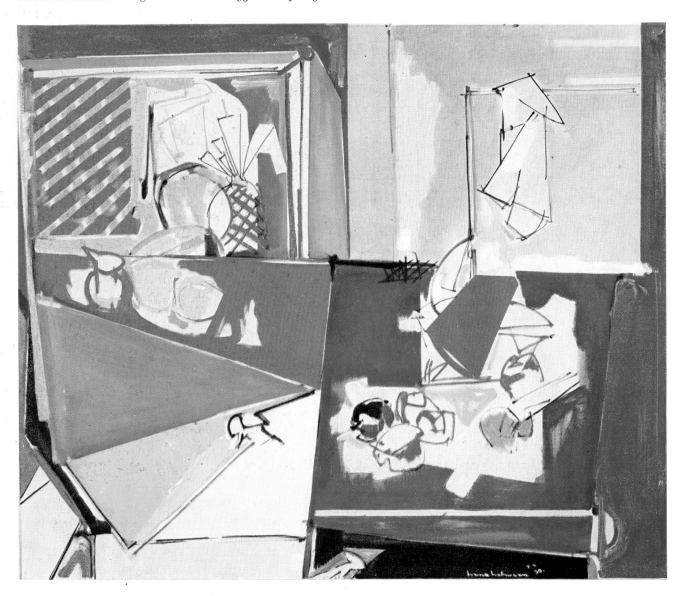

Jon Schueler. Snow Cloud and Blue Sky. 1958. Oil. 80 x 71.

Gift of the Friends of the Whitney Museum of American Art.

Balcomb Greene. Composition: The Storm. 1953–54. Oil. 36¼ x 48.

Charles Schucker.   The Bridge. 1954. Oil. 26 x 83½.

George Mueller.
The Study. 1955. Egg
tempera, casein, and
enamel. 56¾ x 48.

Gift of Mr. and Mrs. Roy R.
Neuberger.

Robert Goodnough.   Seated Figure with Gray. 1956–57. Oil. 57 x 52.

Anonymous gift.

Joseph Glasco.
Portrait of a Poet. 1951.
Oil. 68 x 46.

22 free-form abstraction: painting

Abstract expressionism, sometimes called action painting or the New York school, is the first American-born art movement to affect profoundly every part of the world where modern concepts of art exist, from Paris to Tokyo. It has altered even more profoundly the geography of our own art during the last fifteen years, both by the number of followers it has attracted and by the strong reactions against it which it has inevitably generated. As we have seen in preceding chapters, it has also created a new kind of figurative painting which incorporates some of its methods and attitudes. Few of our living artists have been unaffected by it in one way or another.

Mark Tobey.   Universal Field. 1949. Tempera and pastel. 28 x 44.

Mark Tobey. New Life (Resurrection). 1957. Tempera. 43⅜ x 27¼.

Gift of the Friends of the Whitney Museum of American Art.

Robert Motherwell. The Red Skirt. 1947.

Oil. 48 x 24.

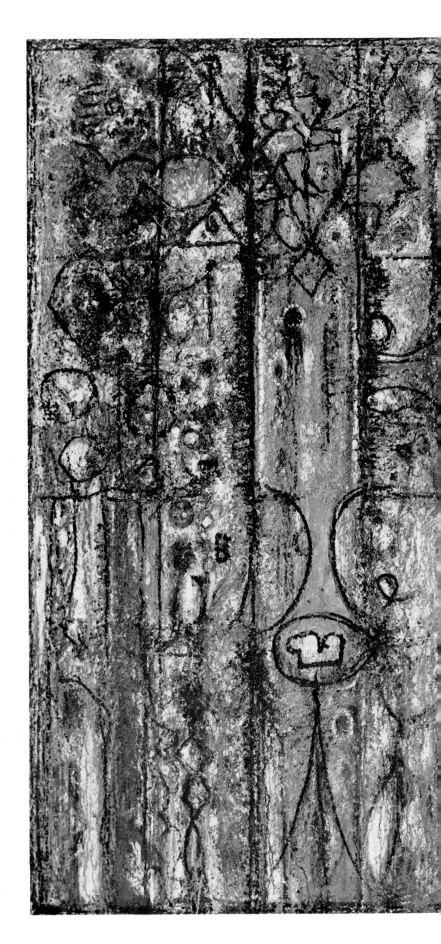

ard Pousette-Dart.   The Magnificent. 1950–51. Oil. 86¼ x 44.

of Mrs. Ethel K. Schwabacher.

Adolph Gottlieb.   The Frozen Sounds, Number 1. 1951. Oil. 36 x 48.

Gift of Mr. and Mrs. Samuel M. Kootz.

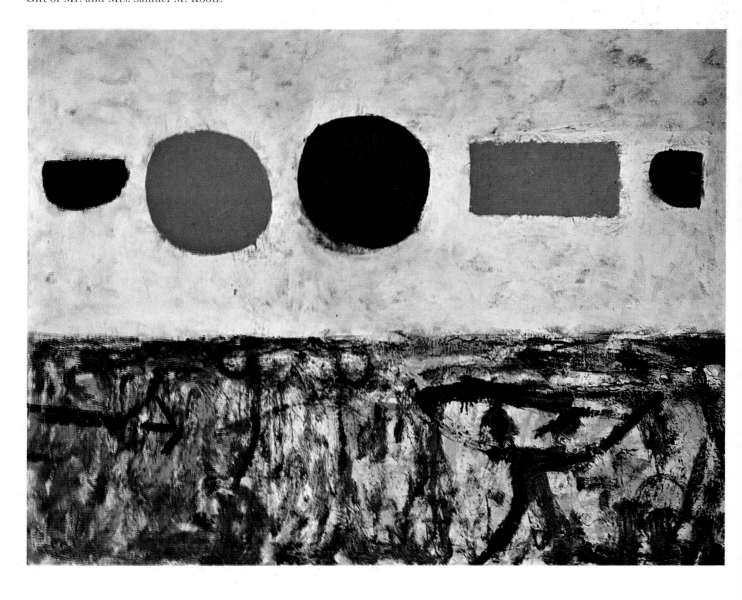

Franz Kline. Mahoning. 1956. Oil. 80 x 100.

Gift of the Friends of the Whitney Museum of American Art.

Kenzo Okada.   Memories. 1957. Oil. 68 x 84½.

Gift of the Friends of the Whitney Museum of American Art.

James Brooks.   Rasalus. 1959. Oil. 66 x 79¾.

Gift of the Friends of the Whitney Museum of American Art.

The sources of abstract expressionism are many. It inherited from earlier forms of abstraction a rejection of subject matter and a belief in the primacy of the medium: A painting is an object to be experienced solely in terms of its own laws, its own structure; it must never be an illustration; the flat plane of the picture must always be preserved. But it broke with cubism and other formal kinds of abstraction by disavowing any aesthetic interest. Instead, it took from surrealism a faith in the guidance of the subconscious mind, and it sought a means to transfer this directly to canvas in the purest and most intense way possible. It found the fantastic imagery of surrealism frivolous, but it adopted the surrealist theory of automatism and applied it in a totally abstract manner, entrusting to the spontaneous and unpremeditated gesture of hand and brush the expression of whatever inner forces moved them. The canvas became, in Harold Rosenberg's definition, a field or battleground on which the artist acted out a drama of his own state of being (hence "action painting"). It discovered sanctions for this approach in the early abstractions of Kandinsky, the later ones of Miro and Matta, but it pushed automatism and an anti-aesthetic bias to more extreme conclusions.

It is apparent that abstract expressionism is a deeply introspective movement, for it is not concerned (at least in theory) with an interpretation of the outer world, but only with the artist's own inner

Paul Burlin.   Red, Red, Not the Same. 1959. Oil. 48½ x 72.

Gift of Sam Jaffe, Milton Lowenthal, Harry Pinkerson, Bernard Reis, and Dr. Samuel Ernest Sussman.

life—although inevitably this is affected by his external experiences. Of all the charges which have been leveled against it, that of "dehumanization" seems the emptiest, for this is an art rooted exclusively in the mind and spirit of man. It has been accused more legitimately of being a private art which fails to communicate readily; its privacy is unquestionable, its degree of communication depends largely on the spectator but is certainly less precise than in paintings which rely on common associations. This element of privacy, which is central to its character, has also made it one of the most abused styles of our day, exploited by a multitude of inept paint manipulators who claim the privilege of the absolute freedom it offers in self-expression without accepting the discipline and rigorous self-examination which have been so plainly involved in the work of its leading practitioners.

As in all movements, generalizations like these seldom apply wholly to any one artist. Gorky, discussed in the preceding chapter, can scarcely be called an abstract expressionist because of his persistent use of natural forms and his aesthetic preoccupations, yet he was an important forerunner in the area of introspection and irrational associations. Mark Tobey stands in a similar relation to the movement, but in his case it was the technical innovation of his "white writing," developed in 1935, which pointed a way toward expression through a personal calligraphy. Tobey himself, though a mystic, has generally been concerned with the interpretation of facts and forces outside himself. Thus *Universal Field* was inspired by his first visit to an airport, when "I sensed the rapidity of communications in this day and attempted to symbolize in space and accent the messages which enliven the world," while in *New Life (Resurrection)* the gray masses symbolize "old earth, before and upon which dance the elemental figurations of new life." So conscious a symbolism, even though private, is alien to abstract expressionism, but Tobey's continuous, threading line, which he derived from Chinese calligraphy and which seems to move with a nearly independent life of its own, anticipates by a decade the linear webs Pollock was to spin.

But it was Jackson Pollock, more than any other single artist, who gave definition to abstract expres-

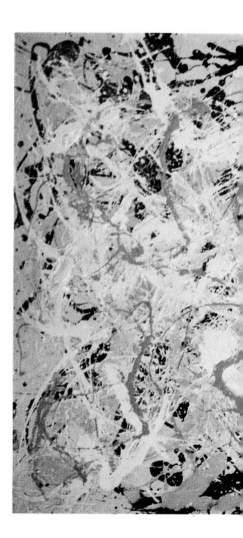

Jackson Pollock. Number 27. 1950. Oil. 49 x 106.

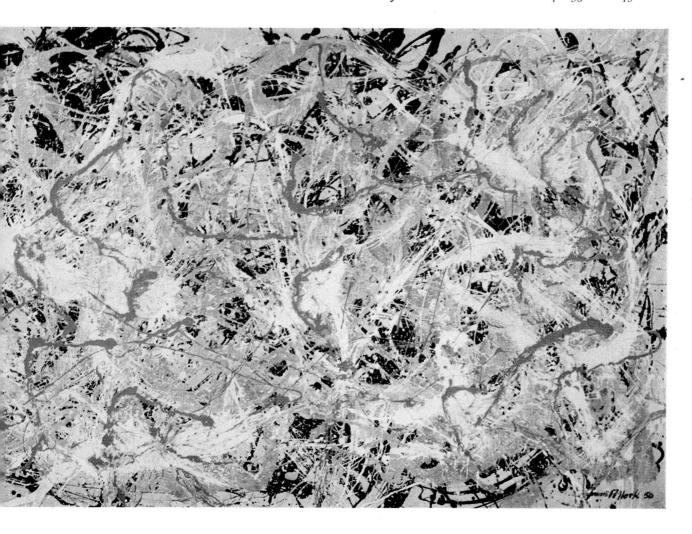

Philip Guston. Dial. 1956. Oil. 72 x 76.

sionism and who established it (in the public's eye, at least) as the most revolutionary of the avant-garde movements. Spreading big canvases on the floor, Pollock applied house paint and metallic pigments from a battery of cans, sometimes flinging or dripping his color on with sticks, sometimes pouring it on directly and letting it run in accidental patterns. Occasionally, he used the more conventional brush and palette knife, but for the most part he found that these hampered the spontaneous gestures of his arm on which he relied. Everything about his method suggests an unbridled spontaneity and automatism, and yet the results were entirely different from what one might have expected. For these pictures have an intensity of rhythm, an ordered complexity, sequences of rest and explosion, and what Alfonso Ossorio aptly called an "immediate splendor." They also have an astonishing variety, ranging from a kind of barbed ferocity to the floating, lyrical mood of *Number 27*, illustrated here. They suggest that a more conscious control of the medium was exercised than Pollock's method would seem to indicate, that accidental effects were incidents upon which he built, and that automatism was less important than the agonizing struggle to imbue line and color alone with a naked violence of feeling.

Pollock's personal style has never been successfully imitated. Hans Hofmann, for one, has had a much wider influence, while Willem de Kooning, soon after his first one-man exhibition, in 1948, became a leading figure in the movement. Some others who joined it during the decade of the 1940's include Robert Motherwell, Richard Pousette-Dart (though somewhat apart from the main line of development), Theodoros Stamos, Adolph Gottlieb, Bradley Walker Tomlin, and Franz Kline. From 1950 on, it expanded more rapidly, but no study has yet been made to establish the precise chronology of its development. All we can attempt here is to point out some of the directions it has taken and how it has been partially transformed by certain artists into a less introspective art with a new orientation toward imagery.

Although abstract expressionism allows the artist complete freedom in the choice of his formal methods, in practice it has established three main devices

Helen Frankenthaler. Blue Territory. 1955. Oil. 113 x 58.

Gift of the Friends of the Whitney Museum of American Art.

which the majority of its practitioners have used either singly or, more often, in various combinations. One of these is a personal calligraphy, like that of Tobey and Pollock. A second is the expressive brush stroke, such as Hofmann's or De Kooning's. A third is the use of amorphous shapes and stains of color, sometimes accidental, sometimes controlled, which was an important element in Gorky's work.

Of these, the calligraphic approach may well be the most difficult; certainly it has attracted fewer artists than the others. About 1948, Adolph Gottlieb began to paint a series of linear canvases which eventually reached a labyrinthine complexity and which appear to have had a considerable influence on Bradley Walker Tomlin's elegant arabesques. During the same years, however, Gottlieb was also experimenting with mysterious floating shapes, like the irregular circles and squares of *The Frozen Sounds, Number 1,* and these eventually became more important to him. It was Franz Kline, starting in 1949, who made the most impressive use of calligraphy by enlarging it to monumental proportions and by limiting his palette to stark black-and-white oppositions. His big canvases, such as *Mahoning,* are drained of any elegance or decorative quality and have the impact of a sledge hammer. By contrast, Kenzo Okada's handsome patterns, with their delicately blurred lines, return calligraphy toward its Oriental sources, though in a purely contemporary manner.

The range of expression through predominantly linear means has proved great, but the range of expression through the character of the brush stroke— its shape, direction, weight, and texture—has proved even greater. James Brooks, in *Rasalus,* for instance, has built a picture almost entirely out of disparate strokes which stand apart from each other, seldom overlapping, barely touching here and there along their ragged edges. They are like sentinels ranged in static ranks and only occasionally breaking into action. Paul Burlin uses nearly as definite a stroke,

Ethel Schwabacher.   Oedipus at Colonos, Number 2. 1959. Oil. 84¾ x 60.

Milton Resnick.
Genie. 1959.
Oil. 104 x 70.

Adja Yunkers.   Tarrasa, XIII. 1958. Pastel. 69 x 48.

Gift of Theodore R. Racoosin.

in a counterpoint with line, but he sets both elements in turbulent motion. They dart about the canvas colliding, stopping, starting again with a restless energy which seems almost to be inherent in the paint itself. Compared with the breadth of treatment in these works, Philip Guston's *Dial* seems withdrawn, complex, and infinitely subtle. It is as if the artist's brush had endlessly probed the surface, searching its way through the most delicate nuances of touch and color until it emerged with the bolder but still strangely tentative areas of red in the center. Though just as delicate, Milton Resnick's *Genie* is more relaxed, more lyrical in feeling. Here the strokes move across each other in a kind of animated scribble, creating a network of pale colors which traps light like an impressionist canvas. Still other handlings are found in the sinuous ascending strokes of Helen Frankenthaler's *Blue Territory* or the arrow-like ones in Jack Tworkov's *Duo, I*, with their variety of weight and transparency.

The third device of abstract expressionism—the use of amorphous or irregular shapes—is apparent in many of the paintings discussed above, but it may be observed even more clearly in work where the character of individual brush strokes is subordinate to the forms they construct. Whether these forms are born from associations in the artist's mind with a specific subject or whether they come from a more general realm of feeling and emotion, the mystery of their incarnation is equal. They seem to grow from the subconscious with a kind of organic in-

Mark Rothko.   Entombment, I. 1946. Gouache.
20⅜ x 25¾.

John Ferren. The Garden. 1954. Oil. 82 x 65¼.

Jack Tworkov.   Duo, I. 1956. Oil. 81¾ x 57¾.

Gift of the Friends of the Whitney Museum of American Art.

224

Enrico Donati. Gore et Mandra. 1957. Oil. 60 x 60.

Theodoros Stamos. High Snow—Low Sun, II. 1957.
Oil. 53½ x 97½.

Gift of the Friends of the Whitney Museum of American Art.

evitability. Sometimes they are extremely simple, like the irregular bands and squares of pulsating color which give Mark Rothko's mature work (later than the painting illustrated) its hypnotic quality. In Adja Yunker's big pastel, *Tarrasa, XIII,* they rise with a more romantic presence—vague and ominous masses which trail off at points into insubstantiality. In Ethel Schwabacher's *Oedipus at Colonos, Number 2* they seem to move and dissolve into each other with the splendor of cloud formations. They may be earthen and heavy, as in some of Robert Motherwell's pictures or Enrico Donati's *Gore et Mandra,* with its massive, textured blocks of paint. Sometimes they are not at all amorphous; Conrad Marca-Relli's collages, for instance, are quite sharp-edged and precise, yet even so are endowed with a strangely symbolic look. Other artists combine in the same canvas fluid and concrete shapes; Theodoros Stamos'

Conrad Marca-Relli.   Junction. 1958. Collage. 56 x 77½.

Gift of the Friends of the Whitney Museum of American Art.

Willem de Kooning. Door to the River. 1960. Oil. 80 x 70.

Gift of the Friends of the Whitney Museum of American Art (and purchase).

High Snow—Low Sun, II breaks two solid black bars with a dark, watery mass and a flamelike eruption of red. Again the pattern may resemble organic shapes of growth, as in John Ferren's *The Garden*, or the configurations of landscape, as in Angelo Ippolito's *Storm*.

The discovery that line, brush motion, abstract shape, and color can embody impulses which are not primarily aesthetic is the singular achievement of abstract expressionism. In its purest form it has demanded of the artist a nearly superhuman degree of introspection and concentration in order to achieve the most direct expression of the deepest part of self. In this process, canvas and paint have assumed a reality which seems ultimate and essentially inexplicable. The artist has been consumed by his art in a kind of mystical union. Perhaps this is one reason for his reluctance to speak of his aims in any other terms than those of the act of painting. "My whole desire is to be as deeply in painting as possible," Jack Tworkov writes, "without holding any prepared position or maintaining any preconceived . . . attitude. To experience, not painting in general, but each particular picture as deeply as possible is my desire." When James Brooks notes that *Rasalus* evolved from "no theme or idea" but required months to bring to unity, or when Milton Resnick says that he named his picture *Genie* "because at some time before it had been finished, the painting itself had a way of looking back at me," they are speaking from the same position. Richard Pousette-Dart has been more explicit: "Art is always mystical in its final meaning, it is structure which stands up by the presence and significance of its own reality. . . . It is my belief that ultimate reality can only be achieved by a passionate, burning devotion to one's work."

There is no law, however, which requires the abstract artist to paint pictures that are subjectless except for the rapport between self and canvas. Pollock, De Kooning, and Hofmann have all broken at times into imagery. Today many painters who remain completely abstract in their approach deal, nevertheless, with specific themes and subjects outside the personal realm. Donati's *Gore et Mandra* was inspired by the mandragora legend and has its dark aura of magic and superstition. Schwabacher's

Oedipus captures precisely the shining mood of Sophocles' description of his death, which "was not with lamentation, or in sickness and suffering, but, above mortal's, wonderful." Other artists have moved a step or two further from pure abstraction and have used a symbolic (rather than naturalistic) imagery to deal with their subjects. Nature and the moods of nature have thus returned to an art which long banished them. Stamos' *High Snow—Low Sun* series is based on thoughts of the equinox; sun, snow, sky, equinoctial line, are all present and recognizable, though in abstract configuration. Sometimes this new imagery creeps in unconsciously, as it did in Helen Frankenthaler's *Blue Territory*, which she painted on for some time before she became aware that the shape of a tree and a "mood-with-landscape" had invaded her work. Or the imagery may start with a conscious object and develop into something different in the process of realization; Ippolito's *Storm* began as a spring landscape of delicate colors, "but as the summer wore on . . . the reds became stronger, the yellows heavier, the painting more rigid, the forms shifted," until it ended as a kind of symbol of the whole "cycle from spring to fall and its effect on me." In their reliance on subconscious impulses released by the act of painting, these artists remain true to the abstract-expressionist approach, but in their acceptance of imagery and their willingness to pursue it even into such traditional fields as landscape painting, they have given the movement a new orientation.

This is more significant than a simple enlargement of subject matter, for it has ruptured the shell of extreme introspection which was both the strength and the limitation of the movement. By turning his eyes outward to other men and to the material aspects of the universe, the artist has opened avenues to larger areas of experience (and perhaps of spiritual truth) than are comprised within the bounds of self. "It is not by neglecting matter but by imbuing it with life that we make apparent the spirit," as Ferren wrote. That this can be done by the abstract and intuitive methods inherent in the movement has already been demonstrated, but the new avenues still remain largely unexplored. Time alone will tell whether they lead to a dead end or a fresh adventure.

Angelo Ippolito. Storm. 1956. Oil. 43 x 50.

Gift of the Friends of the Whitney Museum of American Art.

23 free-form abstraction: sculpture

As long as sculpture remained tied to its traditional techniques of carving and modeling, it was bound by their limitations—by the shape and weight of the block or the structural possibilities of an armature. Although it made a virtue of these necessities and developed a "sculptural" aesthetic out of the nature of its methods and materials, it was never so free as painting, even when, in its great periods, it was stronger. The revolution which ruptured the traditional concepts of sculpture originated abroad with the constructivists (see Chapter 25) and wrought a change that went far beyond their own aims, which were principally formal. Nevertheless, it was they who demonstrated that sculpture could be built directly out of unconventional materials such as metal, plastics, and wire by modern technical methods such as welding, soldering, and brazing. It remained for a younger generation of artists to turn this discovery in a more romantic direction, which has carried sculpture still further from its traditions and has brought it closer to painting in its freedom and variety of effects.

In America, David Smith and Ibram Lassaw were both pioneers in this development from early in the 1930's. It was not until the middle forties, however, when Ferber, Hare, Lipton, and Roszak all joined the trend, that it began to take on the aspects of a movement. It is almost precisely contemporary, therefore, with the development of abstract expressionism in painting—to which, indeed, it is closely related. For purely practical reasons, automatism is less applicable to sculpture than to painting, yet the works of these men seem to have been formed, to some extent, by unpremeditated impulses released in the process of creating. Accidental effects in the drip of molten metal or the color patterns made by the heat of the torch are not unlike those of poured or splattered paint. Moreover, the calligraphy of the painters has its counterpart in the free linear patterns which much of this sculpture describes in space, while the use of amorphous and mysteriously evocative shapes is common to both. Nevertheless, sculpture has its own unique problems and character—even when freed from traditional methods.

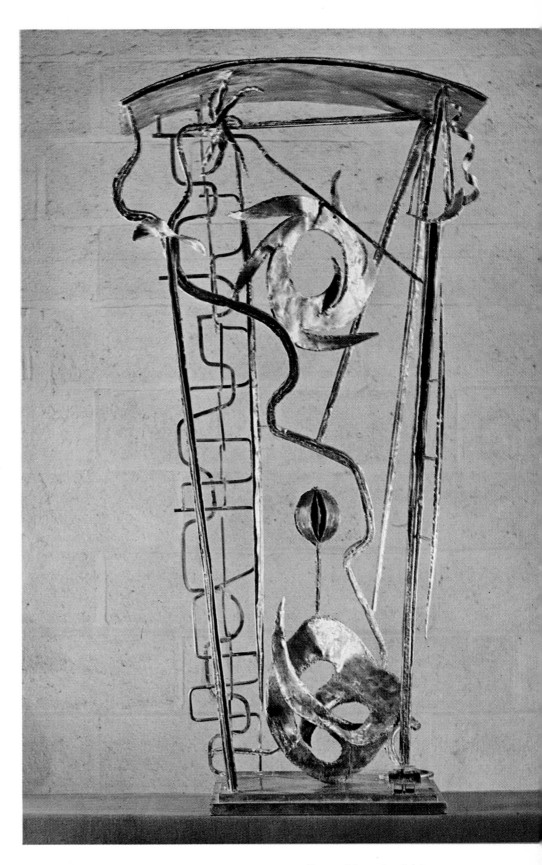

Herbert Ferber. Sun Wheel. 1956. Brass, copper, silver solder. 56¼ high.

Ibram Lassaw. Procession. 1955–56. Wire, copper, various bronzes, silver. 40 long.

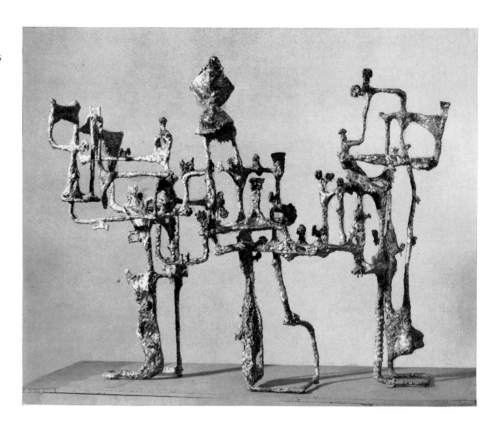

These are inherent not only in its three-dimensional character but also in the range of materials now available. Since every material has its own properties and since these properties carry tactile and psychological associations (e.g., the harshness of steel, the airiness of transparent plastics), the sculptor faces questions of the appropriateness of medium to form which are more complex than in painting, but his technical vocabulary is proportionately wider.

Like certain abstract-expressionist painters, some of these sculptors think and work primarily in terms of the manipulation of their material. Thus Herbert Ferber says of his *Sun Wheel,* "The forms and shapes are chosen, the surfaces used, the directions indicated, in an attempt to animate the space described with excitement and tension." The roof at the top is solely a device "to give a sense of compression to the space." The sun wheel has no symbolic significance; it is used because its whirling, thrusting shape contributes to the dynamic design. Similarly, Lassaw feels that *Procession* "shows a greater facility [than before] in the use of various metals and colors (a growth in the understanding of the nature of these materials and how they want to be shaped)." His title yields no more clue than Ferber's; it was given to the piece only after it was finished, "because it looked to me somewhat like a procession." Yet there can be no doubt that the free forms each of these artists uses have a "meaning" (possibly subconscious) beyond their aesthetic function. The brilliant reflections in Ferber's polished brass and copper, the organic vine and plant forms pushing upward from the pelvic shape below, have their own connotations, as does Lassaw's more subterranean and nodular growth pattern. Lassaw himself is quite conscious of the mysterious forces that shape his art. "My work stems like a plant out of the

David Smith.   Hudson River Landscape. 1951. Steel. 75 long.

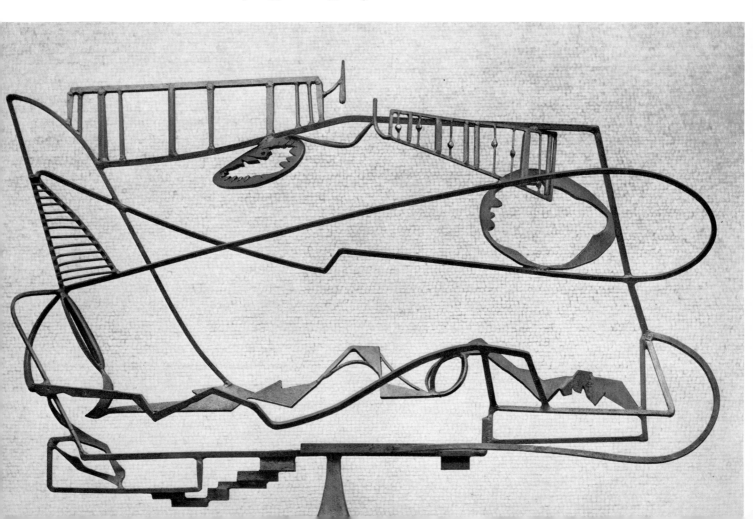

Louise Bourgeois. One and Others. 1955. Painted and stained wood. 20¼ high.

nature of my soil," he wrote. "I feel myself inextricably interwoven both outwardly and inwardly in all events of the universe. There is a growing sense of identification with and participation in the universal process. . . . The cosmos is an organism." His art is the intuitive expression of this organic and spiritual unity.

Other sculptors in the group make franker acknowledgment of the part that consciously chosen subjects play in their work. But they maintain, with justice, that the subject is only a starting point, that the work of art is not simply or even primarily an interpretation of the subject, that it exists on many levels, from the associative to the purely formal. David Smith's *Hudson River Landscape* came, as he wrote in the *College Art Journal* (Winter, 1954), "from dozens of drawings made on a train between Albany and Poughkeepsie. . . . Later, while drawing, I shook a bottle of India ink and it flew over my hand. It looked like my river landscape. I placed my hand on paper. From the image that remained, I traveled with the landscape, drawing other landscapes and their objects, with additions, deductions, directives, which flashed unrecognized into the drawing, elements of which are in the sculpture. Is my sculpture the Hudson River? Or is it the travel and the vision? Or does it matter? The sculpture exists on its own; it is an entity." Seymour Lipton, somewhat like Gorky, often derives his forms from both natural and man-made sources, which become linked by the mysterious process of association and emerge in his art as a unified metaphor. Thus *Sorcerer* appears to be partly a man with arms outstretched in incantation, but it also suggests a primitive totem or instruments of magic. The title of Louise Bourgeois's *One and Others* suggests at first only a study in disparate shapes, which it is; yet the longer one looks at the piece, the more it resembles strange growths pushing or huddling against each other; its aura is secretive and frightening. All of these works are highly organized formally, but they also evoke elusive associations which cannot be completely explained by their ostensible subjects or lack of subjects.

Finally, we have yet another group of sculptors who have moved still further from abstract expressionism in that they use a quite specific imagery and

Seymour Lipton. Sorcerer. 1957. Nickel-silver on monel metal. 60¾ high.

Gift of the Friends of the Whitney Museum of American Art.

Theodore Roszak. Sea Sentinel. 1956. Steel and bronze. 105 high.

236

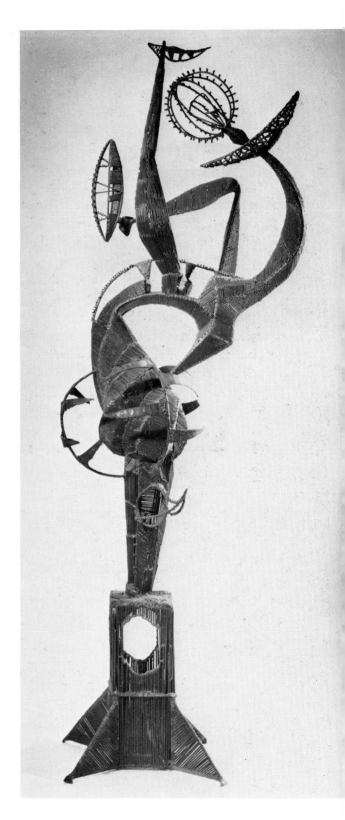

ard Stankiewicz.   Kabuki Dancer. 1956. Steel

cast iron. 80¼ high.

of the Friends of the Whitney Museum of American Art.

David Hare.   Juggler. 1950–51. Steel. 80¼ high.

that their formal methods are consciously related to the communication of the image's significance. Theodore Roszak is a symbolist, who has found in the sharp, cruel aspects of nature—the claw, the thorn, the beak and talon—an expression of one aspect of our age. His use of these natural forms is never naturalistic; they go through a process of metamorphosis and hybridization before they are embodied in the remarkably appropriate medium of brazed and pockmarked steel. One is never in doubt about their allusions, which are direct and forceful; their power comes from the logic of the imagination which has built them into such compelling visions. David Hare is another sculptor who has turned his back on introspection as a principal source of inspiration. "One does not live in a personalized vacuum, but with the whole, great, round, beautiful, terrifying, and joyous earth," he wrote, "and God pity the man who turns his eyes inward and pulls out of himself one cold, infinitely useless lump

after another." He has used a wide variety of techniques, from traditional to modern, and his style has varied nearly as greatly, with *Juggler* representing his more abstract phase. Through it all, however, there runs a direct feeling for his subject and an irrepressible vitality. Several younger sculptors, too, have turned the methods of abstraction to the service of a fairly precise imagery, such as Richard Stankiewicz, who builds witty and sometimes even graceful figures out of refuse from the junkyard (a kind of neo-Dadaism), or James Wines, whose *Monad, I* is inspired by rock formations and symbolizes those elementary beings in nature who embody within themselves the whole universe.

These are some of the artists responsible for endowing sculpture with a versatility it has never had before, a versatility which has permitted it to take part, to nearly the same degree as painting, in the exploration of an intuitive sphere of feeling and expression.

James Wines.   Monad, I. 1960. Bronze. 53½ long.

Gift of the Friends of the Whitney Museum of American Art.

tween intellect and emotion which is at the heart of the classical attitude toward life. In Albers' words:

Art is to present
vision first,
not expression first.
Vision in art is to reveal
our insight—inner sight—
our seeing
the world and life. . . .

A few other American artists have consistently followed this purity of vision. Fritz Glarner's title for all his work is *Relational Painting*. Like Albers, he avoids any variation of texture which might disrupt the flatness and unity of the surface, but he works with a larger repertoire of shapes and has introduced oblique lines into an art that is traditionally rectilinear. These tapering rectangles often seem to overlap and, in conjunction with his colors, set up a dynamic forward-and-backward action within a controlled and shallow depth. Ilya Bolotowsky has remained closest of the three to Mondrian's rigid bands and rectangles, but in recent years he has explored a new area of delicate, closely related colors which have a lyrical and luminous quality. He writes that "the subject matter [of *Large Vertical*] may be defined as calm, monumental, opalescent, counterpoint."

It is a far cry from the aesthetic austerity of these works to the equally geometrical but more romantic and associative painting of such artists as Cleve Gray, Gabor Peterdi, and I. Rice Pereira. Gray, in his *Mosque, Cordova: Number 2,* has handsomely re-explored the vocabulary of cubism, but he has not been content with the emotionally neutral mandolins and wine bottles of the cubists. Instead, he has taken for his subject a mysterious interior and

Ilya Bolotowsky.   Large Vertical 51/59. 1951–59. Oil. 95¼ x 40½.

Gift of Mr. and Mrs. N. E. Waldman.

has made his painting very large, "because I wanted to convey the sensation of being *inside* the mosque —inside a forest of shadows and light that stretches out seemingly to infinity." Peterdi's *Tidal,* though more abstract, is just as closely related to a specific personal experience; it is a conscious attempt "to capture the endless motion of the water, the splashing of the waves as they explode in the sunlight." By using rectangular patches, which have the similarity to each other of waves, and by setting them in rhythmical motion, he has created an abstract diagram, as it were, of the sea's eternal flux, while the variations of color suggest the play of reflections and light. Pereira's forms are also consciously de-

vised symbols. Related to the new concepts of reality forged by modern science, they are "a symbolic geometry as the mind inquires into the intangible . . . a metaphysical approach to human experience as the mind journeys through space and time toward the infinite and a continuum." Her transparent bands of color seem to float lightly in a space which is ambiguous, sometimes as flat as the surface of the canvas, sometimes as vast as eternity. They are interlocked in a poetic order which, though more modern, is as mystical in its own way as the Renaissance concept of the music of the spheres.

These works stand at a pole nearly opposite that of the purists; much formal abstraction falls some-

Cleve Gray.   Mosque, Cordova: Number 2. 1959. Oil. 72 x 96.

Gift of the Friends of the Whitney Museum of American Art.

Fritz Glarner.   Relational Painting. 1949–51. Oil. 65 x 52.

where between the two. This is true of Stuart Davis' recent painting, in which the associative and formal elements have fused more completely than at any time in his earlier period. Then, when he aimed to evoke the atmosphere of Paris, he did so in a relatively naturalistic style, and his most intense formal experiments were exercised on an eggbeater. Now, in *The Paris Bit,* he creates a synthesis of memories and associations but embodies them in an abstract pattern which is as effective upside down as it is right side up. For Davis has become a master of invention, and what he invents are pictorial equivalents of movement, sound, the aura of place and time. Sometimes these equivalents are fragments of recognizable things or forms derived from them; sometimes they are totally abstract (as, for the most part, in *Owh! in San Paõ*). What matters is his ability to compose them in designs of stripped and concentrated power which communicate precisely by color, form, rhythm, and allusion his observation of life, if not its inner meaning. There is, indeed, something a little poker-faced about Davis' paintings; they open a window on the sound of traffic, the beat of jazz, the pulse of city life, but they are stoically reticent about the workings of the heart.

Attilio Salemme's strange art is, by contrast, more introspective. Probably no other artist has ever used so strict a geometry to create so fanciful a world, where hieratic figures built of blocks and triangles enact their obscure dramas and confront each other in situations of unexplained psychological intensity. Yet it is the utter clarity and ordered logic of Salemme's world that makes it so believable—like the one Alice entered through the looking glass. We accept the figures as more than symbols and the geometry as more than a formal device, which indeed it is. In Jimmy Ernst's case geometry disappears entirely and a more surrealist kind of image, although still imbued with great formal clarity, takes its place. Here the image itself seems to have grown subconsciously behind the formal preoccupations, which were, the artist says, the use of white as a color and the development of a continuous movement over the surface. Only later did he recognize, or seem to recognize, "several childhood images—therefore the title *Personal History.*" This, too, is a far step from the strict exclusion of personal associations by the purists, but, as we have seen, few American artists followed that deep and narrow way.

Gabor Peterdi. Tidal. 1955. Oil. 50 x 80.

Gift of Walter Bareiss.

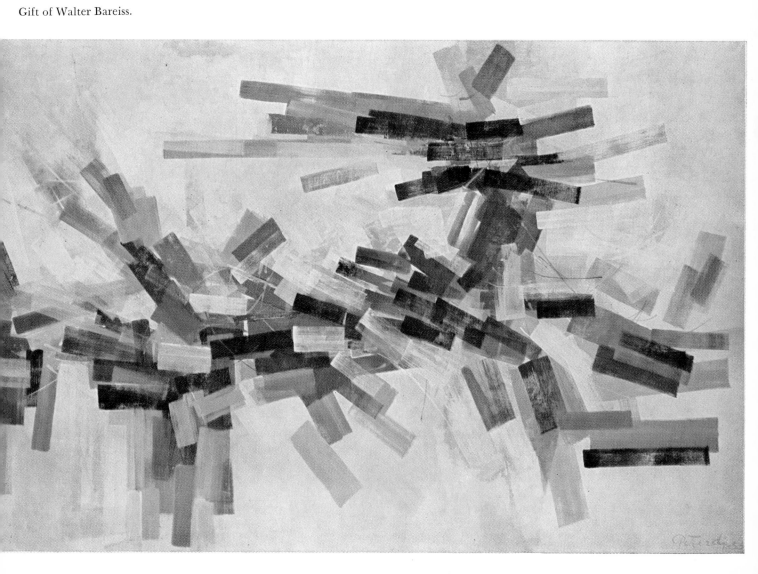

I. Rice Pereira.   Landscape of the Absolute. 1955. Oil. 40 x 50.

Gift of Richard Adler.

Stuart Davis.   Owh! in San Paõ. 1951. Oil. 52¼ x 41¾.

I. Rice Pereira.   Oblique Progression. 1948. Oil. 50 x 40.

Stuart Davis.   The Paris Bit. 1959. Oil. 46 x 60.

Gift of the Friends of the Whitney Museum of American Art.

Attilio Salemme.   Inquisition. 1952. Oil. 40 x 63.

Jimmy Ernst. Personal History. 1949. Oil. 46 x 40.

Juliana Force Purchase.

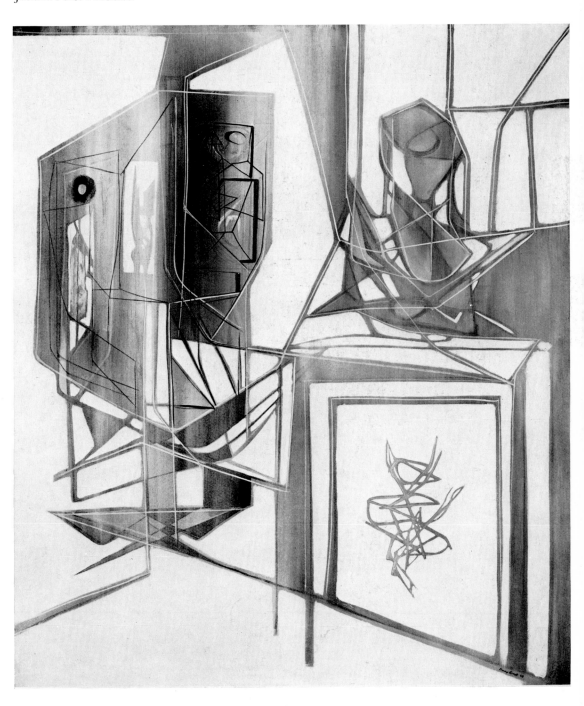

25 formal abstraction: sculpture

José de Rivera.   Construction "Blue and Black." 1951. Painted aluminum. 47 long.

The aesthetic of pure form, espoused by Albers and others in painting, has found more adherents among modern American sculptors. A few of these, such as Raoul Hague and Isamu Noguchi, have used the traditional method of direct carving in stone or wood, but the great majority have adopted various kinds of open, constructed sculpture built of metal, plastics, wire, and other new materials, often polychromed. In this, they all owe some debt to the Russian constructivist movement, born at the time of the first World War and one of whose leaders, Naum Gabo, has been active in America since 1946.

Constructivism derived from cubist collage, which it carried into three dimensions. Its most important contribution, however, was its virtual destruction of mass and volume as the main language of sculpture, its substitution of open or transparent forms, and its treatment of the empty space between them as an important element in the design. It rejected completely the old concept of containment within the block and freed sculpture to move at will in any direction—Gabo even introduced actual motion in his *Kinetic Model* of 1920. Although it started as a semi-abstract movement with recognizable subjects, such as heads, it soon became totally abstract and established a formal aesthetic as rigorous as that of the related movements in painting.

Gabo himself has remained constant to this aesthetic, although his development has been away from the rather mechanistic forms of his youth and toward more fluid designs which suggest, at times, the natural architecture of organic growth. More than any other sculptor in this country, he has made plastics his medium, taking full advantage of their airy transparency and light-conducting qualities. Combined with shining stainless steel wire, they make his *Linear Construction in Space, Number 4* a kind of luminous drawing in the air, a delicate

Naum Gabo.   Linear Construction in Space, Number 4. 1958. Plastic and stainless steel. 40 x 21½ high.

Gift of the Friends of the Whitney Museum of American Art.

pattern which changes at every angle of vision but always flows from part to part with a contained, perpetual motion. José de Rivera has pioneered, since early in the 1940's, in a related but somewhat different direction. Like Gabo's, his constructions turn in upon themselves with a fluid movement, which De Rivera often emphasizes by rotating them on motor-driven turntables. The play of light along their surfaces and edges is also an important element, but De Rivera prefers to work with hard metal and simpler forms, which he shapes with extraordinary subtlety. Theodore Roszak (in the period 1936–45) and the somewhat younger Sidney Gordin are two other artists who have worked in purely formal constructions, although following more the geometrical style of Mondrian than the sinuous one of Gabo and De Rivera. Gordin particularly, with his brightly painted stripes and rectangles, creates a kind of three-dimensional equivalent of neoplasticism in his *Construction, Number 10.*

Our most famous native-born constructivist, Alexander Calder, has been relatively little influenced by European sources. Starting in the 1920's with animated wire figures of circus performers, done for his own amusement, he developed early in the following decade his characteristic mobiles, which were set in action either by cranks and motors or, increasingly, by currents of air that disturbed their sensitive balance. The resulting motion described patterns in space more complex than any sculptor, including Gabo, had attempted before and created a basically new art of changing formal relations. While some of his early work was abstract, much of it was based on natural forms—animals, birds, leaves, or flowers (e.g., *Pomegranate*)—and the motion was precisely calculated to suggest the characteristic movements of his subjects. In recent

Theodore Roszak. Vertical Construction. 1943. Painted wood and plastic. 74 high.

Gift of the artist.

Sidney Gordin.   Construction, Number 10. 1955. Painted steel. 41¼ long.

Alexander Calder. Black, White and 10 Red. 1957. Mobile. Sheet aluminum and steel. About 14 feet long. Gift of the Friends of the Whitney Museum of American Art.

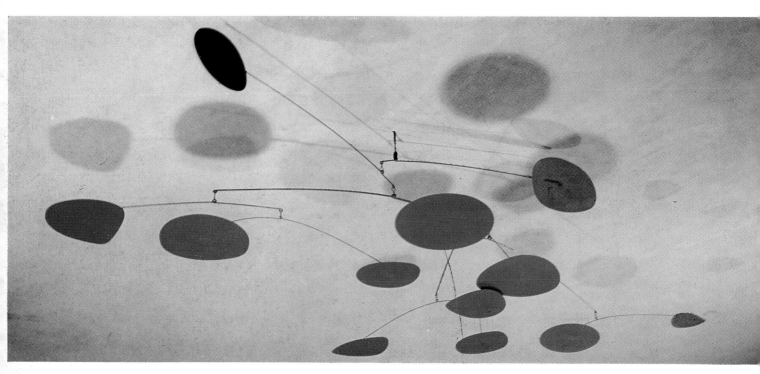

years, Calder has moved in the direction of more purely formal relations, as in *Black, White and 10 Red,* and has explored a wider range of spatial patterns and different tempos, such as the very rapid one of his windmill-like mobile at Litchfield, Connecticut, which rotates violently in a heavy breeze.

Although the techniques of constructivism liberated sculpture from its self-contained volumes, not all abstract sculptors have been willing to sacrifice entirely the monumentality of mass, the sensuous surface, and the tactile values of carved stone or wood. Sometimes they have returned to entirely traditional methods, as Isamu Noguchi did in *Integral,* which he calls "an exercise in integrated or integral carving within the confines of a limiting form. It deals with shadows and subtle sequences." It also deals with the strength of the shaft, the intrinsic beauty of marble, and the tactile beauty of polished surfaces. Raoul Hague is another sculptor who works (exclusively, in his case) with monumental carved forms. These have some association with the human figure, but it is a remote one; basically they are abstract volumes, which flow into each other with a slow and measured rhythm that could hardly have been achieved without the weight and strength of wood or its richness of grain and color.

Another kind of sculpture falls somewhere between carved and constructed works and combines the techniques of both. Gabriel Kohn's *Square Root* is as "pure" aesthetically as Gabo's work; in his own words, it "is formal and my only concern was to arrange my elements in a new and exciting way." Technically, however, it is a hybrid: partly carved (or sawed), partly constructed; partly massive, partly open. Its effect partakes of both methods, for it balances diverse shapes in an extended tension beyond the reach of traditional sculpture, while its roughly cut surfaces preserve some of the latter's strength of volume and texture. Both Noguchi and Louise Nevelson have used a similar combination of techniques. The former's *Humpty Dumpty* is carved with great subtlety of modeling from thin sections of slate, but it is assembled like a construction and the startling interpenetration of forms could not have been achieved in any other way. Nevelson's *Black Majesty* deals also with carved or cut volumes, but she treats them as dis-

Alexander Calder. Pomegranate. 1949. Mobile. Sheet aluminum and steel. About 72 high.

Isamu Noguchi.   Integral. 1959.
Greek marble. 49¼ high.

Gift of the Friends of the Whitney
Museum of American Art.

Gabriel Kohn. Square Root. 1958.
Wood. 40 long.

Raoul Hague. Sawkill Walnut. 1955. 42 high.

Gift of the Friends of the Whitney Museum of American Art.

tinct elements, separating them on their base to establish a rhythm in which the open spaces are as important as the forms themselves. Both of these pieces escape, at least partially, from the purely formal character of the other works in this chapter. Whether Noguchi intended from the beginning to create the droll image of a grotesque dwarf, he has heightened the effect immeasurably by such details as the small opening which peers at one like a beady eye. Certainly Nevelson had a romantic aim as important as her formal one, for this piece was once part of a series called *The Bride of the Black Moon.* "The bride," she explained, "was on a voyage and *Black Majesty* was an image of a continent—identified with Africa. In back of all my work is the image and the symbol. I compose my work pretty much as a poet does, only instead of the word I use the plastic form for my images."

Despite such occasional infusions of imagery and symbolism, our abstract sculpture has been more faithful than our abstract painting to an aesthetic of pure form. Why this should be it is difficult to say, unless it is because sculpture—whether constructed, carved, or modeled—deals inevitably in physical volumes. It cannot closely approach the insubstantial effects of painting—the mists of color, the stains and washes, the lost contours, the blending of shapes. Concrete and three-dimensional by nature, sculpture offers the artist a language of form which is tangible and immediate. Many have responded.

Isamu Noguchi. Humpty Dumpty. 1946. Ribbon slate. 58¾ high.

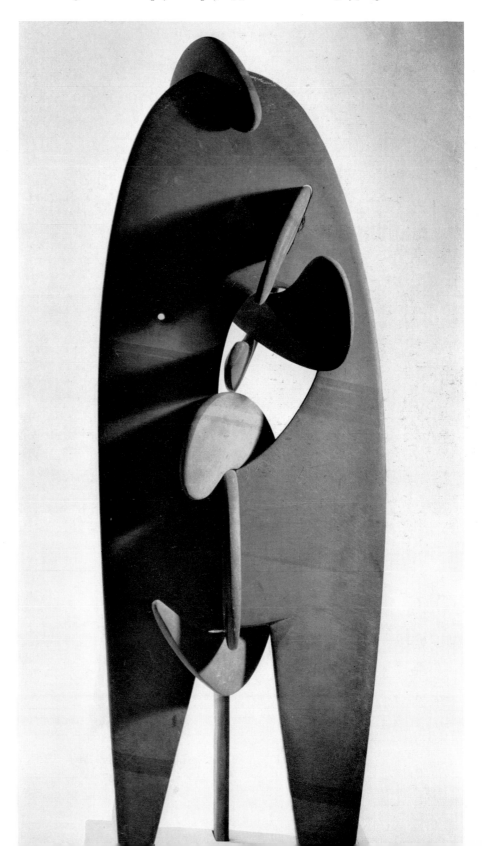

acknowledgments

The publication of this book was made possible by the interest and support of several organizations and individuals. Twelve of the eighty-one color plates were paid for by the Publications Committee of the Friends of the Whitney Museum. The cost of the remaining color plates was defrayed by generous donations from an anonymous foundation in New York, from the Edith and Milton Lowenthal Foundation, Mrs. G. Macculloch Miller, the Roy R. and Marie S. Neuberger Foundation, Inc., the Henry Pearlman Foundation, Inc., Mr. and Mrs. Herbert M. Rothschild, John W. Straus, and Howard Wise. To all of these the Museum is most grateful.

The thorough, accurate doctoral thesis "A History of the Whitney Museum of American Art, 1930–1954," written by Dr. Daty Healy under the auspices of the School of Education of New York University, has been of considerable help in connection with Chapter 2, on the history of the museum.

Quotations of artists' statements in the text were taken from correspondence and questionnaires in the Museum's files, unless otherwise identified. The Museum is indebted to the artists for their cooperation in preparing these explanations of their aims and methods.

A majority of the photographs and color transparencies for the illustrations were made by Oliver Baker. Sixty-five of the color plates were produced by the Capper Engraving Company, four by the Roger Williams Engraving Company. The black-and-white engravings were made by the Capper Engraving Company.

Whitney Museum of American Art

Catalogue of the Collection

Index by Mediums

Exhibitions, 1914–1960

Books Published by the Museum

Friends of the Whitney Museum of American Art

catalogue of the collection

Paintings, sculpture, watercolors, and drawings acquired by the Museum from its founding through December 31, 1960, are listed below. Dimensions of paintings are in inches, height preceding width. The dimensions of watercolors and drawings are sight (measured within the frame or mat opening), unless otherwise noted.

The largest dimension of sculpture is given, in inches. For reliefs, height and width are given, in that order.

Unless otherwise stated, the support for watercolors and drawings is paper.

The term *composition board* is used for fabricated boards, such as Presdwood, Masonite, etc., and *cardboard* for light paper boards, such as academy board.

Dates following titles are inscribed on the works themselves unless enclosed in parentheses. A dash between two dates (1927–30) indicates that the work was executed during these years; a diagonal line (1927/30) that it was worked on again in the latter year.

The figures preceding the decimal point in accession numbers indicate the year of acquisition. For example, 54.17 means that the work was acquired in 1954. All works accessioned in 1931, not identified as purchases, were part of the private collection of Gertrude V. Whitney, which she gave to the Museum on its foundation.

Page references are to illustrations.

In memory of Juliana Force, the Museum acquires each year at least one work by an artist under thirty, designated as a Juliana Force Purchase.

Adler, Samuel M. b. 1898.

INVOCATION. (1952.) Oil on composition board. 42 x 30. Purchase. 53.1.

Albers, Josef. b. 1888.

HOMAGE TO THE SQUARE: "ASCENDING." 1953. Oil on composition board. 43½ x 43½. Purchase. 54.34. (p. 240.)

Albert, Calvin. b. 1918.

GALLEON. (1952.) Lead alloy, bronze, and stainless steel. 36½ high. Gift of Dr. and Mrs. Abram Kanof. 59.1.

PORTRAIT MEMORY. (1954.) Charcoal. 28 x 22. Purchase. 55.13.

Alston, Charles H. b. 1907.

FAMILY. (1955.) Oil on canvas. 48¼ x 35¾. Artists and Students Assistance Fund. 55.47.

Altman, Harold. b. 1924.

STUDY. 1959. Ink. 25 x 37. Sumner Foundation Purchase Award. 60.53.

Amino, Leo. b. 1911.

JUNGLE. 1950. Mahogany. 56 high. Purchase. 52.15.

Anderson, Allan E. 1907–1959.

USKUDAR. (1959.) Oil on canvas. 25 x 30. Gift of Mrs. Allan E. Anderson. 59.4.

Archer, Edmund. b. 1904.

BUYING FLOWERS. 1930. Oil on canvas. 31 x 26. Purchase. 31.89.

ORGANDY COLLAR. (1936.) Oil on canvas. 19 x 16. Purchase. 38.49.

HOWARD PATTERSON OF THE "HARLEM YANKEES." (1940.) Oil on canvas. 34⅛ x 29⅛. Purchase. 42.2. (p. 129.)

Archipenko, Alexander. b. 1887.

TORSO IN SPACE. (1936.) Metalized terra cotta. 50 long. Gift of Mr. and Mrs. Peter A. Rübel. 58.24. (p. 66.)

Aronson, David. b. 1923.

THE JUDGES. (1959.) Pencil. 22 x 30¾ (over-all). Gift of Mr. and Mrs. Chauncey Waddell. 60.39.

Atherton, John. 1900–1952.

OLD BARN, CONNECTICUT. 1942. Oil on canvas. 28 x 40. Purchase. 42.16.

Ault, George C. 1891–1948.

BEATRICE. 1923. Oil on canvas. 18 x 14. Anonymous gift. 60.66.

HUDSON STREET. 1932. Oil on canvas. 24 x 20. Purchase. 33.40.

Avery, Milton. b. 1893.

CLEANING FISH, GASPÉ. (1940.) Oil on canvas. 33¾ x 54. Gift of Mr. and Mrs. Roy R. Neuberger. 50.5.

THE SEINE. 1953. Oil on canvas. 41 x 50. Purchase. 54.33. (p. 188.)

Bacon, Peggy. b. 1895.

BLESSED DAMOZEL. 1925. Pencil. 18 x 14⅝. 31.481.

CITY LIGHTS. 1937. Pastel. 25 x 19⅛. Purchase. 38.18.

MOTHER AND CHILD. (c. 1927.) Pencil. 15¾ x 9. 31.482.

THE UNTILLED FIELD. 1937. Pastel. 19⅛ x 25¼. Gift of Mr. and Mrs. Albert Hackett. 52.29.

VIGNETTE. 1923. Ink. 6⅜ x 6. 31.483.

WILD GARDEN. 1924. Pencil. 22⅛ x 18 (over-all). 31.484.

Bageris, John. b. 1924.

TO GARCÍA LORCA. (1957.) Oil on canvas. 39½ x 50. Gift of The Arts Fund, Inc. 60.6.

Baizerman, Saul. 1889–1957.

SLUMBER. (1948.) Hammered copper. 40 long. Purchase. 48.20. (p. 137.)

Bakos, Jozef G. b. 1891.

SANTA FE CANYON. (1931.) Oil on canvas. 32 x 40. Purchase. 33.1.

Baranik, Rudolf. b. 1920.

SCULPTOR'S STUDIO. (1959.) Oil on canvas. 67 x 49. Gift of Dr. and Mrs. Philip Gold. 60.7.

Barnet, Will. b. 1911.

MALE AND FEMALE. 1954. Oil on canvas. 40 x 32. Anonymous gift through the Federation of Modern Painters and Sculptors, Inc. 55.17.

Barthe, Richmond. b. 1901.

AFRICAN DANCER. 1933. Plaster. 42½ high. Purchase. 33.53.

THE BLACKBERRY WOMAN. 1932. Bronze. 34⅛ high. Purchase. 32.91.

Baskin, Leonard. b. 1922.

OPPRESSED MAN. (1960.) Painted pine. 31 high. Purchase. 60.30. (p. 192.)

TORMENTED MAN. (1956.) Ink. 39½ x 26½ (over-all). Living Arts Foundation Fund. 57.52. (p. 180.)

Baum, Mark. b. 1903.

STREET IN A SMALL TOWN. (1929.) Watercolor. 9½ x 14¼. 31.389.

Baumbach, Harold. b. 1904.

YELLOW LIGHT. 1958. Oil on canvas. 48 x 48. Gift of Mr. and Mrs. J. Seymour Sloan. 59.47.

Baziotes, William. b. 1912.

THE BEACH. 1955. Oil on canvas. 36 x 48. Purchase. 56.12. (p. 201.)

GREEN FORM. (1945–46.) Oil on canvas. 40 x 48. Gift of Mr. and Mrs. Samuel M. Kootz. 49.23.

SEA FORMS. (1951.) Pastel. 38⅛ x 25⅛ (over-all). Purchase. 52.19.

Beal, Gifford. 1879–1956.

FISHERMAN. (1928.) Oil on canvas. 36½ x 48½. 31.92.

LAWN FETE. 1917. Oil on wood. 24 x 36. 31.94.

THE RAG PICKER. (1940's.) Ink. 7⅞ x 10. Purchase. 45.21.
STORM IN GLOUCESTER HARBOR. (1941.) Gouache and ink.
9¾ x 20. Purchase. 42.23.

Beattie, George. b. 1919.
VOLTERRAN LANDSCAPE. 1960. Oil on canvas. 30 x 49¾. Gift
of Mr. and Mrs. Sidney A. Wien. 60.32.

Beatty, John W. 1851–1924.
HILLS OF PLYMOUTH IN SEPTEMBER. 1912. Oil on canvas.
26 x 36. Purchase. 41.44.

Beauchamp, John. b. 1925.
PAINTING. (1951.) Lacquer on composition board. 29⅞ x
40¼. Juliana Force Purchase. 52.1.

Beck, Rosemarie. b. 1923.
NUMBER 3—1954. Oil on canvas. 49¾ x 45¾. Living Arts
Foundation Fund. 55.51.

Beerman, Miriam. b. 1923.
TERRESTRE. 1956. Enamel and oil. 21½ x 25¼. Anonymous
gift. 57.37.

Bell, Cecil C. b. 1906.
ICE SKATERS, CENTRAL PARK. (1934.) Watercolor. 16⅛ x 22¾.
Purchase. 36.18.
RAINY DAY, LOWER MANHATTAN. (1944.) Watercolor on
cardboard. 21½ x 29. Purchase. 45.11.

Bellows, George. 1882–1925.
DEMPSEY AND FIRPO. (1924.) Oil on canvas. 51 x 63¼. Pur-
chase. 31.95. (p. 84.)
FLOATING ICE. (1910.) Oil on canvas. 45 x 63. 31.96. (p. 27.)

Benn, Ben. b. 1884.
MOTHER AND CHILD. 1915. Oil on canvas. 36 x 27. 31.98.

Benrimo, Tom. 1887–1958.
FIGURE IN SPACE. (1951.) Casein and oil on composition
board. 30 x 40. Wildenstein Benefit Purchase Fund. 53.2.

Benton, Thomas Hart. b. 1889.
THE LORD IS MY SHEPHERD. (1926.) Tempera on canvas.
33¼ x 27⅜. Purchase. 31.100. (p. 90.)
Also thirteen drawings.

Berman, Eugene. b. 1899.
PROJECT FOR A PAINTING. 1944. Ink. 14½ x 10⅝ (over-all).
Purchase. 45.18.

Bernstein, Sylvia. b. 1920.
IMPRISONED BOUQUET. (1959.) Watercolor. 24¾ x 36¼. Gift
of the Ruth White Gallery. 60.11.

Berresford, Virginia. b. 1904.
NEW ENGLAND HURRICANE. 1938. Watercolor. 14⅜ x 21. Pur-
chase. 39.25.
THE WAVE. (1938.) Watercolor. 14¼ x 21. Purchase. 39.26.

Biala, Janice.
BLACK INTERIOR. 1955. Oil on canvas. 63¾ x 51⅛. Anonymous gift. 55.44.

Biddle, George. b. 1885.
COW AND CALF. 1931. Charcoal. 8¾ x 12⅜. Purchase. 32.65.
EMPORIUM. (1930.) Watercolor. 17 x 12. Purchase. 32.64.
IN THE BREAKERS. 1933. Watercolor. 19⅜ x 16¼. Purchase.
33.62.
ITALIAN PEASANTS. 1931. Ink. 9 x 12¼. Purchase. 32.66.
WINTER IN TORTILLA FLAT. 1941. Oil on canvas. 25 x 30.
Purchase (and exchange). 44.2.

Billings, Henry. b. 1901.
LEHIGH VALLEY. (c. 1930.) Tempera on composition board.
20 x 25. Purchase. 35.1.

Bilotti, S. F. 1880–1953.
A MODEL. (1935.) Marble. 16 high. Purchase. 36.1.

Bing, Alexander M. 1878–1959.
ABSTRACTION, 1956. Oil on paper. 18½ x 23¾. Purchase.
58.5.

Bischoff, Elmer. b. 1916.
SEATED FIGURE IN GARDEN. 1958. Oil on canvas. 48 x 57. Purchase. 59.2. (p. 174.)

Bishop, Isabel. b. 1902.
NUDE. (1934.) Oil on composition board. 33 x 40. Purchase.
34.11. (p. 75.)
SUBWAY SCENE. (1957–58.) Egg tempera and oil on composi-
tion board. 40 x 28. Purchase. 58.55.
WAITING. (1935.) Ink. 7⅛ x 6. Purchase. 36.31.

Bittleman, Arnold. b. 1933.
RECOLLECTION: SPAIN 1957. (1958.) Ink. 26½ x 39¼. Neysa
McMein Purchase Award. 58.30.

Blaine, Nell. b. 1922.
HARBOR AND GREEN CLOTH, II. 1958. Oil on canvas. 50 x 65.
Neysa McMein Purchase Award. 58.48.

Blanch, Arnold. b. 1896.
BOUQUET. (1920's.) Oil on canvas. 24 x 18. 31.101.
FOUR SHIPS. (1951.) Oil on canvas. 30 x 48. Purchase (and
exchange). 53.9.
GIRL DAYDREAMING. 1934. Oil on canvas. 50 x 36. Purchase.
34.12.
THE PORT OF KINGSTON. (1920's.) Oil on canvas. 22 x 30.
31.106.
PORTRAIT OF A WOMAN. (c. 1929.) Oil on canvas. 36¼ x 25½.
31.104.

Blanch, Lucile. b. 1895.
AUGUST LANDSCAPE. 1932. Oil on canvas. 22 x 28. Purchase.
33.3.
FLOWERS. 1927. Oil on canvas. 22 x 15. 31.110.
HIGH TENSION. 1953. Oil on canvas. 50 x 36. Purchase (and
exchange). 54.32.
Also twelve drawings of circus subjects.

Blatas, Arbit. b. 1908.

WOMAN IN INTERIOR. (1955.) Oil on canvas. 51¼ x 38¼. Gift of Mr. and Mrs. David M. Solinger. 55.49.

Blaustein, Al. b. 1924.

VIEW OF VENICE. (1955.) Oil on composition board. 55½ x 50½. Neysa McMein Purchase Award. 57.31.

Bloch, Julius. b. 1888.

GOSSIP. (1930.) Watercolor and ink. 9¾ x 8½. Purchase. 31.586.

KINGSTON. (1932.) Gouache. 12¾ x 17. Purchase. 32.68.

THE LYNCHING. (1932.) Oil on canvas. 19 x 12. Purchase. 33.28.

ROOMS TO LET. (1930.) Watercolor and ink. 12⅜ x 9. Purchase. 31.587.

SELF-PORTRAIT. (1937.) Oil on canvas. 20 x 16. Purchase. 37.46.

Bloom, Hyman. b. 1913.

THE ANATOMIST. (1953.) Oil on canvas. 70½ x 40½. Purchase. 54.17. (p. 181.)

AUTOPSY. (1953.) Crayon. 54½ x 37½. Purchase. 54.18.

Bluemner, Oscar. 1867–1938.

COMPOSITION. (1931.) Oil on wood. 23 x 30. Purchase. 33.4.

HOUSE AND TREE. Oil on composition board. 15 x 20. Anonymous gift. 58.62.

LAST EVENING OF THE YEAR. (c. 1929.) Oil on wood. 14 x 10. Purchase. 31.115.

NEW ENGLAND LANDSCAPE. Watercolor. 13¾ x 19½. Purchase. 38.8.

OLD CANAL PORT. (1914.) Oil on canvas. 30¼ x 40¼. Purchase. 31.114. (p. 38.)

SLEEP. (1936.) Tempera on composition board. 15 x 20. Purchase. 37.31.

Bluhm, Norman. b. 1920.

THE ANVIL. 1959. Oil on canvas. 84 x 72. Gift of the Friends of the Whitney Museum of American Art. 60.22.

Blum, Jerome. 1884–1956.

THE ROAD AROUND THE ISLAND. (c. 1920.) Oil on canvas. 34 x 46. 31.116.

Blumberg, Yuli. b. 1894.

MAN WITH TORAH. 1957. Oil on canvas. 44 x 36¼. Gift of Hyman N. Glickstein. 58.59.

Blume, Peter. b. 1906.

LIGHT OF THE WORLD. 1932. Oil on composition board. 18 x 20¼. Purchase. 33.5. (p. 107.)

MAN OF SORROWS. 1951. Tempera on canvas. 28 x 24. Purchase. 51.5. (p. 153.)

Bohrod, Aaron. b. 1907.

CHICAGO JUNK YARD. 1935. Gouache on cardboard. 14⅛ x 19. Purchase. 36.11.

CHICAGO STREET IN WINTER. 1939. Gouache on cardboard. 17⅞ x 26⅞. Purchase. 39.17.

LANDSCAPE NEAR CHICAGO. 1934. Oil on composition board. 24 x 32. Purchase. 34.13.

Bolotowsky, Ilya. b. 1907.

BLUE RECTANGLES. 1953. Oil on canvas. 34 x 42. Purchase. 56.1.

LARGE VERTICAL 51/59. 1951–59. Oil on canvas. 95¼ x 40½. Gift of Mr. and Mrs. N. E. Waldman. 59.48. (p. 241.)

Borie, Adolphe. 1877–1934.

BENJAMIN DE LOACHE. (c. 1927.) Charcoal. 11⅞ x 8⅞. Purchase. 35.13.

THE BLACK HAT. (1924.) Oil on canvas. 28¾ x 23½. Purchase. 34.30.

PETER. (c. 1919.) Charcoal. 10 x 6. Purchase. 35.14.

SEATED NUDE. (c. 1920.) Oil on canvas. 39 x 32. Purchase. 31.117.

Bosa, Louis. b. 1905.

HEY, GARÇON! (1951.) Oil on canvas. 12¼ x 22. Gift of Joseph Horwitz. 56.47.

MY FAMILY REUNION. 1950. Oil on canvas. 42½ x 62. Gift of Mr. and Mrs. Alfred Jaretzki, Jr. 54.55.

Bothwell, Dorr. b. 1902.

KEEPSAKE FROM CORSICA. 1950. Oil on canvas. 31 x 21. Gift of Miss Doris Meltzer. 54.56.

Botkin, Henry. b. 1896.

SLEEP. (1950.) Oil on canvas. 30 x 23. Gift of Mr. and Mrs. David M. Solinger. 53.19.

Bouché, Louis. b. 1896.

ARRANGEMENT. 1930. Oil on canvas. 30 x 20. 31.118.

BANTHAM, DEVONSHIRE. 1933. Oil on canvas. 30 x 33. Purchase. 34.14.

STAMFORD HARBOR. 1932. Oil on canvas. 29 x 36¼. Purchase. 33.6. (p. 81.)

Bourgeois, Louise. b. 1911.

ONE AND OTHERS. (1955.) Painted and stained wood. 20¼ high. Purchase. 56.43. (p. 234.)

Bowes, Julian. b. 1894.

GEORGE BELLOWS. (1924.) Bronze. 14 high. Purchase. 31.4.

Boyd, Fiske. b. 1895.

SUBURBAN HOTEL. 1934. Watercolor. 17⅜ x 21⅝. Purchase. 36.13.

Boynton, James W. b. 1928.

AFTERMATH. (1956–57.) Oil on canvas. 60 x 34. Gift of Mr. and Mrs. Allan D. Emil. 58.35.

Braught, Ross. b. 1898.

TROPICAL NIGHT. 1942. Pencil. 18½ x 24. Purchase. 48.11.

Brenson, Theodore. 1893–1959.

NUMBER 17, 1956. Oil on canvas. 51¾ x 40. Gift of Mr. and Mrs. Hudson D. Walker. 58.1.

Brice, William. b. 1921.

FLOWERS AT NIGHT. 1949. Ink and oil. 24 x 18½. Purchase. 51.22.

PINE CONES AND TWIGS. 1947. Charcoal and ink. 16⅞ x 23⅜. Gift of Edith and Milton Lowenthal. 57.48.

Briggs, Ernest. b. 1923.

NUMBER 1107. (1955.) Oil on canvas. 69 x 50½. Gift of the Friends of the Whitney Museum of American Art. 57.20.

Brockman, Ann. 1899–1943.

LOT'S WIFE. (1942.) Oil on canvas. 46 x 36. Purchase. 43.1.

Broderson, Morris. b. 1928.

CRUCIFIXION, II. 1960. Ink, charcoal, chalk, and textile paint. 36 x 28. Purchase. 60.45.

Brodie, Gandy. b. 1925.

END OF WINTER. 1956. Oil on composition board. 47¼ x 57¼. Gift of Mrs. Ethel K. Schwabacher. 56.37.

Brook, Alexander. b. 1898.

BOUQUET, I. (1924.) Oil on canvas. 36 x 20. 31.123.

BOUQUET, II. (1924.) Oil on canvas. 36 x 20. 31.122.

DOING HER HAIR. 1936. Oil on canvas. 18 x 14⅛. Gift of Mr. and Mrs. Albert Hackett. 55.40.

GIRL WITH FLOWER. 1930. Oil on canvas. 34 x 26. 31.124.

MOOD. (1947.) Oil on canvas. 25 x 20. Purchase (and exchange). 53.27. (p. 128.)

MORNING LIGHT. 1936. Oil on canvas. 30 x 40. Purchase. 36.142.

NUDE. (1920's.) Pencil. 17 x 13⅜. 31.502.

THE SENTINELS. (1934.) Oil on canvas. 32 x 48¼. Purchase. 34.15. (p. 79.)

Brooks, James. b. 1906.

NUMBER 27. 1950. Oil on canvas. 37 x 46. Gift of Mr. and Mrs. Roy R. Neuberger. 53.32.

RASALUS. (1959.) Oil on canvas. 66 x 79¾. Gift of the Friends of the Whitney Museum of American Art. 59.39. (p. 214.)

Brown, Carlyle. b. 1919.

THE RED CABINET. 1954. Oil on canvas. 50¾ x 36¾. Purchase. 55.21. (p. 146.)

Brown, Sonia Gordon. b. 1894.

HEAD OF A YOUNG MAN. (1928.) Bronze. 14 high. Purchase. 33.54.

Browne, Byron. b. 1907.

HEAD IN BRONZE. 1952. Bronze. 17 high. Gift of Dr. and Mrs. John Beck. 53.44.

STILL LIFE WITH CITY WINDOW. 1945. Oil on canvas. 47 x 36. Gift of Edith and Milton Lowenthal. 57.16.

WOMAN WITH BIRD. 1948. Oil on canvas. 38 x 30. Gift of Mr. and Mrs. Roy R. Neuberger. 49.1.

Bruce, Edward. 1879–1943.

INDUSTRY. (1932.) Oil on canvas. 28 x 36. Purchase (and exchange). 34.4.

Bruce, Patrick Henry. 1881–1937.

PAINTING. (c. 1930.) Oil on canvas. 35 x 45¾. Anonymous gift. 54.20. (p. 47.)

Buller, Audrey. b. 1902.

TRAGEDY. (1936.) Oil on canvas. 15 x 25. Purchase. 36.151.

Bultman, Fritz. b. 1919.

SLEEPER, NUMBER 2. 1952. Oil on canvas. 30 x 38. Wildenstein Benefit Purchase Fund. 53.3.

Bunce, Louis. b. 1907.

LAVA FIELD. 1953. Oil on canvas. 28 x 36. Gift of Samuel N. Tonkin and Sidney Freedman. 54.57.

Burchfield, Charles. b. 1893.

AN APRIL MOOD. 1946/55. Watercolor. 40 x 54. Gift of Mr. and Mrs. Lawrence A. Fleischman (and purchase). 55.39. (p. 124.)

BEGINNING OF A SNOWSTORM. (1920.) Watercolor and gouache. 17½ x 24½. Purchase. 31.407.

ICE GLARE. 1933. Watercolor. 30¾ x 24¾. Purchase. 33.64. (p. 89.)

THE MARKET AT CHRISTMASTIME. 1941. Watercolor. 25½ x 42½. Purchase. 42.11.

NOONTIDE IN LATE MAY. 1917. Watercolor and gouache. 21⅜ x 17⅜. Purchase. 31.408. (p. 39.)

OLD HOUSE BY CREEK. 1932–38. Oil on canvas. 34½ x 57. Purchase. 39.14. (p. 93.)

OVERHANGING CLOUD IN JULY. 1947/59. Watercolor. 39½ x 35½. Gift of the Friends of the Whitney Museum of American Art. 60.23.

SEPTEMBER ELMS. (1927.) Watercolor. 23⅛ x 32¾. Purchase. 31.409.

SUNFLOWER. 1916. Watercolor. 19½ x 13⅝. Gift of Mr. and Mrs. Lesley G. Sheafer. 55.43.

TALL WHITE SUN. 1917. Watercolor. 22 x 18 (over-all). Purchase. 31.410.

WINTER TWILIGHT. 1930. Oil on composition board. 27¾ x 30½. Purchase. 31.128.

Burkhard, Henri. 1892–1956.

TABLE TOPS. (c. 1928.) Oil on canvas. 50 x 42. 31.135.

Burlin, Paul. b. 1886.

DRAPED FIGURE. (1916.) Pencil. 22⅞ x 16⅞. 31.504.

THE GHOST CITY. (1936.) Oil on canvas. 32¼ x 40. Purchase. 36.152.

RED, RED, NOT THE SAME. (1959.) Oil on canvas. 48½ x 72. Gift of Sam Jaffe, Milton Lowenthal, Harry Pinkerson, Bernard Reis, and Dr. Samuel Ernest Sussman. 60.21. (p. 215.)

YOUNG MAN ALONE WITH HIS FACE. (1944.) Oil on canvas. 39 x 32. Purchase. 45.2.

Burliuk, David. b. 1882.

IN THE SOUTH. 1939. Oil on canvas. 13 x 18. Gift of Juliana Force. 43.6.
REGATTA. (1938.) Oil on canvas. 15 x 19. Purchase. 41.13.
ST. MARK'S PLACE. (1951/52.) Oil on canvas. 26 x 34. Gift of Sidney Elliott Cohn. 54.1.
THE WHITE COW. (c. 1936.) Oil on canvas. 36 x 54. Gift of Samuel N. Tonkin. 49.24.

Burroughs, Betty. b. 1899.

HERBERT WINLOCK. 1931. Terra cotta. 13¾ high. Purchase. 37.51.

Burroughs, Bryson. 1869–1934.

ISLAND OF NAXOS. 1928. Oil on canvas. 40 x 36. Purchase. 31.137.

Cadmus, Paul. b. 1904.

FANTASIA ON A THEME BY DR. S. (1946.) Egg tempera on composition board. 13 x 13. Purchase. 47.1. (p. 140.)
TO THE LYNCHING! (1935.) Pencil and watercolor. 20½ x 15¾. Purchase. 36.32.

Caesar, Doris. b. 1893.

TORSO. (1953.) Bronze. 58 high. Purchase (and exchange). 54.30. (p. 194.)

Calcagno, Lawrence. b. 1916.

SAPAQUE, II. 1955. Oil on canvas. 57½ x 45. Gift of the New York Foundation. 56.2.

Calder, Alexander. b. 1898.

BLACK, WHITE AND 10 RED. 1957. Mobile. Sheet aluminum, steel wire, and rods. About 14 feet long. Gift of the Friends of the Whitney Museum of American Art. 57.36. (p. 256.)
THE MERMAID. (c. 1945.) Watercolor and ink. 18⅛ x 23⅛. Gift of Edith and Milton Lowenthal. 57.49.
POMEGRANATE. (1949.) Mobile. Sheet aluminum and steel, steel wire, and rods. About 72 high, about 68 diameter. Purchase. 50.6. (p. 257.)
YOUNG ONION REARING ON ITS TOES. 1944. Gouache. 31 x 22½. Gift of Mr. and Mrs. Samuel M. Kootz. 51.37.

Callahan, Kenneth. b. 1906.

CASCADE MOUNTAIN LANDSCAPE, NUMBER 12. (c. 1951.) Ink. 20⅝ x 24⅝ (over-all). Gift of the American Academy of Arts and Letters, Childe Hassam Fund. 52.34.
TRANSITION. 1956. Gouache. 19¼ x 25. Living Arts Foundation Fund. 57.50.

Cammarata, Peter. b. 1887.

STILL LIFE. (1926.) Oil on canvas. 28 x 24. 31.138.

Campbell, Blendon R. b. 1872.

ALICE. 1914. Oil on canvas. 27 x 21. 31.139.
ZINNIAS. (1927.) Oil on cardboard. 16¼ x 13. 31.140.

Campbell, Charles. b. 1905.

TEXAS BOUDOIR. (c. 1937.) Watercolor. 15¼ x 19. Purchase. 37.11.

Candell, Victor. b. 1903.

ASCENDANT. (1952.) Oil on canvas. 60 x 32. Purchase. 53.4.

Caparn, Rhys. b. 1909.

A GATHERING OF BIRDS. (1954.) Cast stone. 20½ x 20. Gift of George Claiborne Royall through the Federation of Modern Painters and Sculptors, Inc. 55.18.

Carles, Arthur B. 1882–1952.

BOUQUET ABSTRACTION. (c. 1930.) Oil on canvas. 31¾ x 36. Purchase. 53.41. (p. 113.)

Carone, Nicolas. b. 1917.

PSYCHOMACHIA, II. 1958. Oil on canvas. 63¼ x 76. Gift of Miss Katharine Ordway. 59.19.

Carroll, John. 1892–1959.

PUPPY. (1932.) Oil on canvas. 20 x 24. Purchase. 33.33.

Carter, Clarence Holbrook. b. 1904.

THE GUARDIAN ANGEL. 1936. Watercolor. 21½ x 14½. Purchase. 37.12.
IMMORTAL WATER. 1933. Oil on canvas. 54¼ x 38. Purchase. 33.46.
JULIA MARLOWE'S HOUSE, PORTSMOUTH, OHIO. 1932. Watercolor. 19⅝ x 14¾. Purchase. 33.47.

Castellón, Federico. b. 1914.

THE DARK FIGURE. 1938. Oil on canvas. 17 x 26⅛. Purchase. 42.3. (p. 149.)
REST ON THE FLIGHT INTO EGYPT. (1940.) Ink. 8⅛ x 10½. Purchase. 41.48.

Cavallon, Giorgio. b. 1904.

UNTITLED. 1959. Oil on canvas. 65 x 38. Gift of the Friends of the Whitney Museum of American Art. 60.2.

Celentano, Daniel R. b. 1902.

THE FIRST BORN. (1937.) Oil on canvas. 26 x 24. Purchase. 37.38.

Chaiken, William. b. 1921.

DUSK. 1955. Casein on canvas. 33 x 48. Neysa McMein Purchase Award. 57.18.

Chamberlain, Wynn. b. 1928.

CELEBRATION. 1954–55. Egg tempera on composition board. 55¼ x 28½. Gift of the Pastorale Fund. 59.41.

Chanler, Robert W. 1872–1930.

CARL VAN DOREN. (1920's.) Oil on canvas. 36¼ x 24. 31.150.

Cherney, Marvin. b. 1925.

CLASSICAL NUDE. (1958–59.) Oil on canvas. 42 x 50. Gift of Mr. and Mrs. William Meyers. 60.27.

Childs, Bernard. b. 1910.
THE BIG KNIFE. 1958. Oil on canvas. 35 x 46. Purchase. 60.34.

Cicero, Carmen. b. 1926.
OVER SQUANKUM HILL. 1960. Ink. 20½ x 24⅞. Purchase. 60.55.
PEGASUS. 1957. Oil on canvas. 56 x 72. Gift of the Friends of the Whitney Museum of American Art. 58.27.

Clews, Henry. 1876–1937.
PORTRAIT OF SAM. 1911. Bronze. 12⅛ high. 31.8.

Coiner, Charles T. b. 1898.
ARTICHOKES AND LEMONS. 1932. Watercolor. 21⅛ x 27½ (over-all). Purchase. 36.27.

Coleman, Glenn O. 1887–1932.
THE ARCH. (c. 1927.) Oil on canvas. 30 x 25. 31.153.
DOWNTOWN STREET. (1926.) Oil on canvas. 33 x 44. 31.154. (p. 87.)
GREENWICH VILLAGE VISTA. Gouache. 16⅝ x 12⅛. 31.413.
THE MIRROR. (1927.) Oil on canvas. 30 x 25. 31.155.
THE PIER. Pastel. 14⅞ x 18. Gift of Samuel S. Goldberg. 50.19.
STREET BATHERS. (c. 1906.) Crayon. 11 x 15¾. Purchase. 32.44.

Congdon, William. b. 1912.
PIAZZA SAN MARCO. (1950.) Oil on wood. 20 x 46¼. Gift of Jennifer Conway in memory of Alban Conway. 57.23.
ST. GERMAIN. 1954. Oil on composition board. 48 x 54. Gift of Miss Katharine Ordway. 54.59.

Cook, Howard. b. 1901.
TAXCO BOY. (1932.) Crayon. 17½ x 11½. Purchase. 40.16.

Cook, Robert. b. 1921.
THE DANCER. (1950.) Bronze. 12⅛ high. Gift of Mr. and Mrs. Arthur G. Altschul. 59.23.

Corbett, Edward. b. 1919.
NUMBER 12. 1951. Pastel and charcoal on canvas. 22⅞ x 18 (over-all). Purchase. 54.22.

Corbino, Jon. b. 1905.
LAUGHING ANGEL. (1941.) Gouache and crayon. 33¾ x 22¾. Purchase. 42.12.

Corcos, Lucille. b. 1908.
AFTERNOON AT THE ZOO. 1937. Gouache. 11⅛ x 15½. Purchase. 38.14.

Cornell, Joseph. b. 1903
HÔTEL DU NORD. (c. 1953.) Construction in wood, glass, and paper. 19 x 13¼. Purchase. 57.6.

Cramer, Konrad. b. 1888.
LANDSCAPE. 1932. Oil on composition board. 24 x 32. Purchase. 33.8.
VIADUCT. 1931. Ink. 9⅜ x 14. Purchase. 32.4.

Crampton, Rollin. b. 1896.
CYCLE EAST. (1959.) Oil on canvas. 28 x 39. Purchase. 60.16.

Crawford, Ralston. b. 1906.
STEEL FOUNDRY, COATESVILLE, PA. (1936–37.) Oil on canvas. 32 x 40. Purchase. 37.10.

Crisp, Arthur. b. 1881.
ADAM AND EVE. (c. 1918.) Oil on plaster. 22 x 30. 31.156.

Criss, Francis. b. 1901.
ASTOR PLACE. 1932. Oil on canvas. 32 x 40. Purchase. 33.9.
PATTERN FOR TRACKS. 1933. Egg tempera on composition board. 20½ x 32¾. Purchase. 33.65.

Cunning, John. 1889–1953.
OLD DOCK. (1927.) Oil on canvas. 28 x 25. 31.157.

Curry, John Steuart. 1897–1946.
BAPTISM IN KANSAS. (1928.) Oil on canvas. 40 x 50. 31.159. (p. 91.)
THE FLYING CODONAS. 1932. Tempera and oil on composition board. 36 x 30. Purchase. 33.10.
HEAD OF A NEGRO. (1927.) Pastel. 20¾ x 15¾. Purchase. 35.18.
HORSES RUNNING BEFORE A STORM. 1930. Watercolor and ink. 14 x 19⅞. 31.414.
THE NE'ER-DO-WELL. 1929; incorrectly dated 1930. Oil on canvas. 20 x 26. 31.160.
THE STOCKMAN. (1929.) Oil on canvas. 52 x 40. Purchase. 31.161.

Cushing, Howard G. 1869–1915.
MRS. HARRY PAYNE WHITNEY. 1902. Oil on canvas. 24 x 20. 31.162.

Dasburg, Andrew. b. 1887.
APPLES. (1929.) Oil on canvas. 16⅛ x 24¼. Purchase. 31.163.
LANDSCAPE. 1920. Pencil. 12⅜ x 13⅞. 31.513.
SPRING LANDSCAPE. (c. 1930.) Watercolor. 12 x 15¾. 31.415.
TAXCO. 1933. Watercolor. 14½ x 21½. Purchase. 36.14.
TULIPS. 1934. Crayon. 24 x 17⅞ (over-all). Purchase. 40.15.

Datz, A. Mark. b. 1889.
"HANDS OF FATE." (1946–49.) Oil on canvas. 36 x 26. Purchase (and exchange). 53.34.

Davey, Randall. b. 1887.
THE CANYON. (1919.) Watercolor. 6 x 8. 31.416.
THE COCK FIGHT. (1917.) Ink on cardboard. 6 x 7¾. 31.514.
THE COCK FIGHT. 1917. Ink on cardboard. 6⅝ x 9¼. 31.417.
HURDLE RACE. (1930.) Oil on canvas. 26 x 32. Purchase. 31.164.
PENITENTES. (1919.) Ink. 5⅞ x 7¾. 31.515.
STREET SCENE. 1917. Ink on cardboard. 6¾ x 9⅜. 31.418.

Davidson, Jo. 1883–1952.

DR. ALBERT EINSTEIN. 1934. Bronze. 13¾ high. Purchase. 34.31.

FEMALE TORSO. (1927.) Terra cotta. 22½ high. Purchase. 33.55.

NUDE. 1910. Bronze. 25¼ high. 31.11.

GERTRUDE STEIN. 1920. Bronze. 31 high. Purchase. 54.10. (p. 33.)

GERTRUDE V. WHITNEY. (c. 1917.) Marble. 15 high. Purchase. 54.33. (p. 14.)

GERTRUDE V. WHITNEY. 1942. Terra cotta. 17 high. Purchase. 43.3.

Davies, Arthur B. 1862–1928.

CRESCENDO. (1910.) Oil on canvas. 18 x 40. 31.166. (p. 21.)

CROUCHING NUDE, NUMBER 1. Chalk and charcoal. 12¼ x 9⅝. Purchase. 31.516.

KNEELING NUDE. Crayon and chalk. 12 x 9⅜. Purchase. 31.517.

RECLINING NUDE. Crayon and pencil. 8⅝ x 12⅜. Purchase. 31.518.

SIBYL RETURNING TO CUMAE. (1910.) Oil on canvas. 23 x 28. Purchase. 31.167.

TIPTOEING YOUTH. (1910.) Oil on canvas. 18 x 40. Purchase. 31.168.

TWILIGHT TRAVELING. (1910.) Oil on canvas. 11 x 22. Bequest of Mrs. Sam A. Lewisohn. 54.49.

Davis, Emma Lu. b. 1905.

COCK. (1932.) Painted cherry wood and copper. 12½ high. Purchase. 36.5.

ALICE COMPTON. (1934.) Butternut wood. 11½ high. Purchase. 36.6.

Davis, Stuart. b. 1894.

EARLY AMERICAN LANDSCAPE. 1925. Oil on canvas. 19 x 22. 31.171.

EGG BEATER, NUMBER 2. (1927.) Oil on canvas. 29⅛ x 36. 31.169. (p. 112.)

FLOWER STUDY: COMPOTE. (1928.) Ink. 24¼ x 18⅜. 31.519.

HOUSE AND STREET. (1931.) Oil on canvas. 26 x 42¼. Purchase. 41.3.

NEW ENGLAND STREET. (c. 1929.) Gouache. 8⅞ x 11⅜. 31.421.

OWH! IN SAN PAŌ. 1951. Oil on canvas. 52¼ x 41¾. Purchase. 52.2. (p. 247.)

THE PARIS BIT. 1959. Oil on canvas. 46 x 60. Gift of the Friends of the Whitney Museum of American Art. 59.38. (p. 249.)

PLACE PASDELOUP. (1928.) Oil on canvas. 36¼ x 28¾. 31.170. (p. 111.)

de Creeft, José. b. 1884.

THE CLOUD. (1939.) Greenstone. 13½ high. Purchase. 41.17. (p. 65.)

HIMALAYA. 1942. Beaten lead. 34½ high. Purchase. 43.8. (p. 136.)

Dehn, Adolf. b. 1895.

"BEAUTY IS WHERE YOU FIND IT." 1943. Watercolor. 19⅛ x 27⅝. Purchase. 43.13.

COLD DAY. 1941. Watercolor. 19 x 27⅝. Purchase. 41.52.

THE DARK ONE. 1953. Gouache. 19¾ x 28¼. Gift of Mr. and Mrs. Albert Hackett. 56.29.

OUT STROLLING. 1927. Ink. 11⅞ x 18½. 31.520.

QUINCY BEACH. 1934. Ink. 14¼ x 21¼. Purchase. 36.33.

JIMMY SAVO AND ROPE. 1944. Gouache. 14⅜ x 21⅜. Purchase. 45.12. (p. 166.)

THE SISTERS. 1927. Ink. 13¾ x 18½. 31.521.

WINTER LANDSCAPE. 1931. Ink. 14⅜ x 21¾. Purchase. 35.15.

de Kooning, Willem. b. 1904.

DOOR TO THE RIVER. (1960.) Oil on canvas. 80 x 70. Gift of the Friends of the Whitney Museum of American Art (and purchase). 60.63. (p. 227.)

WOMAN AND BICYCLE. (1952–53.) Oil on canvas. 76½ x 49. Purchase. 55.35. (p. 199.)

de Martelly, John S. b. 1903.

RIDE A COCKHORSE. (c. 1939.) Oil on canvas. 21¾ x 24. Purchase. 42.4.

De Martini, Joseph. b. 1896.

QUARRY BRIDGE. (1942.) Oil on canvas. 36 x 28. Gift of Edith and Milton Lowenthal. 53.47.

Demuth, Charles. 1883–1935.

AUGUST LILIES. 1921. Watercolor. 11¾ x 17⅞. Purchase. 31.422.

BUILDINGS, LANCASTER. 1930. Oil on composition board. 24 x 20. Anonymous gift. 58.63. (p. 52.)

DAISIES. 1918. Watercolor. 17¼ x 11⅜. 31.423.

MY EGYPT. 1927. Oil on composition board. 35¾ x 30. Purchase. 31.172. (p. 53.)

de Rivera, José. b. 1904.

CONSTRUCTION "BLUE AND BLACK." (1951.) Painted aluminum. 47 long. Purchase. 52.16. (p. 252.)

Der Harootian, Koren. b. 1909.

EAGLES OF ARARAT. (1955–56.) Serpentine marble. 58 high. Purchase. 56.22. (p. 135.)

Deshaies, Arthur. b. 1920.

CYCLE OF LOVE: THEN WHAT? (1959.) Conté crayon and dry pigment. 27¾ x 33⅞ (over-all). Gift of the Friends of the Whitney Museum of American Art. 60.64.

Dickinson, Edwin. b. 1891.

THE FOSSIL HUNTERS. 1926–28. Oil on canvas. 96½ x 73¾. Purchase. 58.29. (p. 105.)

Dickinson, Preston. 1891–1930.

HARLEM RIVER. Pastel and ink. 14¾ x 21¼. 31.424.

INDUSTRY. (Before 1924.) Oil on canvas. 30 x 24¼. 31.173. (p. 56.)

INDUSTRY, II. Oil on canvas. 24¾ x 30. Gift of Mr. and Mrs. Alan H. Temple. 57.47.

INTERIOR WITH FLOWERS. (c. 1924.) Oil on canvas. 26 x 20. Gift of Mr. and Mrs. Alan H. Temple. 59.45.

STILL LIFE, BREAD AND FRUIT. Oil on canvas. 30 x 28⅛. 31.174.

STILL LIFE, FLOWERS. (Before 1924.) Oil on canvas. 30 x 20. 31.175.

Diederich, Hunt. 1884–1953.

COCK. Sheet metal. 25½ high. Gift of Mr. and Mrs. Lawrence Rill Schumann. 56.31.

PLAYING DOGS. Bronze. 30¼ long. Purchase. 31.14.

Diller, Burgoyne. b. 1906.

THIRD THEME. (1946–48.) Oil on canvas. 42 x 42. Gift of Miss May Walter. 58.58.

Dirk, Nathaniel. 1895–1961.

BOATS AT REST. (1936.) Watercolor. 14 x 18. Purchase (and exchange). 39.19.

PROMENADE. (1932.) Oil on canvas. 60 x 34. Purchase. 33.11.

Dobkin, Alexander. b. 1908.

THE SUBWAY. (1952/59.) Oil on canvas. 33 x 47¼. Living Arts Foundation Fund. 60.1.

Dodd, Lamar. b. 1909.

EUROPEAN HILLSIDE. 1957. Oil on canvas. 42 x 30. Purchase. 58.7.

Dohanos, Stevan. b. 1907.

PIGEON ROOST. (1933.) Watercolor. 15½ x 18⅞. Purchase. 33.48.

ROSS YARD. 1936. Watercolor. 15⅛ x 20. Purchase. 37.14.

WIRES, NUMBER 3. 1936. Watercolor and ink. 5¾ x 3⅛. Purchase. 37.13.

Donati, Enrico. b. 1909.

GORE ET MANDRA. 1957. Oil on canvas. 60 x 60. Purchase. 58.9. (p. 225.)

Donnelly, Thomas. b. 1893.

FAIRFIELD BEACH. 1935. Gouache. 17⅝ x 29⅜. Purchase. 36.15.

VALHALLA BRIDGE. 1932. Oil on canvas. 22¼ x 34. Purchase. 39.18.

VASE OF FLOWERS. 1930. Ink. 13¾ x 9¼. Purchase. 31.523.

THE VILLAGE. 1932. Watercolor. 7¾ x 15⅛. Purchase. 33.45.

Dove, Arthur G. 1880–1946.

DISTRACTION. (1929.) Oil on canvas. 21 x 30. Anonymous gift. 58.64.

FERRY BOAT WRECK. (1931.) Oil on canvas. 18 x 30. Gift of Mr. and Mrs. Roy R. Neuberger (and purchase). 56.21. (p. 109.)

PLANT FORMS. (1915.) Pastel on canvas. 17¼ x 23⅞. Gift of Mr. and Mrs. Roy R. Neuberger. 51.20. (p. 44.)

Dozier, Otis. b. 1904.

LANDSCAPE. 1940. Gouache on cardboard. 13½ x 10½. Purchase. 40.10.

Driggs, Elsie. b. 1898.

LEAVES. (1926.) Pastel. 12⅞ x 8⅝. 31.427.

PITTSBURGH. (1927.) Oil on canvas. 34¼ x 40. 31.177.

Drumlevitch, Seymour. b. 1923.

CONCA D'ORO. 1951. Oil and lacquer on composition board. 30 x 40. Gift of Mr. and Mrs. Roy R. Neuberger. 54.16.

Duble, Lu. b. 1896.

CAIN. (1953.) Hydrocal. 38 high. Purchase. 53.35.

du Bois, Guy Pène. 1884–1958.

BLONDE AND BRUNETTE. (1915.) Oil on wood. 20 x 15. 31.178.

FATHER AND SON. 1929. Oil on canvas. 21½ x 18. Purchase. 31.179.

JEANNE EAGELS IN "RAIN." 1922. Oil on canvas. 84¾ x 48. Purchase. 31.181.

JULIANA FORCE AT THE WHITNEY STUDIO CLUB. (c. 1920.) Oil on wood. 20 x 15. Gift of Mr. and Mrs. James S. Adams in memory of Philip K. Hutchins. 51.43.

MORNING, PARIS CAFÉ. 1926. Oil on canvas. 36¼ x 28¾. 31.182.

MOTHER AND DAUGHTER. 1928. Oil on canvas. 21¾ x 18. Purchase. 31.183.

WOMAN WITH CIGARETTE. 1929. Oil on canvas. 36¼ x 28¾. 31.187. (p. 70.)

Also nineteen drawings.

Duffy, Edmund. b. 1899.

TWO LITTLE BUTTERCUPS. 1923. Ink and crayon. 20 x 16. 31.543.

Dzubas, Friedel. b. 1915.

YESTERDAY. (1957.) Oil on canvas. 44½ x 108¾. Gift of Mr. and Mrs. David M. Solinger. 59.24.

Eades, Luis. b. 1923.

SURVIVORS. 1959. Oil on canvas. 38 x 54. Neysa McMein Purchase Award. 59.31.

Eberle, Abastenia St. Leger. 1878–1942.

ROLLER SKATING. (Before 1909.) Bronze. 13 high. 31.15.

Edie, Stuart. b. 1908.

GIRL WITH BOOK. 1932. Oil on canvas. 24 x 18. Purchase. 32.21.

COMPOSITION. (1932.) Gouache on cardboard. 7¾ x 9. Purchase. 33.66.

Eilshemius, Louis M. 1864–1941.

DISDAIN. (1917.) Oil on composition board. 25½ x 30. Anonymous gift. 59.42.

FIGURES IN LANDSCAPE. 1906. Oil on canvas. 22½ x 25¾. Gift of Louise Nevelson. 56.14. (p. 31.)

THE FLYING DUTCHMAN. 1908. Oil on composition board. 23½ x 25½. 31.189.

Eilshemius, Louis M. (*continued*)

THE FORSAKEN MILL. (1908.) Oil on composition board. 24 x 28. Purchase. 42.29.

NUDES BY A STREAM. 1907. Oil on composition board. 27 x 22¼. Gift of James N. Rosenberg. 53.8.

Ernst, Jimmy. b. 1920.

CALLIGRAPHICS, NUMBER 2. 1949. Gouache. 21¾ x 16. Purchase. 49.6.

FACE. 1960. Ink. 22 x 29¾ (over-all). Purchase. 60.56.

PERSONAL HISTORY. 1949. Oil on canvas. 46 x 40. Juliana Force Purchase. 50.10. (p. 251.)

Esherick, Wharton. b. 1887.

GOSLINGS. 1927. Boxwood with mahogany base. 20 long. Purchase. 33.43.

Etting, Emlen. b. 1905.

WESTERN RAILWAY. (1936.) Oil on canvas. 30 x 40. Purchase. 36.150.

Evergood, Philip. b. 1901.

LILY AND THE SPARROWS. (1939.) Oil on composition board. 30 x 24. Purchase. 41.42. (p. 103.)

THE NEW LAZARUS. (1927–54.) Oil on canvas. 48 x 83¼. Gift of Joseph H. Hirshhorn. 54.60. (p. 164.)

THROUGH THE MILL. (1940.) Oil and tempera on canvas. 36 x 52. Purchase. 41.24.

VIRGINIA IN THE GROTTO. 1960. Oil on canvas. 50 x 30. Living Arts Foundation Fund. 60.15. (p. 189.)

Faggi, Alfeo. b. 1885.

BLANCHE GUZZI HECHT. 1947. Relief. Bronze. 15¾ x 11¼. Gift of Kalmun Hecht. 48.24.

NUDE. 1933. Crayon. 14⅜ x 9½. Purchase. 42.25.

THREE NUDES. (1911.) Relief. Bronze. 5¼ x 8¼. Purchase. 31.16.

HERVEY WHITE. (1940.) Bronze. 14½ high. Purchase. 42.27.

Farnsworth, Jerry. b. 1895.

MY NEIGHBOR, MISS WILLIAMS. (1942.) Oil on canvas. 20 x 16. Purchase. 42.17.

Fausett, Dean. b. 1913.

LANDSCAPE. 1948. Ink on cardboard. 17 x 27⅞. Purchase (and exchange). 54.47.

MOONLIGHT. (1940.) Oil on canvas. 24 x 36. Purchase. 41.4.

Feininger, Lyonel. 1871–1956.

GELMERODA, VIII. 1921. Oil on canvas. 39¼ x 31¼. Purchase. 53.38. (p. 55.)

MANHATTAN SKYSCRAPERS. 1942. Ink. 21⅜ x 15¼. Purchase (and exchange). 53.54. (p. 173.)

OFF THE COAST. 1942. Watercolor and ink. 11¼ x 17¾. Purchase. 42.35.

Ferber, Herbert. b. 1906.

THE FLAME. 1949. Brass, lead, and soft solder. 65½ high. Purchase. 51.30.

SUN WHEEL. (1956.) Brass, copper, and silver solder. 56¼ high. Purchase. 56.18. (p. 231.)

Ferguson, Duncan. b. 1901.

MALE FIGURE. Bronze. 72 high. Purchase. 32.15.

SQUIRREL. Wood. 17 high. 31.17.

Ferren, John. b. 1905.

THE GARDEN. 1954. Oil on canvas. 82 x 65¼. Purchase. 55.53. (p. 223.)

Fiene, Ernest. b. 1894.

CONCETTA. 1926. Oil on canvas. 40¼ x 30¼. 31.193.

DYCKMAN STREET CHURCH. 1925. Oil on canvas. 26 x 36. 31.194.

HUDSON NAVIGATION BOAT. 1927. Oil on composition board. 38 x 40. 31.199.

NOCTURNE, 34TH STREET. 1932. Oil on canvas. 26 x 36¼. Purchase. 33.12.

POPPIES IN WHITE VASE. (1928.) Gouache. 18⅜ x 11¾. 31.428.

ROSES IN BLUE VASE. (1928.) Gouache. 18⅜ x 12⅜. 31.429.

VARIATIONS ON A THEME: "THE WRECK, NUMBER 2." 1948. Oil on canvas. 34 x 44. Purchase (and exchange). 53.39. (p. 170.)

WRECK AT MONHEGAN ISLAND. 1952. Casein on canvas. 21⅜ x 29⅜. Purchase (and exchange). 53.40.

Fiene, Paul. 1899–1949.

FISH. (1929.) Marble. 10 high. Purchase. 31.18.

RECLINING FIGURE. (1927.) Bronze. 19½ long. Purchase. 31.20.

SNAIL. (1929.) Limestone. 8¾ high. Purchase. 31.21.

Filmus, Tully. b. 1903.

GLADYS. (1944.) Oil on canvas. 30 x 24. Purchase. 45.3.

Finch, Keith. b. 1920.

WALKING FIGURE. (1958.) Oil on composition board. 72 x 48. Purchase. 58.40.

Fine, Perle. b. 1908.

SUB-MARINE. 1948. Gouache. 22¼ x 30¾ (over-all). Purchase. 49.7.

THE TOLLING BELL. (1954.) Oil on canvas. 60 x 54. Gift of Mr. and Mrs. Robert J. Fields. 55.3.

Fink, Don. b. 1923.

BLACK AND WHITE MOUNTAINS. 1956. Oil on canvas. 58¼ x 22. Anonymous gift. 57.38.

Fiore, Joseph. b. 1925.

POLAND SPRING. 1960. Oil on canvas. 79½ x 63¾. Purchase. 60.60.

Flannagan, John B. 1898–1942.

CHIMPANZEE. (1928.) Granite. 14 high. 31.22.

ELEPHANT. (1929–30.) Bluestone. 15 long. 31.24. (p. 62.)

Floch, Joseph. b. 1895.

GREENHOUSE. (1956–57.) Oil on canvas. 32 x 36. Anonymous gift. 59.6.

Foote, John, Jr. b. 1921.

GREAT BEAST, NUMBER 2. 1950. Oil on composition board. 20½ x 30½. Anonymous gift. 57.39.

Forbes, Donald. 1905–1951.

ANVILS AND TRAPPED WHEEL. (1947.) Oil on canvas. 26 x 36. Gift of William Hunter. 52.33.

Foy, Gray. b. 1922.

UPROOTED PLANTS. (1955.) Pencil. 12 x 7½. Neysa McMein Purchase Award. 56.16.

Francis, Sam. b. 1923.

ABSTRACTION. 1959. Oil on canvas. 84 x 50. Bequest of Udo M. Reinach. 60.16.

Franck, Frederick. b. 1909.

BLUE POTS AND JARS. 1958. Oil on canvas. 17 x 34. Gift of Georgette Passedoit. 59.21.

Frankenthaler, Helen. b. 1928.

BLUE TERRITORY. (1955.) Oil on canvas. 113 x 58. Gift of the Friends of the Whitney Museum of American Art. 57.8. (p. 219.)

Frazier, Susan. b. 1900.

THE EAST RIVER. 1932. Gouache. 19¼ x 29¼. Purchase. 36.16.

Free, Karl. 1903–1947.

ARRANGEMENT. Ink. 13½ x 17½. Gift of Henry R. Free. 48.17.

COMPOSITION. (1934.) Ink. 15¾ x 20. Purchase. 35.10.

EPIPHANY. (1932.) Oil on canvas. 30 x 45. Gift of Henry R. Free. 48.13.

LANDSCAPE, OYSTER BAY. 1927. Oil on canvas. 18 x 28. 31.203.

STUDY OF A TREE. (1928.) Watercolor and ink. 14½ x 20. 31.433.

Also six watercolors of circus subjects.

Freed, William. b. 1904.

REPOSE. 1957. Oil on canvas. 42 x 32. Anonymous gift. 59.30.

French, Jared. b. 1905.

ATTEMPTED SUICIDE. (1935.) Pencil and watercolor. 17¾ x 15. Purchase. 36.34.

THE ROPE. (1954.) Egg tempera on paper. 13½ x 14¼. Charles F. Williams Fund. 56.3. (p. 144.)

SUMMER'S ENDING. (1939.) Oil and tempera on canvas. 24¼ x 40¼. Purchase. 39.24.

Friedensohn, Elias. b. 1924.

HEAD AND HANDS. (1958.) Ink. 18 x 14½. Purchase. 59.3.

Fuller, Sue. b. 1914.

STRING CONSTRUCTION, NUMBER 51. (1953.) Plastic thread and aluminum. 33½ x 45½. Purchase. 54.23.

Gabo, Naum. b. 1890.

LINEAR CONSTRUCTION IN SPACE, NUMBER 4. (1958.) Plastic and stainless steel. 40 x 21½ high. Gift of the Friends of the Whitney Museum of American Art. 58.61. (p. 253.)

Gaertner, Carl. 1898–1952.

SPRING COMES ON THE HUDSON. 1944. Oil on composition board. 28 x 47¾. Purchase. 45.4.

Gallatin, A. E. 1881–1952.

COMPOSITION. 1941–45. Oil on canvas. 50 x 20. Gift of Mrs. W. Floyd Nichols and Mrs. B. Langdon Tyler. 53.24.

Ganso, Emil. 1895–1941.

FACTORIES. 1936. Gouache. 14⅜ x 21⅞. Purchase. 37.16.

GERTIE. (c. 1928.) Oil on canvas. 40 x 34. 31.205.

GIRL RECLINING. (1930.) Ink. 13⅞ x 19¼. Purchase. 31.544.

SEATED NUDE. (1939.) Crayon and chalk. 19½ x 14½. Purchase (and exchange). 54.12.

STILL LIFE. (1931.) Oil on canvas. 31 x 25. 31.210.

Gatch, Lee. b. 1902.

JUMPING JOY. (1952.) Oil on canvas. 31½ x 31½. Gift of Mr. and Mrs. Roy R. Neuberger. 52.14. (p. 186.)

Gerald, Elizabeth Bart. b. 1907.

SPRING AT THE OLD HOUSE. 1942. Oil on canvas. 30 x 35. Purchase. 42.19.

Gershoy, Eugenie. b. 1905.

FIGURE. (1930.) Alabaster. 17¼ high. Purchase. 31.27.

LILA. 1933. Artificial stone. 56 long. Purchase. 33.56.

MARKET, GRANADA. 1932. Ink. 7⅞ x 10½. Purchase. 32.37.

PORT OF PALMA. 1932. Ink. 6⅛ x 9⅜. Purchase. 32.38.

STANDING FIGURE. (1932.) Terra cotta. 16½ high. Purchase. 32.72.

STREET IN ANDALUSIA. 1932. Ink. 7¾ x 10 (over-all). Purchase. 32.39.

Gikow, Ruth. b. 1914.

THE BLIND MUSICIAN. (1957.) Oil on composition board. 22 x 32. Anonymous gift. 57.40.

Glackens, William J. 1870–1938.

FÊTE DE SUQUET. (1932.) Oil on canvas. 25¾ x 32. Purchase. 33.13.

GIRL IN BLACK AND WHITE. 1914. Oil on canvas. 32 x 26. Gift of the Glackens Family. 38.53.

HAMMERSTEIN'S ROOF GARDEN. (c. 1901.) Oil on canvas. 30 x 25. Purchase. 53.46. (p. 23.)

PARADE, WASHINGTON SQUARE. (1912.) Oil on canvas. 26 x 31. 31.215.

"THEN THERE WAS A LIVELY LITTLE FIGHT." (1914.) Illustration for *Collier's*, June 6, 1914. Crayon and watercolor. 10⅛ x 14¼. Purchase. 31.545.

Glarner, Fritz. b. 1899.

RELATIONAL PAINTING. 1949–51. Oil on canvas. 65 x 52. Purchase. 52.3. (p. 243.)

Glasco, Joseph. b. 1925.

PORTRAIT OF A POET. 1951. Oil on canvas. 68 x 46. Purchase. 52.4. (p. 207.)

Goff, Lloyd Lózes. b. 1917.

TEXAS OIL FIRE. 1938. Watercolor and ink. 18⅜ x 24. Purchase. 38.15.

Goldthwaite, Anne. c. 1870–1944.

4 RUE DE CHEVREUSE, PARIS. (1908.) Oil on canvas. 29 x 23¾. 31.218.

Gonzalez, Xavier. b. 1898.

LANDSCAPE, NUMBER 9. (1950.) Watercolor and casein. 21½ x 30. Purchase. 51.23.

Goodnough, Robert. b. 1917.

SEATED FIGURE WITH GRAY. (1956–57.) Oil on canvas. 57 x 52. Anonymous gift. 57.33. (p. 206.)

Gordin, Sidney. b. 1918.

CONSTRUCTION, NUMBER 10. (1955.) Painted steel. 41¼ long. Purchase. 56.10. (p. 255.)

19–59. 1959. Welded steel. 34¾ long. Purchase (and exchange). 60.62.

Gorky, Arshile. 1904–1948.

THE ARTIST AND HIS MOTHER. 1926–29. Oil on canvas. 60 x 50. Gift of Julien Levy for Maro and Natasha Gorky in memory of their father. 50.17. (p. 114.)

THE BETROTHAL, II. 1947. Oil on canvas. 50¾ x 38. Purchase. 50.3. (p. 200.)

DRAWING. 1946. Pencil and crayon. 18½ x 24½. Gift of Mr. and Mrs. Wolfgang S. Schwabacher. 50.18.

PAINTING. 1936–37. Oil on canvas. 38 x 48. Purchase. 37.39. (p. 115.)

Gottlieb, Adolph. b. 1903.

THE FROZEN SOUNDS, NUMBER 1. 1951. Oil on canvas. 36 x 48. Gift of Mr. and Mrs. Samuel M. Kootz. 57.3. (p. 211.)

UNSTILL LIFE. 1952. Oil on canvas. 36 x 48. Gift of Mr. and Mrs. Alfred Jaretzki, Jr. 56.25.

VIGIL. 1948. Oil on canvas. 36 x 48. Purchase. 49.2.

VOYAGER'S RETURN. 1946. Watercolor and gouache. 25½ x 19⅝. Gift of Mr. and Mrs. Samuel M. Kootz. 51.38.

Gottlieb, Harry. b. 1895.

DUCK FARM. (1952.) Oil on canvas. 24 x 30. Purchase (and exchange). 54.37.

JAVANESE DANCER. (1932.) Gouache. 27⅝ x 19½. Purchase. 32.55.

WINTER AT THE MAVERICK. 1923. Oil on canvas. 24 x 30¼. 31.226.

Graham, Ellwood. b. 1911.

HYPERBOLE. (1950.) Watercolor. 19¾ x 19¾. Gift of Mr. and Mrs. Ansley K. Salz. 51.2.

KINSHIP. (1950.) Oil on composition board. 21⅞ x 28. Gift of Mr. and Mrs. Ansley K. Salz. 51.1.

Graham, John D. b. 1887.

HEAD OF A WOMAN. 1926. Oil on canvas. 22 x 18. 31.228.

MONA ANNA UXOR DE ADOLFO RAVENATO. 1947. Ink, pencil, and chalk. 22¼ x 17⅝. Gift of the Friends of the Whitney Museum of American Art. 60.65.

Graves, Morris. b. 1910.

BIRD IN THE SPIRIT. (c. 1940–41.) Gouache. 21½ x 42 (overall). Gift of the Friends of the Whitney Museum of American Art. 59.9. (p. 155.)

FLIGHT OF PLOVER. 1955. Oil on composition board. 36 x 48. Gift of Mr. and Mrs. Roy R. Neuberger. 56.4. (p. 156.)

JOURNEY. 1943. Gouache and watercolor. 22¼ x 30⅛. Purchase. 45.14.

Gray, Cleve. b. 1918.

MOSQUE, CORDOVA: NUMBER 2. 1959. Oil on canvas. 72 x 96. Gift of the Friends of the Whitney Museum of American Art. 60.24. (p. 242.)

Greco, Robert. b. 1923.

HERMETIC RETREATS. (1951.) Oil on canvas. 40 x 30. Juliana Force Purchase. 52.5.

Greenbaum, Dorothea. b. 1893.

DROWNED GIRL. (1950.) Tennessee marble. 9 x 9½. Purchase. 58.33. (p. 137.)

GIRL WITH TOWEL. (1943.) Plaster. 63¼ high. Purchase. 43.9.

Greene, Balcomb. b. 1904.

COMPOSITION: THE STORM. (1953–54.) Oil on canvas. 36¼ x 48. Purchase. 55.4. (p. 204.)

THIS ARCHITECTURAL WORLD. 1945. Oil on canvas. 30 x 47¾. Purchase. 46.1.

Greene, Stephen. b. 1918.

THE BURIAL. (1947.) Oil on canvas. 42 x 55. Purchase. 49.16. (p. 147.)

Greitzer, Jack J. b. 1910.

STILL LIFE UNITY. 1931. Watercolor. 12⅞ x 17⅞. Purchase. 36.17.

Grillo, John. b. 1917.

METAMORPHOSIS, II. (1956–57.) Oil on canvas. 42 x 48. Anonymous gift. 57.22.

Grippe, Peter. b. 1912.

THREE FURIES, II. 1955–56. Bronze. 14 high. Purchase. 57.44.

Gropper, William. b. 1897.

FARMERS' REVOLT. (1933.) Ink. 16 x 19. Purchase. 33.73. (p. 101.)

FINISHERS. (1933.) Ink. 16 x 19⅛. Purchase. 33.74.

OLD TREE AND OLD PEOPLE. (1939.) Oil on canvas. 20 x 22¼. Purchase. 39.21.

Gross, Chaim. b. 1904.

ACROBATIC DANCERS. 1942. Ebony. 39¾ high. Purchase. 42.28.

ACROBATS. (1935.) Pencil. 17⅞ x 10¾. Purchase. 36.35.

SISTERS. (1946.) Ink and pencil. 21 x 10. Gift of Mrs. Chaim Gross. 58.51.

SISTERS. (1946.) Italian pink marble. 41 high. Purchase. 58.45. (p. 196.)

SNAKE AND BIRDS. 1954. Lignum vitae. 60 high. Purchase. 58.44.

Gross, Sidney. b. 1921.

OASIS. (1954.) Oil on canvas. 42 x 50. Gift of Dr. Julius Lempert through the Federation of Modern Painters and Sculptors, Inc. 55.22.

VICTORY, 1945. (1945.) Tempera and oil on canvas. 26 x 40. Purchase. 46.2.

Grosz, George. 1893–1959.

APPROACHING STORM. 1940. Oil on composition board. 16¼ x 20¼. Purchase. 41.25.

COUPLE. (1934.) Watercolor. 25¼ x 17¾. Purchase. 36.18. (p. 101.)

THE PAINTER OF THE HOLE. (1947.) Watercolor. 23⅜ x 17¼. Purchase. 48.8.

PEACE, II. (1946.) Oil on canvas. 47 x 33¼. Purchase. 47.2. (p. 167.)

WAVING THE FLAG. (1947–48.) Watercolor. 25 x 18. Purchase (and exchange). 54.9. (p. 166.)

Guglielmi, Louis. 1906–1956.

CITYSCAPE WITH FIGURES. 1949. Oil on canvas. 26 x 20. Gift of Mrs. Edith Gregor Halpert in memory of Juliana Force. 49.11.

TERROR IN BROOKLYN. 1941. Oil on canvas. 34 x 30. Purchase. 32.34. (p. 152.)

Gussow, Bernar. b. 1881.

SUBWAY STAIRS. Oil on composition board. 25 x 30. Purchase. 42.5.

Guston, Philip. b. 1912.

DIAL. 1956. Oil on canvas. 72 x 76. Purchase. 56.44. (p. 218.)

Gwathmey, Robert. b. 1903.

FIELD FLOWERS. 1946. Oil on canvas. 37⅝ x 25¾. Gift of Mr. and Mrs. Sidney Elliott Cohn. 56.34.

SOWING. (1949.) Oil on canvas. 36 x 40. Purchase. 49.17. (p. 160.)

Hague, Raoul. b. 1905.

SAWKILL WALNUT. (1955.) 42 high. Gift of the Friends of the Whitney Museum of American Art. 57.35. (p. 260.)

Hall, Carl. b. 1922.

CRADLES. 1947. Oil on canvas. 24 x 35¾. Purchase. 48.1.

Halpert, Samuel. 1884–1930.

BROOKLYN BRIDGE. 1913. Oil on canvas. 34 x 42. Gift of Mr. and Mrs. Benjamin Halpert. 54.2. (p. 36.)

FRUIT. Oil on canvas. 24 x 20. 31.230.

NOTRE DAME, PARIS. Oil on canvas. 18¼ x 22. 31.231.

Harari, Hananiah. b. 1912.

DIAGRAMS IN LANDSCAPE. 1942. Oil on canvas. 29 x 46. Purchase. 42.30.

Hardy, Tom. b. 1921.

PORCUPINE. (1955.) Steel wire, nickel-silver, and brass. 37¾ long. Gift of the Howard W. Lipman Foundation, Inc. 60.57.

Hare, David. b. 1917.

HEAD OF AN ANIMAL. (1955.) Steel and iron. 65½ high. Purchase. 57.45.

JUGGLER. (1950–51.) Steel. 80¼ high. Purchase. 51.34. (p. 237.)

Harkavy, Minna. b. 1895.

THE LAST PRAYER. (1949.) Bronze. 18 high. Purchase. 50.7.

Harmon, Lily. b. 1913.

LONESOME PINES. (1956.) Oil on canvas. 30 x 40. Purchase. 57.4.

Harriton, Abraham. b. 1893.

NEW YORK WATERFRONT. 1936. Gouache. 21¼ x 27¼. Purchase. 36.19.

SUNSET AND STORM OVER PROVINCETOWN. (1955.) Oil on canvas. 20 x 28. Gift of David A. Teichman. 59.26.

Hart, George O. ("Pop"). 1868–1933.

THE BAHAMAS. (c. 1918.) Watercolor. 13½ x 21½. Purchase. 32.7.

Hartigan, Grace. b. 1922.

GRAND STREET BRIDES. 1954. Oil on canvas. 72 x 102½. Anonymous gift. 55.27. (p. 184.)

Hartl, Léon. b. 1889.

BOUQUET CÉLESTE. 1926. Oil on canvas. 22 x 18. 31.233.

DAISIES AND RED TABLE SCARF. 1926. Oil on canvas. 60¼ x 30¼. 31.234.

PRIMROSES. 1926. Oil on canvas. 32 x 22¼. 31.236.

RAYON DE SOLEIL. 1926. Oil on canvas. 22 x 18. 31.237.

Hartley, Marsden. 1877–1943.

FORMS ABSTRACTED. (1913.) Oil on canvas. 39½ x 31¾. Gift of Mr. and Mrs. Hudson D. Walker (and exchange). 52.37.

GRANITE BY THE SEA. (1937.) Oil on composition board. 20 x 28. Purchase. 42.31.

THE OLD BARS, DOGTOWN. (1936.) Oil on composition board. 18 x 24. Purchase. 37.26. (p. 41.)

PAINTING, NUMBER 5. (1914–15.) Oil on canvas. 39½ x 31¾. Anonymous gift. 58.65. (p. 43.)

Hartman, Bertram. b. 1882.

MARK ISLAND. 1928. Oil on canvas. 20 x 30. Purchase. 31.239.

SAILING VESSEL. 1927. Watercolor. 14⅝ x 22⅛. Purchase. 31.436.

TELEPHONE BUILDING. (1928.) Watercolor. 22⅛ x 14⅝. Purchase. 31.435.

Hartman, Rosella. b. 1894.

LANDSCAPE. 1930. Ink. 15⅝ x 19¾. Purchase. 31.592.

PHEASANT. 1932. Oil on composition board. 23¾ x 20. Purchase. 33.51.

SNARLING. (1944.) Ink. 12¾ x 17¼. Purchase. 45.22.

TIGER LILIES. (1928.) Crayon. 16⅞ x 18½. 31.547.

Harwood, Janet Compere. b. 1934.

FOREST. (1959.) Ink. 20¼ x 26½ (over-all). Purchase. 60.35.

Harwood, Stuart. b. 1923.

WINGED FIGURE. (1954–56.) Chestnut. 84 high. Gift of William Helburn. 56.27.

Haseltine, Herbert. b. 1877.

MEADOWBROOK TEAM. (1909.) Bronze. 68 long. 31.33.

UN PUYAZO. 1912. Bronze. 22 long. 31.34.

Hatofsky, Julius. b. 1922.

LA PUSH, II. 1959. Oil on canvas. 72 x 60. Anonymous gift. 59.20.

Hauck, Fred. 1905–1960.

THE GYRES. (1960.) Oil on canvas. 48¼ x 40. Anonymous gift. 60.50.

Haucke, Frederick. b. 1908.

THE FLOWER. 1941. Watercolor. 11¼ x 13⅝. Purchase. 41.50.

Hayter, Stanley William. b. 1901.

OPHELIA. 1948. Oil on canvas. 35¾ x 41⅝. Purchase. 52.7.

WORK IN PROGRESS. 1946. Colored ink on cardboard. 27¾ x 21½. Purchase. 49.9.

Hebald, Milton. b. 1917.

WOMAN WITH BIRDS. (1947.) Teakwood. 47¼ high. Purchase. 48.5.

Heidenreich, Charles. b. 1901.

MANHATTAN WINDOW, NUMBER 2. (1951.) Watercolor. 30¼ x 21¾. Gift of Harry Salpeter. 54.6.

Heliker, John. b. 1909.

FROM CRANBERRY ISLE. (1956.) Oil on canvas. 30 x 40¼. Gift of the Friends of the Whitney Museum of American Art. 57.28. (p. 186.)

OF MAINE. (1953.) Oil on composition board. 15¾ x 28½. Purchase. 53.49.

ROCKS. 1942. Oil on canvas. 25 x 18. Purchase. 42.32.

THE SOUND. 1941. Watercolor and ink. 9½ x 12½. Purchase. 41.51.

STUDY. (1950.) Pastel and gesso on cardboard. 15 x 23. Purchase. 50.9.

Henri, Robert. 1865–1929.

LAUGHING CHILD. (1907.) Oil on canvas. 24 x 20. 31.240.

GEORGE LUKS PLAYING BASEBALL. 1904. Ink. 7 x 4⅜ (over-all). Gift of Mr. and Mrs. Edward W. Root. 42.37.

STORM TIDE. (1903.) Oil on canvas. 26 x 32. Purchase. 31.242. (p. 22.)

Henry, Everett.

CARRIAGE. Watercolor. 18⅝ x 25⅝. 31.437.

Hering, Harry. b. 1887.

CLEAR AND COLD. 1926. Oil on canvas. 33¼ x 38¼. 31.243.

Higgins, Eugene. 1874–1958.

DESTRUCTION. (1932.) Watercolor. 14¼ x 20¾. Purchase. 33.67.

OVERLABOR. (1931–32.) Oil on canvas. 30 x 40. Purchase. 32.17.

Hirsch, Joseph. b. 1910.

MOONLIGHT. (1937.) Oil on canvas. 24¾ x 17¾. Purchase. 43.2.

THE PRISONER. (1942.) Oil on canvas. 44 x 30¼. Gift of Edith and Milton Lowenthal. 53.48.

THE SENATOR. (1941.) Oil on canvas. 16 x 32. Purchase. 42.6.

Hirsch, Stefan. b. 1899.

PIC OF ORIZABA. 1932. Oil on canvas. 29¼ x 39¼. Purchase. 33.14.

Hoff, Margo.

THE CLOWN. 1956. Oil on canvas. 40 x 30. Gift of Mr. and Mrs. Allan D. Emil. 56.24.

Hofmann, Hans. b. 1880.

CONSTRUCTION. 1948. Oil on paper. 16¾ x 13¾. Purchase. 50.4.

FANTASIA IN BLUE. 1954. Oil on canvas. 60 x 52. Gift of the Friends of the Whitney Museum of American Art. 57.21.

MAGENTA AND BLUE. 1950. Oil on canvas. 48 x 58. Purchase. 50.20. (p. 202.)

Holzhauer, Emil. b. 1887.

GIRL RESTING. 1931. Watercolor. 15 x 22. Purchase. 31.588.

Hondius, Gerrit. b. 1891.

CIRCUS FOLKS. (1932.) Oil on canvas. 54 x 34. Purchase. 33.15.

Hopper, Edward. b. 1882.

EARLY SUNDAY MORNING. (1930.) Oil on canvas. 35 x 60. Purchase. 31.426. (p. 88.)

EL PALACIO. (1946.) Watercolor. 20¾ x 28⅝. Purchase (and exchange). 50.2.

HOUSE ON PAMET RIVER. (1934.) Watercolor. 19¾ x 24⅞. Purchase. 36.20. (p. 89.)

SECOND-STORY SUNLIGHT. (1960.) Oil on canvas. 40 x 50. Gift of the Friends of the Whitney Museum of American Art (and purchase). 60.54. (p. 127.)

SEVEN A.M. (1948.) Oil on canvas. 30 x 40. Purchase (and exchange). 50.8. (p. 126.)

Horter, Earl. 1881–1940.

GLOUCESTER. 1932. Oil on canvas. 17 x 25. Purchase. 33.16.

GLOUCESTER. (1932.) Pastel. 9¾ x 14⅞. Purchase. 35.4.

GLOUCESTER DOCKS. 1935. Watercolor. 16½ x 22⅛. Purchase. 36.21.

SEASCAPE. (c. 1927.) Watercolor. 13 x 17½. 31.439.

Houmère, Walter. b. 1895.

PRELUDE TO INVASION. 1943. Oil on composition board. 23¾ x 29⅝. Purchase. 45.5.

House, James, Jr. b. 1902.

NEGRO HEAD. 1931. Wood. 11¾ high. Purchase. 32.73.

Howard, Cecil. 1888–1956.

JO DAVIDSON. (1934.) Bronze. 18 high. Purchase. 37.48.
FIGURE. (1928–30.) Limestone. 71 high. Gift of Mrs. Harry Payne Whitney. 41.1.
LEANING FIGURE. (c. 1929.) Bronze. 31 high. 31.37.
MOTHER AND CHILD. (1918.) Limestone. 22 high. 31.38.

Howland, Isabella. b. 1895.

RODEO. (1930.) Oil on canvas. 20 x 25. Purchase. 31.247.

Hultberg, John. b. 1922.

NIGHT STILL LIFE. 1954. Oil on canvas. 38¼ x 51. Purchase. 55.5.

Hunt, Richard. b. 1935.

EXTENDING HORIZONTAL FORM. (1958.) Steel. 57 long. Gift of the Friends of the Whitney Museum of American Art. 58.53.

Ipcar, Dahlov. b. 1917.

GENTLING THE COLT. (1941.) Oil on canvas. 30 x 44¼. Anonymous gift. 55.30.

Ippolito, Angelo. b. 1922.

STORM. 1956. Oil on canvas. 43 x 50. Gift of the Friends of the Whitney Museum of American Art. 57.11. (p. 229.)

Jamieson, Mitchell. b. 1915.

FIRST COMMUNION. 1948. Colored ink and crayon on cardboard. 15⅛ x 21⅜. Purchase. 49.10.

Jenkins, Paul. b. 1923.

DIVINING ROD. (1956.) Oil on canvas. 54 x 38. Gift of Thomas Ryder Rudel. 56.45.

Jenks, Jo. b. 1904.

YOUNG GOAT. (1933.) Brazilian onyx. 19 long. Purchase. 33.57.

Johnson, Buffie. b. 1912.

BLACK SPRING. 1958. Oil on canvas. 62 x 45. Anonymous gift. 60.51.

Johnston, Ynez. b. 1920.

BREAKWATER. (1952.) Casein and ink. 16⅜ x 28⅜. Purchase. 52.20.

Jones, Joe. b. 1909.

AMERICAN FARM. (1936.) Oil and tempera on canvas. 30 x 40. Purchase. 36.144.

Kahn, Wolf. b. 1927.

LARGE OLIVE GROVE. (1957–58.) Oil on canvas. 47½ x 54¾. Gift of the Friends of the Whitney Museum of American Art. 59.10.

Kamihira, Ben. b. 1925.

THE COUCH. (1960.) Oil on canvas. 63 x 79¼. Sumner Foundation Purchase Award. 60.49. (p. 132.)

Kane, John. 1860–1934.

PANTHER HOLLOW. (1930–31.) Oil on canvas. 20 x 29. Purchase. 35.2. (p. 29.)

Kantor, Morris. b. 1896.

LAUREL. (1929.) Oil on canvas. 30 x 25. Purchase. 31.251.
NUDE. (1930.) Gouache. 12½ x 17¾. Purchase. 31.440.
THE RACE TRACK. (1933.) Pencil. 14½ x 21½. Purchase. 35.6.
SKYROCKET. 1933. Oil on canvas. 28 x 24. Purchase. 34.16. (p. 108.)
STILL LIFE. (1932.) Crayon and pencil. 16 x 22. Purchase. 34.8.
STORM. 1944. Oil and egg tempera on composition board. 27⅞ x 36. Purchase (and exchange). 52.9.

Karfiol, Bernard. 1886–1952.

BOY BATHERS. 1916. Oil on canvas. 28 x 36. Purchase (and exchange). 54.19. (p. 35.)
BOYS AND PONIES. (1927.) Oil on canvas. 36 x 27¼. Purchase. 31.253.
FISHING VILLAGE. (c. 1930.) Oil on canvas. 30 x 40. Purchase. 33.41.
HILDA. 1929. Oil on canvas. 35 x 55. Purchase. 31.254.
STANDING FIGURE. (1926.) Ink. 17⅞ x 12⅞. Purchase. 33.42.

Katzman, Herbert. b. 1923.

TWO NUDES BEFORE JAPANESE SCREEN. 1952. Oil on composition board. 76 x 43. Juliana Force Purchase. 53.5. (p. 176.)

Kaufmann, Robert D. 1913–1959.

CASTLE AT DAWN. 1958. Oil on canvas. 50 x 62. Gift of Walter A. Weiss. 60.41.

Kaz, Nathaniel. b. 1917.

CYRANO. 1950. Bronze. 34¼ high. Wildenstein Benefit Purchase Fund. 53.17. (p. 195.)

Kearns, James. b. 1924.

CAT'S CRADLE. 1959. Oil on composition board. 60 x 48. Neysa McMein Purchase Award. 60.18.
FALLEN ANGEL. 1956. Crayon and oil. 26 x 38. Anonymous gift. 58.8.
BEN SHAHN. (1957–58.) Bronze. 10 high. Gift of the Howard W. Lipman Foundation, Inc. 60.58.

Keller, Henry G. 1869–1949.

BIRD ROCK, CALIFORNIA. (1925.) Watercolor and charcoal. 27½ x 20⅛. Purchase. 33.49.

Kelly, Ellsworth. b. 1923.

ATLANTIC. (1956.) Oil on canvas. 80 x 114. Purchase. 57.9.

Kelly, Leon. b. 1901.

Boy Giving a Mollusk to the Poet. 1954. Lead pencil and colored pencils. 46½ x 34½. Purchase. 54.27.

Departure Through the Umbrellas. 1944. Oil on canvas. 22⅛ x 28. Gift of Briggs Buchanan. 46.7.

Head of a Young Man. (1928.) Ink. 3½ x 6¾. Purchase. 41.31.

Magic Bird. 1945. Ink. 9¼ x 9¾. Purchase. 46.15.

Man Genuflecting. 1956. Ink. 24⅝ x 18¾ (over-all). Purchase. 59.18.

Kent, Adaline. 1900–1957.

Citadel. 1955. Terra cotta. 13 high. Purchase. 58.56.

Kent, Rockwell. b. 1882.

The Kathleen. (1923.) Ink. 6⅞ x 7⅝ (over-all). 31.548.

Man and Boy. 1918. Ink. 6 x 7⅜. 31.549.

Man and Boy Sawing Wood. 1919. Ink. 6¾ x 9¾. 31.550.

Old Man. (1919.) Ink. 6½ x 8½. 31.551.

Puffin Rock, Ireland. 1926–27. Oil on wood. 24 x 29¾. 31.256.

Shadows of Evening. 1921–23. Oil on canvas. 38 x 44. 31.257. (p. 68.)

Shepherdess. 1927. Watercolor. 9¾ x 13¾ (over-all). 31.441.

The Trapper. 1921. Oil on canvas. 34 x 44. Purchase. 31.258.

Kepes, Gyorgy. b. 1906.

Tender Space. (1959.) Oil, casein, glue, and sand on canvas. 59¾ x 59¾. Anonymous gift. 60.14.

Kienbusch, William. b. 1914.

Red Vine, Autumn, Dogtown. 1956. Oil on canvas. 41 x 56½. Gift of the Friends of the Whitney Museum of American Art. 58.19. (p. 177.)

Twin Pine. 1950. Casein. 25¾ x 38¾. Purchase. 51.24.

Kingman, Dong. b. 1911.

The El and Snow. (1946.) Watercolor. 21 x 29⅜. Purchase. 47.9.

Kinigstein, Jonah. b. 1923.

Baroque Altar. (1954.) Oil on composition board. 50¾ x 34½. Gift of Mr. and Mrs. Roy R. Neuberger. 56.8.

The Monsters, Number 2. (1954.) Gouache. 17⅛ x 23⅛. Purchase. 54.24.

Kirschenbaum, Jules. b. 1930.

The City. 1953. Watercolor. 22 x 30¼. Neysa McMein Purchase Award. 56.23.

Study for "The Triumph of the Birds." 1956. Ink. 18¾ x 35¾. Gift of Harry Salpeter. 59.34.

Kittredge, Kraemer. b. 1905.

Tubs at Chain-o-Mines. (1939.) Watercolor. 17¼ x 20¼. Gift of Juliana Force. 41.10.

Kline, Franz. b. 1910.

Mahoning. (1956.) Oil on canvas. 80 x 100. Gift of the Friends of the Whitney Museum of American Art. 57.10. (p. 212.)

Klitgaard, Georgina. b. 1893.

Bouquet. (1928.) Watercolor. 24 x 17⅞. 31.442.

Ice House, Nantucket. (1930.) Watercolor. 13½ x 19¾. 31.444.

Luther's Farm. (1929.) Oil on canvas. 32 x 40¼. Purchase. 31.259.

Knaths, Karl. b. 1891.

Duck Flight. (1948.) Oil on canvas. 40 x 30. Purchase. 49.18. (p. 185.)

Mexican Platter. (1946.) Oil on canvas. 42 x 48. Gift of the Phillips Collection. 58.3.

Winter Wharf. (1955.) Oil on canvas. 40 x 50. Gift of Mr. and Mrs. Roy R. Neuberger. 58.2.

Koehler, Florence. 1861–1944.

Still Life. Gouache. 17¾ x 23¾. Gift of Mrs. Henry D. Sharpe. 48.16.

Koerner, Henry. b. 1915.

Vanity Fair. (1946.) Oil on composition board. 36 x 42. Purchase. 48.2. (p. 142.)

Kohn, Gabriel. b. 1910.

Square Root. 1958. Wood. 40 long. Purchase. 60.20. (p. 259.)

Konzal, Joseph. b. 1905.

Rain God. 1959. Copper and brass. 59 high. Gift of Mr. and Mrs. Alfred Hecht. 60.36.

Kopman, Benjamin. b. 1887.

In a Gallery. 1950. Oil on canvas. 28 x 22. Gift of Sidney Elliott Cohn (and purchase). 54.43.

Portrait of a Man. 1912. Oil on canvas. 30 x 26. 31.261.

Koppe, Richard. b. 1916.

Trio. 1954. Watercolor and ink. 21¾ x 29⅞. Purchase. 54.25.

Krasner, Lee.

The Guardian. (1960.) Oil on canvas. 53 x 58. Gift of Uris Brothers Foundation, Inc. 60.61.

Kreis, Henry. b. 1899.

In Pensive Mood. (1935.) Tennessee marble. 28 high. Purchase. 38.9.

Kroll, Leon. b. 1884.

Anne. (1930.) Oil on canvas. 18 x 15. Purchase. 31.263.

Head. (1934.) Charcoal. 15¾ x 10⅞. Purchase. 34.9.

Nude in a Blue Chair. (1930.) Oil on canvas. 48¼ x 36¼. Purchase. 31.264.

A Road Through Willows. (1933.) Oil on canvas. 26 x 42. Purchase. 34.17. (p. 78.)

Kuehne, Max. b. 1880.

Diamond Hill. 1919. Oil on canvas. 31 x 36. 31.266.

Main Street, Gloucester. (1929.) Oil on canvas. 24 x 30. 31.268.

Kuhn, Walt. 1877–1949.

THE BLUE CLOWN. 1931. Oil on canvas. 30 x 25. Purchase. 32.25. (p. 77.)

CLOWN IN HIS DRESSING ROOM. 1943. Oil on canvas. 72 x 32. Anonymous gift. 50.1.

MUSICAL CLOWN. 1938. Oil on canvas. 40 x 30. Purchase. 43.10.

Kuniyoshi, Yasuo. 1890–1953.

CAFÉ. 1937. Oil on canvas. 16 x 12⅛. Purchase. 37.40.

CHILD. (1923.) Oil on canvas. 30 x 24. Gift of Mrs. Edith Gregor Halpert. 55.1.

DAMP PLACE. 1923. Ink. 13¾ x 18¾. 31.554.

DELIVERANCE. (1947.) Oil on canvas. 40 x 30. Purchase. 48.7. (p.182.)

DELIVERANCE (sketch). (1947.) Pencil. 16½ x 13½. Anonymous gift. 58.11.

DELIVERANCE (sketch). (1947.) Pencil. 16½ x 13½. Anonymous gift. 58.12.

DESERT WOMAN. (1943.) 16 x 11⅞. Casein on composition board. Gift of Mr. and Mrs. Allan D. Emil. 56.35.

FAKIRS (sketch). (1951.) Pencil. 16½ x 13¼. Anonymous gift. 58.13.

FAKIRS (sketch). (1951.) Pencil. 16 x 12. Anonymous gift. 58.14.

FAKIRS (sketch). (1951.) Pencil. 14¼ x 12. Anonymous gift. 58.15.

FARMER'S DAUGHTER WITH THREE COWS. 1922. Ink. 12¾ x 18¾. Gift of Mrs. Edith Gregor Halpert. 57.1.

I'M TIRED. 1938. Oil on canvas. 40¼ x 31. Purchase. 39.12. (p. 80.)

JUGGLER. (1952.) Ink on cardboard. 22 x 28. Purchase. 53.37. (p. 183.)

LADY SLIPPER. 1924. Ink. 20 x 13¾. 31.555.

LANDSCAPE. (1924.) Oil on canvas. 20 x 30. Purchase. 31.271.

LANDSCAPE. (1930's.) Pencil. 13 x 16½. Anonymous gift. 58.17.

NUDE. (1930's.) Pencil. 16½ x 13½. Anonymous gift. 58.18.

SLEEPING BEAUTY. 1924. Ink and pencil. 14 x 19¾. Gift of Mrs. Edith Gregor Halpert. 54.54. (p. 106.)

STREET SCENE. (1920's.) Pencil. 13 x 16½. Anonymous gift. 58.16.

THE SWIMMER. 1924. Ink. 14¾ x 17⅞. Gift of Mr. and Mrs. Charles J. Liebman. 48.18.

THE TWIST LOAF. 1930. Oil on canvas. 30⅛ x 42¼. Purchase. 31.272.

Kupferman, Lawrence. b. 1909.

MICROSCOPIC PATH OF LIFE. (1949.) Casein. 24¼ x 39½. Purchase. 51.25.

Lachaise, Gaston. 1882–1935.

DOLPHIN FOUNTAIN. 1924. Bronze. 39 long. 31.41.

JULIANA FORCE. (1934.) Bronze. 12 high. Anonymous gift. 53.51.

HEAD. (1923–24.) Marble. 16¾ high. Purchase. 41.54.

HEAD. 1928. Bronze, nickel plated. 13¼ high. Purchase. 31.42.

HEAD OF A WOMAN. 1923. Bronze. 13½ high. Bequest of Mrs. Sam A. Lewisohn. 54.50.

HEAD OF A WOMAN. (Between 1922–32.) Pencil. 19⅝ x 14⅜. Purchase. 38.43.

MAN WALKING. 1933. Bronze. 23¼ high. Purchase. 33.58.

NUDE, NUMBER 1. Pencil. 10½ x 8. Purchase. 32.1.

NUDE, NUMBER 2. Pencil. 10⅝ x 7. Purchase. 32.2.

NUDE WITH DRAPERY. (Between 1922–32.) Pencil. 18⅝ x 11⅝. Purchase. 38.44.

SEAL. 1921. Bronze. 14¼ long. Purchase. 31.43.

SEATED NUDE. (Between 1932–35.) Pencil. 23¾ x 18. Purchase. 38.45.

STANDING NUDE. (Between 1922–32.) Pencil. 17¾ x 11¾. Purchase. 38.46.

STANDING WOMAN. 1912–27. Bronze. 70 high. Purchase. 36.91. (p. 60.)

TORSO. (1930.) Bronze. 11½ high. Purchase. 58.4. (p. 64.)

Lahey, Richard. b. 1893.

HEAD OF JOAN. (1931.) Oil on composition board. 23¾ x 19¾. Purchase. 31.273.

Laning, Edward. b. 1906.

FOURTEENTH STREET. 1931. Tempera on canvas. 30 x 40. Purchase. 33.17.

PASSAGE TO INDIA. 1935. Pair of drawings, *Central Pacific* and *Union Pacific*. Pencil and ink. 12 x 27 each. Purchase. 36.36.

Lasker, Joe. b. 1919.

NAPLES. (1952.) Oil on canvas. 34¾ x 51. Purchase. 53.50. (p. 162.)

Lassaw, Ibram. b. 1913.

PROCESSION. (1955–56.) Wire, copper, various bronzes, and silver. 40 long. Purchase (and exchange). 56.19. (p. 232.)

Laufman, Sidney. b. 1891.

THE ORCHARD. (1928.) Oil on canvas. 23½ x 36. Purchase. 31.275.

Laurent, Robert. b. 1890.

THE AWAKENING. (1931.) Bronze. 55 long. Purchase. 31.44.

DUCK. (1926.) Wood. 14½ long. Purchase. 31.45.

THE FLAME. (c. 1917.) Wood. 18 high. Gift of Bartlett Arkell. 42.1. (p. 63.)

KNEELING FIGURE. (1935.) Bronze. 23½ high. Purchase. 36.2. (p. 62.)

Lawrence, Jacob. b. 1917.

TOMBSTONES. 1942. Gouache. 28¾ x 20½. Purchase. 43.14.

WAR SERIES. 1946–47. Fourteen panels. Egg tempera on composition board. 20 x 16 each. Gift of Mr. and Mrs. Roy R. Neuberger. 51.6–19. (p. 161.)

Lawson, Ernest. 1873–1939.

FISHERMEN. (1911.) Oil on canvas. 25¼ x 30. 31.277.

Lawson, Ernest. (*continued*)

HIGH BRIDGE. (1934.) Oil on canvas. 30 x 40. Purchase. 34.18. (p. 70.)

WINTER ON THE RIVER. 1907. Oil on canvas. 33 x 40. 31.280.

Lebrun, Rico. b. 1900.

MAN IN HELMET. (1949.) Ink and casein. 24¼ x 18½. Purchase. 52.24.

RUNNING FIGURE. 1948. Ink. 18¾ x 24⅜. Purchase. 48.12.

WOOD OF THE HOLY CROSS. 1948. Oil and casein on canvas. 80 x 30. Purchase. 53.10. (p. 178.)

Lee, Arthur. 1881–1961.

ETHIOPIAN. 1912. Bronze. 28 high. 31.49.

RHYTHM. Before 1930. Bronze. 73½ high. Purchase. 33.59.

L'Engle, William. 1884–1957.

SIX-DAY BICYCLE RACE. 1935. Oil on canvas. 30 x 40. Gift of Mrs. William L'Engle. 58.49.

Leslie, Alfred. b. 1927.

COLLAGE WITH STRIPES. 1956. Paper, oil paint, and ink. 29¼ x 18½. Anonymous gift. 57.32.

Levee, John. b. 1924.

JULY VI, 1956. Oil on canvas. 52 x 64. Gift of Mr. and Mrs. Jack I. Poses. 57.34.

Levi, Julian. b. 1900.

CAPE COD MORNING. (1944.) Gouache. 14 x 18⅞. Purchase. 45.16.

SHIPBOTTOM FISHERY. (1937.) Oil on canvas. 22 x 32. Purchase. 37.41.

Levine, Jack. b. 1915.

GANGSTER FUNERAL. (1952–53.) Oil on canvas. 63 x 72. Purchase. 53.42. (p. 159.)

Liberte, L. Jean. b. 1896.

MOTHER AND CHILD. 1932. Oil on paper. 14½ x 19½. Purchase. 32.69.

MOTHER LORE. (c. 1932.) Oil on paper. 19½ x 14⅝. Purchase. 33.32.

Lindner, Richard. b. 1901.

SUNDAY AFTERNOON. 1954. Pencil and watercolor. 25 x 19. Gift of the Friends of the Whitney Museum of American Art. 60.3.

Lipchitz, Jacques. b. 1891.

SACRIFICE, II. (1948/52.) Bronze. 49¼ high. Purchase. 52.27. (p. 191.)

Lipman-Wulf, Peter. b. 1905.

THE DANCING COUPLE. (1949.) Ebony. 68 high. Gift of Paul Gouary. 55.50.

Lipton, Seymour. b. 1903.

SORCERER. (1957.) Nickel-silver on monel metal. 60¾ high. Gift of the Friends of the Whitney Museum of American Art. 58.25. (p. 235.)

THUNDERBIRD. (1951–52.) Bronze on steel. 36½ long. Wildenstein Benefit Purchase Fund. 53.18.

Locke, Charles. b. 1899.

THE HARBOR. 1940. Oil on canvas. 29 x 38. Gift of Mrs. Harry Payne Whitney. 41.5.

HARBOR TRAFFIC. 1940. Ink. 13¼ x 19¼. Purchase. 42.26.

THE TERRACE. (1933.) Ink and crayon. 11⅞ x 19⅝. Purchase. 33.75.

THE TUG. (1939.) Oil on canvas. 36 x 45. Gift of Mrs. Reginald Marsh. 59.7.

VERMONT LANDSCAPE. (1935.) Ink. 8⅞ x 14⅝. Purchase. 43.17.

Lockwood, Ward. b. 1894.

AFTER SPRING RAINS. (1929.) Oil on canvas. 18 x 24. 31.283.

BOAT IN PORT. (1939.) Watercolor. 13½ x 19½. Purchase. 40.8.

SOUTHWEST, NUMBER 4. (1954.) Casein on cardboard. 24¾ x 30¾. Purchase (and exchange). 54.31.

Lorian, Dolia. 1909–1952.

VIEW OF THE EAST RIVER. (c. 1950.) Oil on canvas. 40 x 45. Gift of the Estate of Dolia Lorian. 52.38.

Luce, Molly. b. 1896.

HORSE POWER. 1941. Oil on canvas. 22 x 28. Purchase. 41.43.

THE ZOO. 1926. Oil on canvas. 15 x 18. 31.284.

Lucioni, Luigi. b. 1900.

JO. 1931. Oil on canvas. 20 x 18. Purchase. 31.285.

TWO WILLOWS. (1936.) Oil on canvas. 18¼ x 23. Purchase. 38.1.

VICTORIAN STILL LIFE. 1931. Oil on canvas. 11½ x 17¼. Purchase. 32.28.

Lucius, Florence.

STANDING FIGURE. (1920's.) Bronze. 31½ high. 31.50.

Ludins, Eugene. b. 1904.

LANDSCAPE. 1930. Oil on canvas. 30¼ x 33. Purchase. 31.286.

Luks, George. 1867–1933.

ARMISTICE NIGHT. 1918. Oil on canvas. 37 x 68¾. Anonymous gift. 54.58. (p. 26.)

MAN IN A GREEN HAT. 1920. Gouache on cardboard. 18¼ x 14⅞. 31.450.

MAURICE PRENDERGAST. (c. 1904.) Pencil. 10 x 6¾ (over-all). Gift of Mr. and Mrs. Edward W. Root. 42.38.

MRS. GAMLEY. (1930.) Oil on canvas. 66 x 48. Purchase. 31.289. (p. 69.)

OLD WOMAN WITH WHITE PITCHER. (1926.) Oil on canvas. 30 x 25. Gift of Mr. and Mrs. Lesley G. Sheafer. 55.45.

PLUCKING CHICKENS. (c. 1915.) Watercolor. 19⅞ x 13¾. Purchase. 31.451.
ROSIE. (1919.) Oil on canvas. 31 x 26¼. 31.287.
WOMAN WITH GOOSE. (1907.) Oil on wood. 20 x 16. 31.288.

McCarter, Henry. 1866–1942.
EVENING STAR. (1942.) Oil on canvas. 30 x 36. Gift of the Estate of Henry McCarter. 45.1.

McChesney, Robert. b. 1913.
MOUNTAIN SERIES, NUMBER 2. 1953. Oil on canvas. 38 x 53. Purchase. 55.6.

Macdonald-Wright, Stanton. b. 1890.
"CONCEPTION." SYNCHROMY. (1915.) Oil on canvas. 30 x 24. Gift of George F. Of. 52.40.
"ORIENTAL." SYNCHROMY IN BLUE-GREEN. 1918. Oil on canvas. 36 x 50. Purchase. 52.8. (p. 48.)

McFee, Henry Lee. 1886–1953.
CROW WITH PEACHES. (1928.) Oil on canvas. 30¼ x 24⅛. Purchase. 31.301.
FRUIT AND CRUMPLED PAPER. (1931.) Pencil. 17 x 16⅞. Purchase. 33.39.
HOUSE TOPS. (1931.) Pencil. 19⅞ x 16⅞. Purchase. 33.76.
NEGRO GIRL. (1931.) Oil on canvas. 24⅛ x 20¼. Purchase. 33.18.
NEGRO HEAD. (1935.) Pencil. 14½ x 11½. Purchase. 36.136.
RED FIELDS IN VIRGINIA (1928–29.) Oil on canvas. 24 x 30. Purchase. 31.302.
STILL LIFE, ORANGES. (1934.) Oil on canvas. 40 x 30. Purchase. 34.25.

MacIver, Loren. b. 1909.
VENICE. (1949.) Oil on canvas. 59 x 93. Purchase. 49.19. (p. 187.)

McLaughlin, Gerald. b. 1925.
THE EMPRESS. (1956.) Oil on composition board. 48 x 92. Purchase. 57.19. (p. 154.)

McNeil, George. b. 1908.
ASTOR. 1958. Oil on canvas. 66 x 66. Anonymous gift. 59.17.

Madson, Jack. b. 1927.
PURSUIT, NUMBER 3. 1956. Oil on canvas. 35 x 54. Juliana Force Purchase. 57.15.

Mager, Gus. 1878–1956.
WRESTLERS. (1933.) Oil on canvas. 29½ x 49. Purchase. 33.36.

Maldarelli, Oronzio. b. 1893.
CARESS. (1944.) Burgundy marble. 27½ high. Purchase. 46.8.
LINDA WU. 1946. Saravezza marble. 17 high. Purchase. 47.6.

Mandel, Howard. b. 1917.
THE BLESSING. 1952. Casein on composition board. 19¾ x 24. Wildenstein Benefit Purchase Fund. 53.23.

Mangravite, Peppino. b. 1896.
ABDUCTION OF A BEAUTIFUL LADY. (1935.) Gouache. 17½ x 11½. Purchase. 36.135.
BERENICE. (1944.) Ink. 11 x 11½. Purchase. 45.24.
CITY PEOPLE IN THE COUNTRY. (1936.) Oil on canvas. 25½ x 39½. Purchase. 36.145.
FROM FIRE BY FIRE. 1951. Gouache. 24¾ x 17⅛. Purchase (and exchange). 54.44.

Manso, Leo. b. 1914.
HOMAGE TO TURNER. (1955.) Oil on canvas. 28 x 40. Gift of Mr. and Mrs. Victor S. Riesenfeld. 56.6.

Marca-Relli, Conrad. b. 1913.
JUNCTION. (1958.) Collage of painted canvas. 56 x 77½. Gift of the Friends of the Whitney Museum of American Art. 59.11. (p. 226.)

Marcus, Marcia. b. 1928.
SEATED SELF-PORTRAIT. 1960. Oil on canvas. 54 x 50. Neysa McMein Purchase Award. 60.46.

Margo, Boris. b. 1902.
FROM THE OTHER SIDE OF THE BRIDGE. (1945/47.) Oil on canvas. 50 x 50. Purchase. 48.3.

Margoulies, Berta. b. 1907.
MINE DISASTER. 1942. Bronze. 28½ long. Purchase. 45.10.

Margules, De Hirsh. b. 1899.
PORTRAIT OF JOSEPH STELLA. 1943. Watercolor. 25 x 19¼. Gift of the artist in memory of Juliana Force. 49.13.

Marin, John. 1870–1953.
DEER ISLAND, MAINE. 1923. Watercolor. 17½ x 13⅞ (over-all). Purchase. 31.589.
MOVEMENT, BOAT, SEA, ROCKS, AND SKY, MAINE. 1941. Watercolor. 15¼ x 21¾ (over-all). Purchase. 42.36.
REGION OF BROOKLYN BRIDGE FANTASY. 1932. Watercolor. 18¾ x 22¼. Purchase. 49.8. (p. 40.)
SEA PIECE. 1951. Oil on canvas. 22 x 28. Gift of the Friends of the Whitney Museum of American Art. 57.29. (p. 172.)
SUNSET. 1914. Watercolor. 16½ x 19¼ (over-all). Purchase. 31.452. (p. 36.)
WHITE HORSES, SEA MOVEMENT OFF DEER ISLE, MAINE. 1926. Watercolor. 15¼ x 19¾. Anonymous gift. 54.61.

Marsh, Reginald. 1898–1954.
ALEXANDER BROOK. (1929.) Oil on canvas. 24 x 20. 31.291.
CONEY ISLAND BEACH, NUMBER 1. 1943. Watercolor and ink. 21½ x 29½. Purchase. 43.15.
GIRL WALKING. (1944.) Ink. 21⅞ x 15. Purchase. 45.19.
HUMAN POOL TABLES. 1938. Egg tempera on composition board. 29¾ x 40. Gift of Mrs. Reginald Marsh and William Benton. 55.34. (p. 95.)
LINER. 1940. Watercolor. 15¼ x 22¾ (over-all). Purchase. 40.9.
LOCOMOTIVE, NUMBER 2. 1929. Watercolor. 13½ x 19½. 31.453.

Marsh, Reginald. (*continued*)

NEW DODGEM. 1940. Watercolor. 40¼ x 26¾. Anonymous gift. 53.21.

SELF-PORTRAIT. 1927. Oil on canvas. 24 x 20. 31.292.

TWENTY-CENT MOVIE. 1936. Egg tempera on composition board. 30 x 40. Purchase. 37.43.

WHITE TOWER HAMBURGER. 1945. Ink. 26¼ x 39¾. Anonymous gift. 53.22. (p. 130.)

WHY NOT USE THE "L"? 1930. Egg tempera on canvas. 36 x 48. Purchase. 31.293. (p. 94.)

Martin, Fletcher. b. 1904.

CHERRY TWICE. (1946.) Oil on canvas. 72 x 40. Artists and Students Assistance Fund. 55.48.

Martin, Keith. b. 1911.

EDGE OF THE CITY. 1954. Collage of paper on paper mounted on composition board. 24 x 36. Anonymous gift. 60.5.

Martinelli, Ezio. b. 1913.

DEMIURGE. (1954.) Bronze. 18 long. Purchase. 55.26.

Marx, Robert E. b. 1925.

PROCESSION. 1955. Oil on canvas. 40 x 60. Bequest of Robert D. Kaufmann. 60.40.

Mason, Alice Trumbull. b. 1904.

MEMORIAL. 1958–59. Oil on composition board. 36 x 28. Gift of Jonathan Alden Trumbull.

Mattson, Henry. b. 1887.

EVENTIDE. (c. 1946.) Oil on canvas. 27 x 36. Purchase (and exchange). 53.25. (p. 125.)

MARINE. (1933.) Oil on canvas. 25 x 30. Purchase. 34.3.

MOONLIT LANDSCAPE. (1934.) Oil on canvas. 25 x 30. Purchase. 34.19.

PORTRAIT OF THE ARTIST. (1936.) Oil on canvas. 32 x 22. Purchase. 37.27.

QUINCES. (1936.) Oil on canvas. 32 x 22. Purchase. 36.146.

SPRING. (1937.) Oil on canvas. 36 x 48. Purchase (and exchange). 39.23.

Matulka, Jan. b. 1892.

ARRANGEMENT WITH PHONOGRAPH. (1929.) Oil on canvas. 30 x 40. 31.298.

STILL LIFE WITH LILIES. (c. 1926.) Oil on canvas. 30 x 25. 31.299.

Maurer, A. H. 1868–1932.

AN ARRANGEMENT. (1901.) Oil on cardboard. 36 x 31⅞. Gift of Mr. and Mrs. Hudson D. Walker. 50.13.

FLOWERS. (c. 1912.) Oil on cardboard. 21¼ x 18. 31.300.

TWIN HEADS. (c. 1930.) Oil on canvas. 26⅜ x 18. Gift of Mr. and Mrs. Hudson D. Walker (and exchange). 53.28. (p. 38.)

Mecklem, Austin. 1894–1951.

TOMPKINS' COVE. 1934. Oil on canvas. 24 x 34. Purchase. 34.20.

VALLEY, WINTER. 1936. Watercolor. 13¾ x 20¾. Purchase. 36.22.

Menkes, Zygmunt. b. 1896.

THE PAINTER. (1954.) Oil on canvas. 44¾ x 37. Gift of Mr. and Mrs. Alfred Jaretzki, Jr. 55.41.

Meo, Salvatore Samuel. b. 1920.

ROMA—1956. Collage of paper, various pigments and metals on burlap. 38 x 52. Anonymous gift. 57.41.

Meyer, Anne Norton. d. 1958.

HEAD OF A YOUNG WOMAN. (1940.) Oil on canvas. 16 x 12. Purchase. 40.21.

Meyer, Felicia. b. 1913.

VERMONT HILLSIDE. (1940.) Oil on canvas. 28 x 34. Purchase. 41.6.

Meyer, Herbert. 1882–1960.

GLIMPSE OF THE METOWEE. 1935. Oil on canvas. 25 x 30. Purchase. 36.9.

SUMMER IN PAWLET. (1932.) Oil on canvas. 28 x 36. Purchase. 32.29.

Midener, Walter. b. 1912.

GIRL WITH MANTILLA. (1953.) Terra cotta. 18⅛ high. Gift of Mr. and Mrs. Paul Mazur. 55.33.

Miller, Harriette G. b. 1892.

BEACON FALLS. (1936.) Watercolor. 13½ x 19½. Purchase. 38.48.

Miller, Kenneth Hayes. 1876–1952.

AT A COUNTRY HORSE SHOW. 1935. Pencil, crayon, and watercolor. 19⅞ x 16¾. Purchase. 36.37.

BOX PARTY. 1936. Oil and tempera on canvas. 60 x 46. Purchase. 36.147.

BY THE POND. (c. 1912.) Oil on composition board. 16⅝ x 11½. Gift of Mrs. Grant Sanger. 55.16.

ON FOURTEENTH STREET. 1932. Ink and crayon. 12 x 15. Purchase. 45.20.

ROCKS AND SEA. (c. 1916/44.) Oil on canvas. 25 x 30. Gift of Mrs. Howard C. Smith, Jr. 54.40.

SHOPPER. 1928. Oil on canvas. 41 x 33. Purchase. 31.305. (p. 73.)

TWO NUDES. (1916.) Ink. 9½ x 7. 31.556.

Also a collection of sketches.

Millman, Edward. b. 1907.

GRAY TERRAIN. (1954.) Oil on canvas. 40 x 26. Anonymous gift. 58.10.

Mintz, Harry. b. 1907.

FAÇADE. (1954.) Oil on wood. 30 x 23. Anonymous gift. 57.42.

Mitchell, Bruce. b. 1908.

STORMY DAY, BLOCK ISLAND. (1945.) Gouache. 16½ x 27⅞. Gift of Leonard Pfeiffer. 46.11.

Mitchell, Joan. b. 1926.

HEMLOCK. (1956.) Oil on canvas. 91 x 80. Gift of the Friends of the Whitney Museum of American Art. 58.20.

Moffett, Langston.
House on the Bay. (1941.) Oil on canvas. 21¾ x 29¾. Purchase. 42.21.

Moffett, Ross. b. 1888.
Provincetown Wharf. (1932.) Oil on canvas. 30 x 40. Purchase. 33.19.

Moholy-Nagy, László. 1895–1946.
Space Modulator. 1938–40. Oil on canvas. 47 x 47. Gift of Mrs. Sibyl Moholy-Nagy. 55.31. (p. 116.)

Moir, Robert. b. 1917.
Mother and Child. (1950.) Limestone. 23 high. Purchase. 52.18.

Moller, Hans. b. 1905.
Collage, Number 116E. 1954. Paper, gouache, and ink. 29¼ x 39½. Purchase. 55.7.

Moore, Bruce. b. 1905.
Panther. 1929. Bronze. 42½ long. Purchase. 31.55.

More, Hermon. b. 1887.
Rocky Hillside. (1934.) Oil on canvas. 32 x 42. Purchase. 35.16. (p. 76.)

Morgan, Herbert. b. 1907.
Armistice Day, Place de la Mairie. (1927.) Oil on canvas. 36 x 36. 31.311.

Morgan, Maud. b. 1903.
Turkey. (1937.) Oil on canvas. 26 x 18. Purchase. 38.50.

Morgan, Randall. b. 1920.
Port at Night. (1954.) Oil on composition board. 28 x 44. Charles F. Williams Fund. 55.19.

Morris, Carl. b. 1911.
River Reflection. 1954. Ink and casein. 19⅜ x 24¾. Gift of the New York Foundation. 56.38.
Stone Matrix. 1957. Oil on canvas. 32 x 72. Purchase. 59.15.

Morris, George L. K. b. 1905.
Nautical Composition. 1937/42. Oil on canvas. 51 x 35. Purchase. 43.11. (p. 117.)

Morris, Kyle. b. 1918.
Evening 1957 Montauk, Number 1. Oil on canvas. 59¾ x 58. Living Arts Foundation Fund. 57.51.
Turbulence. 1958. Oil on canvas. 60 x 72. Gift of Mr. and Mrs. Samuel M. Kootz. 59.46.

Morrison, George. b. 1919.
The Antagonist. 1956. Oil on canvas. 34 x 50. Gift of Mrs. Helen Meredith Norcross. 57.26.

Moselsio, Simon. b. 1890.
Javanese Dancer. 1933. Bronze. 57¾ high. Purchase. 36.3.

Motherwell, Robert. b. 1915.
The Red Skirt. 1947. Oil on composition board. 48 x 24. Purchase. 49.3. (p. 210.)

Moy, Seong. b. 1921.
Susanna and the Elders. (1956.) Oil on canvas. 40 x 50. Gift of Mrs. Helen Meredith Norcross. 57.27.

Mueller, George. b. 1929.
The Study. 1955. Egg tempera, casein, and enamel on composition board. 56¾ x 48. Gift of Mr. and Mrs. Roy R. Neuberger. 55.25. (p. 205.)

Murch, Walter. b. 1907.
Governor, II. (1952.) Oil on paper. 40⅜ x 17¾. Wildenstein Benefit Purchase Fund. 53.11. (p. 143.)

Myers, Jerome. 1867–1940.
Children at Play. (c. 1917.) Pen and pencil. 4½ x 7⅝. Purchase. 31.557.
East Side Market. (1936.) Oil on canvas. 25 x 30. Purchase (and exchange). 41.36.
First Avenue Corner. (c. 1925.) Watercolor and crayon. 7⅝ x 10. Purchase. 31.455.
Self-Portrait. (1912.) Charcoal and chalk. 14 x 11⅛. Purchase. 31.558.
Summer Night, East Side Park. (1919.) Oil on canvas. 25 x 30. Purchase. 31.313. (p. 26.)

Nakian, Reuben. b. 1897.
Animal Study, I. (c. 1921.) Crayon. 10⅛ x 16⅝. 31.559.
Animal Study, II. (c. 1921.) Crayon. 10 x 15. 31.560.
Bull and Cow. (c. 1921.) Crayon. 10 x 15. 31.561.
Bull Crouching. (c. 1921.) Crayon. 8 x 12⅜. 31.562.
Cow and Heifer. (c. 1921.) Crayon. 10 x 15. 31.563.
The Lap Dog. 1927. Terra cotta. 10½ long. 31.56.
Seal. 1930. Bronze. 17¼ high. Purchase. 31.57.

Nevelson, Louise. b. 1900.
Black Majesty. (1955.) Painted wood. 32 long. Gift of Mr. and Mrs. Ben Mildwoff through the Federation of Modern Painters and Sculptors, Inc. 56.11. (p. 259.)

Newman, Daniel. b. 1929.
Early Spring Mountain. (1958.) Oil on composition board. 53¼ x 48. Gift of Alvin M. Greenstein. 59.16.

Nicolaides, Kimon. 1892–1938.
Two Heads. Colored ink. 7¾ x 6⅝. 31.564.

Niese, Henry. b. 1924.
The Ambry. (1955.) Oil on composition board. 66 x 48. Gift of the Sumner Foundation for the Arts, Inc. 60.12.
Window Still Life. (1956–58.) Oil on composition board. 39¾ x 29¾. Neysa McMein Purchase Award. 59.5.

Nivola, Constantino. b. 1911.
Deus. (1953.) Sand and plaster. 63¾ x 34½. Purchase. 55.12.

Noguchi, Isamu. b. 1904.

HUMPTY DUMPTY. (1946.) Ribbon slate. 58¾ high. Purchase. 47.7. (p. 261.)

INTEGRAL. 1959. Greek marble. 49¼ high. Gift of the Friends of the Whitney Museum of American Art. 60.25. (p. 258.)

RUTH PARKS. 1929. Bronze. 16¾ high. Purchase. 31.58.

Okada, Kenzo. b. 1902.

MEMORIES. (1957.) Oil on canvas. 68 x 84½. Gift of the Friends of the Whitney Museum of American Art. 58.23. (p. 213.)

Okamura, Arthur. b. 1932.

BLACK HEATH. (1959.) Ink. 21⅛ x 29¼. Neysa McMein Purchase Award. 60.28.

O'Keeffe, Georgia. b. 1887.

ABSTRACTION. (1926.) Oil on canvas. 30 x 18. Purchase. 58.43. (p. 49.)

THE MOUNTAIN, NEW MEXICO. (1931.) Oil on canvas. 30 x 36. Purchase. 32.14.

SINGLE LILY WITH RED. 1928. Oil on wood. 12 x 6¼. Purchase. 33.29.

THE WHITE FLOWER. (1931.) Oil on canvas. 30 x 36. Purchase. 32.26. (p. 57.)

Olsen, Earle. b. 1926.

ORANGE FLOWERS. (1955.) Pastel. 20½ x 27¾. Neysa McMein Purchase Award. 56.32.

Orr, Elliot. b. 1904.

THE JOURNEY. 1940. Oil on canvas. 10⅜ x 14½. Anonymous gift. 53.45.

Osborne. b. 1909.

SUMMETROS. 1956. Oil on canvas. 73 x 56. Gift of Mr. and Mrs. Hyman N. Glickstein. 59.49.

Oscar, Charles. b. 1923.

SCULPTOR'S STUDIO. (1956.) Tempera. 42 x 34. Gift of the New York Foundation. 56.39.

Ossorio, Alfonso. b. 1916.

NUMBER 14—1953. Casein on cardboard. 60 x 38. Purchase. 55.8.

Osver, Arthur. b. 1912.

BIG WITHALACOOCHEE. 1955. Oil on canvas. 54½ x 50¾. Living Arts Foundation Fund. 55.52.

Pace, Stephen. b. 1918.

NUMBER 58-07. (1958.) Oil on canvas. 66 x 89½. Anonymous gift. 59.29.

Pachner, William. b. 1915.

TERMINAL, NUMBER 1. 1959–60. Oil on canvas. 50 x 47¾. Purchase. 60.19.

Palmer, William C. b. 1906.

COON RIVER. 1933. Ink. 14⅜ x 18¾. Purchase. 33.77.

DUST, DROUGHT, AND DESTRUCTION. 1934. Egg tempera on composition board. 24 x 30. Purchase. 34.22.

Papsdorf, Fred. b. 1887.

FREIGHT YARD. 1938. Oil on canvas. 17¼ x 24. Purchase. 41.18.

Park, David. 1911–1960.

FOUR MEN. 1958. Oil on canvas. 57 x 92. Gift of an anonymous foundation. 59.27. (p. 175.)

Parker, Bill. b. 1922.

COMPOSITION. 1955. Gouache. 38⅛ x 27½. Anonymous gift. 57.43.

Parker, Ray. b. 1922.

UNTITLED. (1956.) Oil on canvas. 83 x 49. Gift of the Uris Brothers Foundation, Inc. 58.57.

Parker, Robert Andrew. b. 1927.

MARSEILLES, NIGHT. 1955. Watercolor and ink. 28½ x 17¼ (over-all). Gift of the New York Foundation. 56.40.

Parsons, Betty.

ISLANDS IN GREECE. 1953. Gouache. 21½ x 28. Gift of Miss Katharine Ordway. 55.23.

Parsons, Lloyd. b. 1893.

CHIPMAN'S CREEK. (1936.) Oil on canvas. 20 x 30. Purchase. 37.28.

Pearlstein, Philip. b. 1924.

ROCK MOUND. (1958.) Oil on canvas. 44 x 52. Gift of the Friends of the Whitney Museum of American Art. 58.54.

UPROOTED TREE. (1956.) Wash drawing. 17¾ x 21⅜. Gift of John Preston in memory of Morgan O. Preston, 1918–1944. 58.6.

Peirce, Waldo. b. 1884.

AFTER THE SHOW. 1933. Oil on canvas. 32¼ x 46. Purchase. 34.23.

Pereira, I. Rice. b. 1907.

LANDSCAPE OF THE ABSOLUTE. (1955.) Oil on canvas. 40 x 50. Gift of Richard Adler. 56.15. (p. 246.)

OBLIQUE PROGRESSION. 1948. Oil on canvas. 50 x 40. Purchase. 48.22. (p. 248.)

Perkins, Harley. b. 1883.

FIORD, NORWAY. 1930. Watercolor. 14⅝ x 21⅝. Purchase. 32.62.

STILL LIFE. (1926.) Oil on canvas. 20 x 24. 31.315.

Perlin, Bernard. b. 1918.

THE JACKET. 1951. Casein tempera on cardboard. 28¼ x 19¾. Wildenstein Benefit Purchase Fund. 53.20. (p. 144.)

Persons, Simmons. b. 1906.

PLEASANT INTRODUCTION. (1937.) Watercolor. 15⅝ x 19½. Purchase. 38.18.

Peterdi, Gabor. b. 1915.

TIDAL. 1955. Oil on canvas. 50 x 80. Gift of Walter Bareiss. 56.7. (p. 245.)

VERTICAL GARDEN, I. 1959. Ink and watercolor. 39½ x 25¾. Gift of the Friends of the Whitney Museum of American Art. 60.4.

Philipp, Robert. b. 1895.

FRUIT. (1932.) Pastel. 17¼ x 23¼. Purchase. 32.53.

Phillips, Blanche. b. 1908.

TWO WHO WALK TOGETHER. (1956–57.) Brass. 32 high. Gift of Mrs. Blanche C. Levine in memory of Lillian Claster. 57.25.

Phillips, James. b. 1929.

WOMAN WITH FLOWERS. 1955. Oil on canvas. 17 x 21. Neysa McMein Purchase Award. 56.33.

Phillips, Marjorie. b. 1895.

AUTUMN AFTERNOON. (1948.) Oil on canvas. 36 x 27. Purchase (and exchange). 48.15.

Picken, George. b. 1898.

BUILDING THE EAST RIVER DRIVE. 1939. Oil on canvas. 20 x 40. Purchase. 42.14.

MILFORD BEACH, LONG ISLAND SOUND. 1930. Watercolor. 13¼ x 19⅜. Purchase. 32.19.

Pickett, Joseph. 1848–1918.

CORYELL'S FERRY, 1776. (Probably between 1914–18.) Oil on canvas. 37½ x 48¼. Purchase. 31.316. (p. 30.)

Pippin, Horace. 1888–1946.

THE BUFFALO HUNT. 1933. Oil on canvas. 21¼ x 31. Purchase. 41.27.

Pittman, Hobson. b. 1900.

THE WIDOW. (1937.) Oil on canvas. 15 x 25. Purchase. 38.51.

Plate, Walter. b. 1925.

COMPOSITION. 1954. Oil on composition board. 48 x 70. Gift of Mr. and Mrs. Jacob M. Kaplan. 58.41.

STILL LIFE. (1954.) Oil on composition board. 36 x 48¼. Juliana Force Purchase. 55.9.

Polasek, Albin. b. 1879.

HEAD OF A MAN. 1920. Bronze. 14¼ high. 31.67.

Pollack, Reginald. b. 1924.

BLUE LANDSCAPE. 1957. Oil on canvas. 37½ x 59. Gift of the Friends of the Whitney Museum of American Art. 59.12.

Pollet, Joseph. b. 1897.

BEN'S BEAN-POLES. (1925.) Oil on canvas. 40½ x 30. 31.318.

BLACK WALNUTS. (1945.) Oil on canvas. 30 x 40. Purchase (and exchange). 52.30.

MIDSUMMER. (1925.) Oil on canvas. 40 x 60. 31.319.

NEIGHBOR GREEN. (1928.) Oil on canvas. 40 x 60. Purchase. 31.320.

RED BARN. (1927.) Oil on canvas. 20 x 24. 31.321.

Pollock, Jackson. 1912–1956.

NUMBER 27. 1950. Oil on canvas. 49 x 106. Purchase. 53.12. (pp. 216–17.)

Poor, Anne. b. 1918.

THREE MUSICIANS. (1951.) Oil on canvas. 20 x 22⅞. Gift of Mr. and Mrs. Leo Simon. 52.12.

Poor, Henry Varnum. b. 1888.

AUTUMN FRUIT. (1932.) Oil on wood. 18 x 26½. Purchase. 33.20. (p. 78.)

BESSIE. (1939.) Oil on wood. 10⅜ x 13¾. Purchase. 39.22.

Porter, David. b. 1912.

THE CLOUAGE CLAN, II. (1957.) Oil on canvas. 40¾ x 49½. Gift of Bernard Davis. 58.50.

Pousette-Dart, Richard. b. 1916.

THE MAGNIFICENT. 1950–51. Oil on canvas. 86¼ x 44. Gift of Mrs. Ethel K. Schwabacher. 53.43. (p. 210.)

Pozzatti, Rudy. b. 1925.

XANADU. 1954. Oil on canvas. 34 x 44. Anonymous gift. 60.8.

Prendergast, Charles. 1868–1948.

WORLD'S FAIR. 1939. Tempera and gold leaf on composition board. 24 x 27½. Purchase. 49.12.

Prendergast, Maurice. 1859–1924.

ALONG THE SEINE. 1892. Oil on canvas. 13 x 9½. Purchase. 39.27.

BATHING BEACH. (c. 1912.) Watercolor and pastel. 13½ x 19½. 31.456.

CENTRAL PARK, 1900. Watercolor. 14 x 21¾. Purchase. 32.41.

CENTRAL PARK, 1901. Watercolor. 14⅛ x 21¾. Purchase. 32.42. (p. 21.)

CINERARIAS AND FRUIT. (1915.) Oil on canvas. 21 x 27. Purchase. 32.48.

THE COVE. (1916.) Oil on canvas. 28 x 39¾. 31.322.

DIEPPE. 1892. Oil on canvas. 13 x 9¾. Purchase. 39.28.

MAY DAY, CENTRAL PARK. (c. 1901.) Watercolor. 14⅜ x 21⅝. Purchase (and exchange). 48.19.

THE PROMENADE. (1913.) Oil on canvas. 30 x 34. Bequest of Alexander M. Bing. 60.10. (p. 32.)

PROMENADE, GLOUCESTER. (c. 1918.) Oil on canvas. 26 x 34. 31.323.

Presser, Josef. b. 1911.

THE BLACK HORSE. 1931. Charcoal and pastel on parchment. 14⅛ x 19. Purchase. 31.566.

Presser, Josef. (*continued*)

THE BROWN HORSE. 1930. Charcoal and pastel on parchment. 14 x 18¾. Purchase. 31.567.

Prestopino, Gregorio. b. 1907.

GLITTER, NUMBER 3. (1951.) Watercolor, pastel, crayon, and ink. 29⅞ x 26 (over-all). Purchase. 52.21.

WINTER. (1945.) Oil on canvas. 20¼ x 30¼. Purchase. 46.3.

Pribble, Easton. b. 1917.

PINE WOODS. 1955. Oil on canvas. 36¾ x 56¼. Anonymous gift (and purchase). 55.20.

Prophet, N. Elizabeth. b. 1890.

CONGOLAIS. (1931.) Wood. 16¾ high. Purchase. 32.83.

Quanchi, Leo. b. 1892.

PURPLE PASSAGE. (1956.) Oil on canvas. 32 x 20¼. Purchase (and exchange). 56.46.

Quinn, Edmond Thomas. 1868–1929.

LEON KROLL. 1924. Bronze. 10¾ high. Purchase. 42.8.

Quirt, Walter. b. 1902.

MUTATION. (1940.) Oil on canvas. 30 x 40. Purchase. 42.34.

Racz, Andre. b. 1916.

SUNFLOWER. 1959. Ink. 36¼ x 26⅛ (over-all). Gift of the Friends of the Whitney Museum of American Art. 59.43.

Rasmusson, Daniel. b. 1913.

DEATH COMES FOR THE HERO. (1937.) Ink. 8½ x 11½. Purchase. 37.34.

PIETÀ. 1937. Ink. 9⅜ x 11¾. Purchase. 37.33.

Rattner, Abraham. b. 1895.

THE EMPEROR. (1944.) Oil on canvas. 28¾ x 23¾. Purchase. 45.6.

SONG OF ESTHER. 1958. Oil on composition board. 60 x 48. Gift of the Friends of the Whitney Museum of American Art. 58.36. (p. 171.)

Ray, Man. b. 1890.

FIVE FIGURES. 1914. Oil on canvas. 36 x 32. Gift of Mrs. Katharine Kuh. 56.36.

WOMAN ASLEEP. 1913. Oil on canvas. 12 x 16. Purchase. 33.30.

Reder, Bernard. b. 1897.

ADAM AND EVE. 1957. Bronze. 43½ high. Purchase. 59.35. (p. 193.)

WOMAN AND DOG. 1956. Ink. 25¼ x 18¼. Purchase. 58.14.

Refregier, Anton. b. 1905.

THE STAIRCASE. 1949. Tempera on canvas. 45 x 28¼. Purchase. 49.20. (p. 163.)

Reinhardt, Ad. b. 1913.

NUMBER 17—1953. Oil and tempera on canvas. 77¾ x 77¾. Purchase. 55.36.

NUMBER 18—1948–49. Oil on canvas. 40 x 60. Purchase. 53.13.

Reinhardt, Siegfried. b. 1925.

CRUCIFIXION. 1953. Oil on composition board. 28 x 45½. Gift of William Benton. 55.2.

Resnick, Milton. b. 1917.

GENIE. 1959. Oil on canvas. 104 x 70. Purchase. 60.31. (p. 221.)

LOW GATE. 1957. Oil on canvas. 76 x 68½. Gift of Mr. and Mrs. Guy A. Weill. 60.67.

Reynal, Jeanne. b. 1903.

OGO. (1952–53.) Mosaic. 52 x 60. Purchase. 54.45.

Ribak, Louis. b. 1903.

CORRAL IN WINTER. (1952–53.) Oil on canvas. 32 x 40. Purchase (and exchange). 54.15.

HOME RELIEF STATION. (1935–36.) Oil on canvas. 28 x 36. Purchase. 36.148.

UNTIMELY CLOUDS. 1933. Gouache. 16½ x 21½. Purchase. 34.1.

WHITE CLIFFS. (1955.) Oil on composition board. 18 x 37. Gift of Mr. and Mrs. Saul Rosen. 56.26.

Richardson, Dean. b. 1931.

MOTORISTS. 1957. Oil on canvas. 53 x 78½. Purchase. 60.29.

Rivers, Larry. b. 1923.

DOUBLE PORTRAIT OF BIRDIE. (1955.) Oil on canvas. 70¾ x 82½. Anonymous gift. 56.9.

Robinson, Boardman. 1876–1952.

AMBASSADOR HARVEY, STUDY NUMBER 1. (1921.) Crayon and gouache. 19¼ x 14. 31.568.

AMBASSADOR HARVEY, STUDY NUMBER 2. 1921. Ink. 24 x 8. 31.569.

THE CLUB. 1917. Oil and crayon on paper. 13½ x 18. 31.457.

DRAPED NUDE. 1923. Pencil and watercolor. 13⅜ x 9¼. 31.570.

PORTRAIT. (1918.) Crayon and ink. 12¼ x 8¾. 31.571.

ELSA WERTMAN. 1940. Illustration for Edgar Lee Masters' *Spoon River Anthology*. Casein. 13¾ x 10½. Purchase. 42.24.

Robus, Hugo. b. 1885.

DESPAIR. (1927.) Bronze. 12 high. Purchase. 40.23. (p. 64.)

Rocklin, Raymond. b. 1922.

EVOCATION. (1958.) Brass. 66 high. Gift of the Friends of the Whitney Museum of American Art. 58.39.

Rohland, Caroline S. b. 1885.

AT THE THEATRE. (1930.) Pastel. 16 x 18½. 31.458.

COTTON PICKERS. (1939.) Pastel. 24 x 18½. Purchase. 41.12.

LUNCHEON. (1930.) Pastel. 16 x 21. Purchase. 31.459.

Rohland, Paul. 1884–1949.

GARDEN OF MANSION. (1931.) Watercolor. 20 x 26. Purchase. 31.460.

THE MANSION. (1931.) Oil on canvas. 27 x 34. Purchase. 33.21.

PEONIES. (1930.) Oil on canvas. 30 x 24. 31.331.

TREES. (1929.) Watercolor. 12¾ x 16⅜. 31.461.

Rollo, Jo. b. 1904.

HEAD. 1932. Crayon. 6⅞ x 6¼. Purchase. 32.45.

Romano, Umberto. b. 1906.

MAN REACHES FOR THE UNKNOWN. (1959.) Oil on canvas. 84 x 52. Gift of Mr. and Mrs. Jacquin D. Bierman. 59.32.

Rosati, James. b. 1912.

INTERIOR CASTLE, NUMBER 1. (1959.) Sheet metal. 26 high. Gift of the Friends of the Whitney Museum of American Art. 60.26.

Rose, Herman. b. 1909.

PORTRAIT OF AN ARTIST. 1958. Oil on canvas. 25 x 25. Gift of Mr. and Mrs. Charles H. Renthal. 60.37.

STREET SCENE. (c. 1945.) Oil on canvas. 13¼ x 14¼. Gift of Bernard S. Needle. 58.60.

Rosen, Charles. 1878–1950.

CAR SHOPS. (1932.) Oil on canvas. 20 x 40. Purchase. 33.22.

OLD FERRY SLIP. (1931.) Oil on canvas. 24 x 30. Purchase. 31.334.

TREES. (1942.) Oil on canvas. 40 x 30. Gift of friends of the artist. 43.4.

Roszak, Theodore. b. 1907.

FISHERMAN'S BRIDE. (1934.) Oil on canvas. 29 x 27. Purchase. 34.24.

SEA SENTINEL. (1956.) Steel and bronze. 105 high. Purchase. 56.28. (p. 236.)

STUDY FOR "THE FURIES." (1950.) Ink. 25 x 38¾. Purchase. 51.29. (p. 154.)

THORN BLOSSOM. (1948.) Steel and nickel-silver. 33½ high. Purchase. 48.6.

VERTICAL CONSTRUCTION. (1943.) Painted wood and plastic. 74 high. Gift of the artist. 57.7. (p. 254.)

Rothko, Mark. b. 1903.

BAPTISMAL SCENE. (1945.) Watercolor. 19⅞ x 14. Purchase. 46.12.

ENTOMBMENT, I. (1946.) Gouache. 20⅜ x 25¾. Purchase. 47.10. (p. 222.)

Rothschild, Lincoln. b. 1902.

MOTHER AND CHILD. (1931.) Wood. 26 high. Purchase. 31.71.

Ruellan, Andrée. b. 1905.

BOY IN ARMCHAIR. (1928.) Pencil. 16⅜ x 10⅛ (over-all). Purchase. 31.572.

GIRL READING. (1928.) Pencil. 16⅜ x 10⅛ (over-all). Purchase. 31.573.

SIDE SHOW. (1938.) Charcoal and crayon. 14⅜ x 19½. Purchase. 38.16.

THE VAGRANT. (1939.) Charcoal. 15¼ x 11⅜. Purchase. 41.40.

Ruggles, Carl. b. 1876.

THE POOL, ROARING BRANCH. (1932.) Oil on paper. 19¼ x 15¼ (over-all). Purchase. 32.32.

TRUMPET FLOWER. 1940. Watercolor. 10 x 8. Purchase. 40.5.

Rumsey, Charles Cary. 1879–1922.

PAGAN KIN. Bronze. 12⅝ high. 31.72.

Russell, Alfred. b. 1920.

LA RUE DE NEVERS. (1949.) Oil on canvas. 40 x 26. Purchase. 50.21.

ORPHIC COMPOSITION. 1952. Ink. 22 x 29⅝. Purchase. 54.28.

Russell, Morgan. 1886–1953.

FOUR PART SYNCHROMY, NUMBER 7. 1914–15. Oil on canvas. 15⅜ x 11½. Gift of the artist in memory of Gertrude V. Whitney. 51.33. (p. 46.)

Ryan, Anne. 1889–1954.

GOLD COLLAGE. (1953.) Paper and cloth. 23⅝ x 29½. Purchase. 54.26.

Saalburg, Allen. b. 1899.

Eight gouache sketches for sets for the film *Green Pastures*. (c. 1935.) Purchase. 37.1–8.

Sage, Kay. b. 1898.

NO PASSING. 1954. Oil on canvas. 51¼ x 38. Purchase. 55.10. (p. 151.)

Salemme, Attilio. 1911–1955.

INQUISITION. 1952. Oil on canvas. 40 x 63. Purchase. 53.26. (p. 250.)

Salemme, Lucia Autorino. b. 1919.

NIGHT IN THE CLAIRVOYANT CITY. 1951. Gouache and ink. 18⅛ x 22⅞. Purchase. 51.26.

Santo, Patsy. b. 1893.

WINTER QUIET. 1940. Oil on canvas. 18 x 24. Purchase. 40.4.

Sardeau, Hélène. b. 1899.

MOTHER AND CHILD. 1933. Walnut. 19 high. Purchase. 33.60.

Sato, Tadashi. b. 1923.

SUBMERGED ROCKS. 1958. Oil on canvas. 36 x 42. Neysa McMein Purchase Award. 59.8.

Sawyer, Helen. b. 1900.

FLORIDA BOUQUETS. (1942.) Oil on canvas. 25 x 30. Purchase. 42.22.

Scaravaglione, Concetta. b. 1900.

GROUP. (1935.) Mahogany. 24¼ high. Purchase. 36.4.

STANDING FIGURE. (1931.) Mahogany. 26¼ high. Purchase. 32.16.

Schanker, Louis. b. 1903.

DARK NATURE THEME. 1945. Casein. 22¼ x 30¾ (over-all). Purchase. 46.13.

Schmidt, Katherine. b. 1898.

BROE AND MCDONALD LISTEN IN. 1937. Oil on canvas. 30 x 24. Purchase (and exchange). 50.15. (p. 96.)

LAUREL AND PINK FLOWER. (1930.) Oil on canvas. 30 x 24. 31.335.

ON THE ROCKS. 1941. Maroger medium on canvas. 18 x 36. Purchase (and exchange). 50.16.

QUINCE IN BOWL. 1925. Pencil and watercolor. 9 x 13. 31.574.

THE SNAKE. 1932. Oil on canvas. 20 x 36. Purchase. 33.23.

THE WHITE FACTORY. (1928.) Oil on canvas. 24 x 30. 31.336.

Schnabel, Day. b. 1905.

TRANSFORMATIONS. (1956.) Sienna marble. 19¾ high. Purchase. 57.24.

Schnakenberg, Henry. b. 1892.

AIR PLANTS, PORTO RICO. (1927.) Oil on canvas. 30¼ x 36¼. 31.337.

CONVERSATION. 1930. Oil on canvas. 50¼ x 36. Purchase. 31.338. (p. 74.)

FOREST CARPET. (1924.) Watercolor. 11¾ x 15¾. 31.463.

ICE PATTERN. (1948.) Watercolor. 14¼ x 21⅜. Purchase. 53.30.

LANDSCAPE WITH MOUNTAIN. (1927.) Watercolor. 13¾ x 19⅝. 31.464.

MEMORIAL TO SUMMER. (1949.) Oil on canvas. 50 x 19. Purchase. 53.29.

NEAR THE QUARRY. (1930.) Watercolor 13½ x 19½. Purchase. 31.465.

THE PALISADES. (1941.) Oil on canvas. 36 x 50. Purchase. 41.53.

THE POOL'S EDGE. (1931.) Watercolor. 16 x 19⅜. Purchase. 31.466.

SHELL AND LEMONS. (1929.) Oil on canvas. 20 x 24. 31.341.

S.S. SAN LORENZO. (1926.) Watercolor. 13⅝ x 19⅝. 31.467.

Schnitzler, Max. b. 1903.

1942. Oil on canvas. 60 x 78. Gift of Mr. and Mrs. Harry Singer and Family. 60.52.

Schrag, Karl. b. 1912.

MONTSERRAT. (1958.) Casein on cardboard. 38 x 26. Gift of the Friends of the Whitney Museum of American Art. 59.37.

Schreiber, Georges. b. 1904.

SECOND BALCONY. 1936. Watercolor. 19⅛ x 29. Purchase. 36.23.

Schucker, Charles. b. 1914.

THE BRIDGE. 1954. Oil on canvas. 26 x 83½. Purchase. 55.11. (p. 205.)

Schueler, Jon. b. 1916.

SNOW CLOUD AND BLUE SKY. 1958. Oil on canvas. 80 x 71. Gift of the Friends of the Whitney Museum of American Art. 58.37. (p. 203.)

Schwabacher, Ethel. b. 1903.

ODE, I. (1951.) Oil on canvas. 36 x 30. Purchase. 53.33.

OEDIPUS AT COLONOS, NUMBER 2. (1959.) Oil on canvas. 84¾ x 60. Purchase. 59.36. (p. 220.)

Schwartz, Manfred. b. 1909.

PROCESSIONAL. (1952–53.) Oil on canvas. 36 x 36. Gift of Mrs. Leo Simon. 53.55.

Seliger, Charles. b. 1926.

FLORAL. 1950. Tempera and ink. 18 x 13¾. Purchase. 51.27.

Seligmann, Kurt. b. 1900.

THE BALCONY, I. 1949–50. Oil on canvas. 33 x 48. Purchase. 53.52. (p. 149.)

PERSEUS. 1946. Ink, egg tempera, and gouache. 23¼ x 32. Wildenstein Benefit Purchase Fund. 53.14.

Sennhauser, John. b. 1907.

EMOTIVE, NUMBER 15. 1950. Watercolor and casein. 19⅞ x 25⅞ (over-all). Purchase. 51.28.

Shahn, Ben. b. 1898.

CHERUBS AND CHILDREN. (1944.) Tempera on composition board. 15 x 22⅞. Purchase. 45.17.

CONVERSATIONS. (1958.) Watercolor. 39¼ x 27. Gift of the Friends of the Whitney Museum of American Art. 58.21. (p. 158.)

EVERYMAN. (1954.) Tempera on composition board. 72 x 24. Purchase. 56.5. (p. 165.)

THE PASSION OF SACCO AND VANZETTI. (1931–32.) From the Sacco-Vanzetti series of 23 paintings. Tempera on canvas. 84½ x 48. Gift of Edith and Milton Lowenthal in memory of Juliana Force. 49.22. (p. 99.)

RECONSTRUCTION. (1945.) Tempera on composition board. 26 x 39. Purchase. 46.4.

SCOTTS RUN, WEST VIRGINIA. 1937. Tempera on cardboard. 22¼ x 27⅞. Purchase. 38.11. (p. 102.)

Shapiro, Liza. 1909–1959.

CRUCIFIXION. (1958.) Oil. gouache, watercolor, wax, and ink on cardboard. 30 x 27. Gift of Dr. Mortimer F. Shapiro. 60.38.

Shaw, Charles. b. 1892.

VIVE LA BAGATELLE! 1955. Oil on composition board. 28¾ x 36½. Gift through the Federation of Modern Painters and Sculptors, Inc. 55.46.

Sheeler, Charles. b. 1883.

ARCHITECTURAL CADENCES. 1954. Oil on canvas. 25 x 35. Purchase. 54.35. (p. 138.)

BUCKS COUNTY BARN. 1923. Tempera and crayon. 19¼ x 25½. 31.468. (p. 54.)

CHRYSANTHEMUMS. 1912. Oil on canvas. 24 x 20. Gift of the artist. 55.24.

INTERIOR. 1926. Oil on canvas. 33 x 22. 31.344.

INTERIOR, BUCKS COUNTY BARN. 1932. Crayon. 15 x 18¾. Purchase. 33.78.

PERTAINING TO YACHTS AND YACHTING. (c. 1922.) Crayon. 19 x 24¼ (over-all). Purchase. 48.4.

RIVER ROUGE PLANT. 1932. Oil on canvas. 20 x 24⅛. Purchase. 32.43. (p. 54.)

Sheets, Millard. b. 1907.

BLACK HORSE. 1934. Watercolor. 14½ x 22. Purchase. 36.24.

Sherman, Sarai. b. 1922.

THE CENTAURS. (1959.) Oil on canvas. 54 x 56. Gift of Dr. and Mrs. Frank Ross De Luca. 60.9.

MEZZADRO. (1954.) Oil on canvas. 35½ x 51¼. Gift of Max Toberoff. 56.17.

Shiff, Madeline.

WILTZ AT WORK. 1932. Oil on canvas. 18 x 15. Purchase. 32.51.

Shinn, Everett. 1876–1953.

BAL TABARIN. 1902. Pastel. 13¾ x 18. Gift of Mr. and Mrs. Albert Hackett. 55.38.

GIRL DRESSING. 1906. Crayon. 15½ x 10¼. Purchase. 35.3.

NUDE BENDING. 1907. Crayon. 10⅝ x 13⅞. 31.576.

REVUE. 1908. Oil on canvas. 18 x 24. 31.346. (p. 24.)

SEINE EMBANKMENT. 1903. Pastel. 26¾ x 39½. Gift of Mr. and Mrs. Arthur G. Altschul. 59.33.

Simkhovitch, Helena. b. 1908.

ISABEL BOLTON. 1951. Brass. 14½ high. Gift through the Federation of Modern Painters and Sculptors, Inc. 56.13.

Simpson-Middleman.
　Simpson, Marshall. 1900–1958.
　Middleman, Roslynn. b. 1929.

NIMBUS. (1953.) Oil on composition board. 33¾ x 22¾. Gift of Samuel S. Goldberg. 55.14.

Siporin, Mitchell. b. 1910.

DANCERS BY THE CLOCK. 1949. Oil on canvas. 40½ x 60⅛. Purchase. 50.22. (p. 168.)

EARTHQUAKE. 1941. Casein on cardboard. 23⅞ x 34. Purchase. 41.41.

FLASHBACK TO CARTHAGE. 1946. Casein. 18⅞ x 23⅞ (over-all). Purchase. 47.11.

HAYMARKET SERIES: THE STOOL PIGEONS, MR. AND MRS. WILLIAM SELIGER. (1933–34.) Ink on cardboard. 21⅜ x 14¼. Anonymous gift. 51.21.

Sloan, John. 1871–1951.

BACKYARDS, GREENWICH VILLAGE. 1914. Oil on canvas. 26 x 32. Purchase. 36.153. (p. 25.)

BEFORE HER MAKERS AND HER JUDGE. (1913.) Illustration for *The Masses,* August, 1913. Crayon. 16½ x 25. Purchase. 36.38.

THE BLUE SEA—CLASSIC. 1918. Oil on canvas. 24 x 30. Purchase (and exchange). 51.39.

CHARLOTTE IN RED COAT. (1951.) Tempera and oil on composition board. 30 x 24. Gift of Mrs. John Sloan. 52.31.

DOLLY WITH A BLACK BOW. (1907.) Oil on canvas. 32 x 26. Gift of Miss Amelia Elizabeth White. 59.28.

KITCHEN AND BATH. (1912.) Oil on composition board. 24 x 20. Gift of Mr. and Mrs. Albert Hackett. 60.44.

MODEL IN DRESSING ROOM. (1933.) Tempera and oil on composition board. 36 x 30. Permanent loan from Mrs. John Sloan. 1.60.

NUDE. 1931. Pencil. 7⅜ x 9⅛. Gift of Mrs. John Sloan. 51.42.

NUDE AND NINE APPLES. 1937. Tempera and oil on composition board. 24 x 30. Purchase (and exchange). 51.41. (p. 72.)

THE PICNIC GROUNDS. (1906/07.) Oil on canvas. 24 x 36. Purchase. 41.34. (p. 24.)

PORTRAIT. 1934. Tempera and oil on wood. 36 x 24. Gift of Miss Amelia Elizabeth White. 52.13.

RIDERS IN THE HILLS. 1946. Tempera and oil on composition board. 19⅝ x 20. Gift of Mrs. John Sloan. 52.32.

ROMANY MARIE. (1920.) Oil on canvas. 24 x 20. Purchase (and exchange). 51.40.

SIXTH AVENUE ELEVATED AT THIRD STREET. (1928.) Oil on canvas. 30 x 40. Purchase. 36.154. (p. 86.)

Slobodkina, Esphyr. b. 1914.

COMPOSITION WITH WHITE OVALS. 1952. Oil on composition board. 34½ x 20¾. Wildenstein Benefit Purchase Fund. 53.6.

Smith, David. b. 1906.

COCKFIGHT—VARIATION. 1945. Steel. 34 high. Purchase. 46.9. (p. 195.)

HUDSON RIVER LANDSCAPE. 1951. Steel. 75 long. Purchase. 54.14. (p. 233.)

Smith, Judson. b. 1880.

ALONG THE HUDSON. 1930. Oil on composition board. 47½ x 60. Purchase. 31.349.

Smith, Pamela Coleman.

THE WAVE. 1903. Watercolor. 10¼ x 17¾ (over-all). Gift of Mrs. Sidney N. Heller. 60.42.

Solman, Joseph. b. 1909.

THE RED SHAWL. (1950.) Oil on composition board. 16 x 24. Gift of Mr. and Mrs. Jack I. Poses. 54.4.

Solomon, Hyde. b. 1911.

Vermont Autumn. (1956.) Oil on canvas. 48 x 59. Gift of Mrs. Henry J. Fuller. 57.5.

Soyer, Isaac. b. 1907.

Employment Agency. 1937. Oil on canvas. 34¼ x 45. Purchase. 37.44. (p. 100.)

Soyer, Moses. b. 1899.

Girl in Orange Sweater. 1953. Oil on canvas. 30 x 24. Purchase (and exchange). 54.5. (p. 128.)

Soyer, Raphael. b. 1899.

The Brown Sweater. (1952.) Oil on canvas. 50 x 34. Purchase (and exchange). 53.53. (p. 131.)

Office Girls. 1936. Oil on canvas. 26 x 24. Purchase. 36.149. (p. 97.)

Sleeping Girl. Pencil. 17 x 14. 31.576.

Speicher, Eugene. b. 1883.

Fira Barchak. (1929.) Oil on canvas. 64 x 42. Purchase. 31.358.

Bending Figure. (1921.) Ink. 10⅞ x 6¼. 31.577.

The Danish Girl. (1939.) Oil on canvas. 19½ x 18¼. Gift of Mrs. Harry Payne Whitney. 41.37.

Girl's Head (1925.) Oil on canvas. 20¼ x 16¼. Purchase. 31.356.

Head of a Girl. (1929.) Pencil. 10 x 9⅛. Purchase. 31.578.

Lucia. (1931.) Oil on canvas. 23 x 28. Purchase. 33.25.

Marianna. (1937.) Oil on canvas. 45½ x 35½. Purchase. 37.45. (p. 71.)

Murray Bay Landscape. (1933.) Oil on canvas. 27 x 35. Purchase. 34.28.

Nude. (1921.) Crayon. 11¾ x 8⅛. 31.579.

Plate of Fruit. (1928.) Pencil. 8½ x 13⅛. Purchase. 34.29.

Portrait. (1928.) Crayon. 10¾ x 8¾. 31.580.

Portrait of a Girl. (1925.) Oil on canvas. 18 x 16. 31.357.

Spring Bouquet. (1925.) Oil on canvas. 20¼ x 15. 31.359.

Winter Rye, Yankeetown. (1940.) Oil on canvas. 17 x 22. Purchase. 41.23.

Spencer, Niles. 1893–1952.

Apartment Tower. 1944. Oil on canvas. 32 x 24. Gift of Mr. and Mrs. Alan H. Temple. 55.42. (p. 139.)

The Green Table. 1930. Oil on canvas. 50 x 40. Purchase. 31.361. (p. 82.)

Seventh Avenue. (1927.) Oil on canvas. 30¼ x 36. 31.363.

Sponsler, Edwin E. b. 1907.

Pasture. 1952. Ink. 8⅝ x 29⅞. Purchase. 54.29.

Spruance, Benton. b. 1904.

The Philatelists. 1935. Oil on canvas. 16¼ x 20. Purchase. 36.8.

Spruce, Everett. b. 1908.

Brushy Hillside. (1957.) Oil on composition board. 24 x 30. Purchase. 58.34. (p. 188.)

Squier, Jack. b. 1927.

Oracle. 1958. Bronze. 29½ high. Juliana Force Purchase. 58.46.

Stamos, Theodoros. b. 1922.

Ancestral Worship. 1947. Pastel, gouache, and ink. 17½ x 23⅜. Purchase. 48.9.

Greek Orison. (1952.) Oil on canvas. 67 x 27. Purchase. 53.15.

High Snow—Low Sun, II. (1957.) Oil on canvas. 53½ x 97½. Gift of the Friends of the Whitney Museum of American Art. 57.30. (p. 225.)

Stankiewicz, Richard. b. 1922.

Kabuki Dancer. (1956.) Steel and cast iron. 80¼ high. Gift of the Friends of the Whitney Museum of American Art. 57.12. (p. 237.)

Steiger, Harwood. b. 1900.

Indian Summer. (1936.) Watercolor. 23⅛ x 17¾. Purchase. 36.25.

Steinberg, Saul. b. 1914.

Railroad Station. 1952. Ink. 19½ x 24 (over-all). Gift of Mr. and Mrs. Carl L. Selden. 59.44.

Stella, Joseph. 1877–1946.

The Brooklyn Bridge: Variation on an Old Theme. (1939.) Oil on canvas. 70 x 42. Purchase. 42.15. (p. 51.)

Der Rosenkavalier. (c. 1915.) Oil on canvas. 24 x 30. Gift of George F. Of. 52.39.

Louis Eilshemius. Pencil. 28⅜ x 21⅝. 31.581.

Nativity. Pastel. 37 x 19⅛ (over-all). 31.469.

Sketch for Brooklyn Bridge. Pastel. 21 x 17½. Gift of Miss Rose Fried. 52.36.

Still Life. Oil on canvas. 15 x 24¼. Gift of Mr. and Mrs. N. E. Waldman. 58.52.

Still Life, Fruit. Gouache. 21 x 29. 31.470.

Steppat, Leo. b. 1910.

Bull. (1952.) Bronze. 33 high. Gift of Robert D. Kaufmann. 54.46.

Sterne, Hedda. b. 1916.

New York, N.Y., 1955. Oil on canvas. 36⅛ x 60⅛. Anonymous gift. 56.20.

Sterne, Maurice. 1878–1957.

Bali Bazaar. (1913–14.) Oil on canvas. 36½ x 39. Purchase. 54.13. (p. 37.)

The Bomb Thrower. (1910/14.) Bronze. 12 high. Bequest of Mrs. Sam A. Lewisohn. 54.51. (p. 58.)

Composition, XIX. (1952.) Ink and chalk. 19½ x 23½. Purchase. 54.38.

Seascape, Provincetown. (1945.) Oil on canvas. 20 x 27. Bequest of Mrs. Sam A. Lewisohn. 54.52.

Stevens, Edward John, Jr. b. 1923.

Still Life with Jungle Objects. 1944. Watercolor and gouache. 21⅝ x 17¾. Purchase. 45.23.

Strombotne, James. b. 1934.

THE GROUP. 1960. Oil on canvas. 48 x 60. Juliana Force Purchase. 60.47.

Stuempfig, Walter. b. 1914.

THE FALLS OF THE SCHUYLKILL. 1953. Oil on canvas. 18¼ x 22¼. Long-term loan from the Henry Ward Ranger Fund through the National Academy of Design. 54.39.

FORNANCE STREET. (1956.) Oil on canvas. 26 x 30. Gift of William Inge. 58.47.

JUDGMENT OF PARIS. 1943. Oil on canvas. 28 x 36⅛. Purchase. 43.12.

Swarz, Sahl. b. 1912.

TREE OF ORACLES. (1957.) Bronze. 53½ high. Living Arts Foundation Fund. 57.46.

Tack, Augustus Vincent. 1870–1949.

BEFORE EGYPT. (c. 1930–35.) Oil on canvas mounted on composition board. Canvas: 16¾ x 36½; board: 26 x 45. Gift of Duncan Phillips. 60.13.

Takal, Peter. b. 1905.

THE APPLE TREE. 1954. Ink. 16 x 23. Purchase. 54.48.

PROFILE OF A CITY. 1956. Ink. 43½ x 27¾. Anonymous gift. 58.32.

Talbot, William. b. 1918.

STEEL SCULPTURE. (1950.) Stainless steel and steel. 39½ high. Purchase. 51.31.

Tam, Reuben. 1916.

A SPAN OF THE SEA. 1958. Oil on canvas. 40½ x 47½. Gift of the Friends of the Whitney Museum of American Art. 58.38.

Tanguy, Yves. 1900–1955.

FEAR. (1949.) Oil on canvas. 60 x 40. Purchase. 49.21. (p. 150.)

Taylor, John W. b. 1897.

STILL LIFE. (1930.) Watercolor. 19⅝ x 14½. Purchase. 31.472.

Teichman, Sabina. b. 1905.

TIVOLI. (1957.) Oil on canvas. 43⅞ x 22. Gift of Mr. and Mrs. Arthur Murray. 57.17.

Thon, William. b. 1906.

MIDNIGHT QUARRY. (1952.) Watercolor. 26½ x 40. Wildenstein Benefit Purchase Fund. 53.16.

Tobey, Mark. b. 1890.

NEW LIFE (RESURRECTION). (1957.) Tempera on cardboard. 43⅜ x 27¼. Gift of the Friends of the Whitney Museum of American Art. 59.13. (p. 209.)

ODALISQUE. 1927. Oil on canvas. 48 x 28. Gift of Mr. and Mrs. John Rogers, Jr., in memory of Juliana Force. 50.14.

SALE. 1943. Tempera on composition board. 18 x 29⅞. Gift of Mr. and Mrs. David M. Solinger. 52.11.

UNIVERSAL FIELD. 1949. Tempera and pastel on cardboard. 28 x 44. Purchase. 50.24. (p. 208.)

Tofel, Jennings. 1891–1959.

HAGAR. (1931.) Oil on canvas. 25½ x 32. Purchase. 32.8.

Tomlin, Bradley Walker. 1899–1953.

SELF-PORTRAIT. (1932.) Oil on canvas. 17 x 14. Gift of Henry Ittleson, Jr. 55.28.

STILL LIFE. (1939.) Oil on canvas. 34 x 46. Purchase. 42.10. (p. 118.)

Toney, Anthony. b. 1913.

PROCESSION. (1954–55.) Oil on canvas. 72 x 48. Gift of Mr. and Mrs. N. E. Waldman. 56.30.

Tooker, George. b. 1920.

THE SUBWAY. (1950.) Egg tempera on composition board. 18⅛ x 36⅛. Juliana Force Purchase. 50.23. (p. 141.)

Tovish, Harold. b. 1921.

SEATED WOMAN, I. 1953. Bronze. 10¾ high. Gift of the Alexander Schilling Fund. 54.36.

Townley, Hugh. b. 1923.

GOLEM. (1956.) Maple, walnut, ebano, and amaranth. 40 high. Gift of the New York Foundation. 56.41.

Trunk, Herman, Jr. b. 1899.

MOUNT VERNON. 1932. Oil on canvas. 34 x 46. Purchase. 33.26.

Tschacbasov, Nahum. b. 1899.

THE CLOWN. 1948. Oil and casein on composition board. 44 x 27. Gift of Samuel B. Cohn in memory of Juliana Force. 49.14.

THE MATRIARCH. 1949. Oil on composition board. 44 x 27. Gift of Samuel S. Goldberg in memory of Juliana Force. 49.15.

Tucker, Allen. 1866–1939.

BAKER'S ISLAND. 1921. Oil on canvas. 25 x 34. 31.367.

LANDSCAPE. 1919. Oil on canvas. 25 x 30. 31.368.

THE ORANGE DRESS. (1929.) Oil on canvas. 72¼ x 25. Purchase. 31.369.

SPRING TREES. Watercolor. 13⅜ x 19¼. Purchase. 31.473.

WASHINGTON CROSSING THE DELAWARE. (1931.) Oil on canvas. 20 x 36. Purchase. 33.35.

Turnbull, James B. b. 1909.

BIRTH OF A SHARECROPPER. 1939. Watercolor. 20⅞ x 28⅞. Purchase. 43.16.

Twiggs, Russell. b. 1898.

UNDER THE TREE. 1957. Oil on paper mounted on composition board. 42¼ x 36⅝. Purchase. 58.26.

Tworkov, Jack. b. 1900.

DUO, I. 1956. Oil on canvas. 81¾ x 57¾. Gift of the Friends of the Whitney Museum of American Art. 58.22. (p. 224.)

Vagis, Polygnotos. b. 1894.

HEAD OF WOMAN. 1931. Bronze. 11¼ high. Purchase. 31.75.

SNAKE. 1942. Bronze. 29½ long. Gift of George Harrison. 60.59.

Varian, Dorothy. b. 1895.

PLANTS AND ARTICHOKES. (1928.) Oil on canvas. 20 x 22. 31.371.

PORTRAIT OF A LIVING ROOM. (1944.) Oil on canvas. 40 x 30. Purchase. 45.7.

STILL LIFE WITH DUCK DECOY. (1937.) Oil on canvas. 36 x 27. Purchase. 41.35.

WILLOW FARM. 1935. Oil on paper. 15 x 22. Purchase. 37.47.

Vickrey, Robert. b. 1926.

THE LABYRINTH. 1951. Casein on composition board. 32 x 48. Juliana Force Purchase. 52.6. (p. 145.)

Visser't Hooft, Martha. b. 1906.

CRY OF THE JUKE BOX. 1951–52. Oil on canvas. 48 x 34. Wildenstein Benefit Purchase Fund. 53.7.

von Wicht, John. b. 1888.

HARBOR FESTIVITY. 1951. Watercolor and casein on cardboard. 28¼ x 20⅜ (over-all). Purchase. 52.22.

ON BLUE. 1954. Oil on canvas. 51 x 37. Gift of Mrs. Leo Simon through the Federation of Modern Painters and Sculptors, Inc. 55.15.

Vytlacil, Vaclav. b. 1892.

SEA AND ROCKS. 1954. Oil and crayon. 20¼ x 30½. Gift of Dr. Nina Bleiberg. 55.32.

Walkowitz, Abraham. b. 1880.

ISADORA DUNCAN, NUMBER 10. (c. 1909.) Watercolor and ink. 9½ x 6¾. Purchase. 32.20.

FROM MY WINDOW. (1930.) Oil on canvas. 40¼ x 26. Gift of the artist in memory of Gertrude V. Whitney. 51.3.

NEW YORK. 1917. Watercolor, ink, and pencil. 30⅝ x 21¾. Gift of the artist in memory of Juliana Force. 51.35. (p. 46.)

WINTER. (1915.) Oil on canvas. 16 x 20. 31.372.

Also a collection of watercolors and drawings.

Walters, Carl. b. 1883.

BULL. 1927. Glazed pottery. 15½ long. Purchase. 31.76.

STALLION. 1924. Glazed pottery. 10⅜ long. 31.77.

WHALE. 1938. Glazed pottery. 23 long. Purchase. 38.26.

Wasey, Jane. b. 1912.

BATHER. (1945.) Butternut wood. 52½ high. Purchase. 46.10.

JULIANA FORCE. (1947.) Bronze. 13¾ high. Anonymous gift. 54.42.

Watkins, Franklin C. b. 1894.

THE CRUCIFIXION. (1931.) Oil on canvas. 10 x 7. Purchase. 31.373.

THE SIDEBOARD. 1941. Oil on canvas. 30½ x 36¼. Purchase. 41.22. (p. 122.)

SOLILOQUY. (1932.) Oil on canvas. 25¼ x 30¼. Purchase. 34.26. (p. 106.)

Watson, Nan.

FRUIT IN BLUE JAR. Oil on canvas. 18¼ x 18¼. 31.376.

FRUIT IN RED BOWL. Oil on canvas. 18 x 30¼. 31.377.

LILIES. Oil on canvas. 18 x 12. 31.378.

YELLOW ROSE WITH FRUIT. Oil on canvas. 18 x 21¾. 31.379.

Weber, Max. b. 1881.

ADORATION OF THE MOON. 1944. Oil on canvas. 48 x 32. Purchase. 46.5. (p. 179.)

CHINESE RESTAURANT. 1915. Oil on canvas. 40 x 48. Purchase. 31.382. (p. 45.)

GAILLARDIAS. (1933.) Oil on canvas. 38¼ x 17. Purchase. 34.27.

LISTENING. 1930. Gouache. 5¾ x 4⅛. Purchase. 31.476.

THE RED CAP. 1930. Gouache. 4¼ x 5 (over-all). Purchase. 31.477.

SUMMER. 1911. Gouache on cardboard. 24⅛ x 18½. Purchase. 33.71. (p. 34.)

Webster, Tom.

DAINTY ANGIE. Ink. 12 x 9. 31.582.

Weinberg, Elbert. b. 1928.

ANGEL OF DEATH. (1957–58.) Bronze. 25 high. Purchase. 59.23.

Werner, Nat. b. 1907.

CONQUISTADOR. (1949.) Black walnut. 28½ high. Gift of Mr. and Mrs. Jack I. Poses. 54.7.

FORBIDDEN FRUIT. (1952.) Marble. 11 high. Gift of Mr. and Mrs. Jack I. Poses. 54.8.

Weschler, Anita.

A TIME TO DIE. 1945. Cement. 21 long. Anonymous gift. 57.14.

AT SUMMER'S FULL. 1957. Plastic resins on fiber glass. 27½ x 21½. Gift of Mr. and Mrs. Roy R. Neuberger. 57.13.

Wheeler, George Bernard.

THE SPHINX. 1924. Ink. 21½ x 27⅝. Purchase. 32.52.

Wheeler, Steve. b. 1912.

LAUGHING BOY ROLLING. 1946. Oil on canvas. 36 x 45. Purchase. 47.3.

Wheelock, Warren. 1880–1960.

ETERNAL MOTHER. 1927. Relief. Wood. 48 x 20. Purchase. 33.61.

White, Charles. b. 1918.

PREACHER. 1952. Ink on cardboard. 21⅜ x 29⅜. Purchase. 52.25.

Whitney, Gertrude V. 1877–1942.

CHINOISE. (1914.) Limestone. 61¼ high. 31.79.

DESPAIR. (1912.) Tennessee stone. 10 high. 31.80.

FOUNTAIN. 1913. Bronze. 42 high. 31.78.

HEAD FOR TITANIC MEMORIAL. 1924. Marble. 12¾ high. 31.81.

MOTHER AND CHILD. (1935.) Marble. 34 high. Gift of Mrs. G. Macculloch Miller. 54.41. (p. 59.)

Whorf, John. 1903–1959.
RAINY DAY. (1932.) Watercolor. 15 x 20¼. Purchase. 33.72.

Wickey, Harry. b. 1892.
THE OLD WRESTLER. 1938. Bronze. 19¾ high. 41.2.

Wilde, John. b. 1919.
MYSELF ILLUSTRATING HOW A SQUARE WITH POINTS A AND H IS ALWAYS IN MY VISION. 1947. Pencil. 13⅜ x 9⅝. Purchase. 52.26.

Wiley, William T. b. 1937.
TIME TABLE. 1959. Oil on canvas. 66 x 67. Juliana Force Purchase. 60.48.

Williams, Walter. b. 1920.
POULTRY MARKET. 1953. Oil on canvas. 46 x 38. Purchase. 55.29.

Wilson, Sol. b. 1896.
BULKHEADS. (1950.) Oil on canvas. 30 x 40. Purchase. 53.31.

Wiltz, Arnold. 1889–1937.
FIREMEN'S HALL. 1931. Oil on canvas. 24 x 30. Purchase. 37.32.

RECONSTRUCTION. 1932. Oil on canvas. 23 x 31. Purchase. 33.27.

THE WASTE CHANNEL. 1929. Watercolor. 13⅜ x 19¼. Purchase. 31.479.

Wines, James. b. 1932.
MONAD, I. 1960. Bronze. 53½ long. Gift of the Friends of the Whitney Museum of American Art. 60.33. (p. 238.)

Wolfe, Jack. b. 1924.
DOWNFALL. (1955.) Oil on canvas. 72 x 46. Purchase. 57.2.

Wood, Grant. 1892–1942.
DINNER FOR THRESHERS. 1933. Two studies for right and left sections of the painting. Pencil. 17¾ x 26¾ each. Purchase. 33.79; 33.80. (pp. 92 and 93.)

Wood-Thomas, Alan. b. 1920.
EXECUTION. 1949. Ink. 20⅛ x 17⅞. Anonymous gift. 50.12.
FIGURE. 1949. Ink. 18 x 21¼. Anonymous gift. 50.11.

Wyeth, Andrew. b. 1917.
SPOOL BED. (1947.) Watercolor. 20⅝ x 28¾. Purchase. 48.10.

Yarrow, William. 1891–1941.
TILE-ROOFED HOUSES. Watercolor. 14⅜ x 19⅛. Purchase. 31.480.

Yerxa, Thomas. b. 1923.
DESERTED WAREHOUSE. 1958. Oil on canvas. 40 x 48. Neysa McMein Purchase Award. 58.42.

Young, Mahonri M. 1877–1957.
GIRL DRESSING. (c. 1911.) Charcoal and pastel. 16⅝ x 10¾. 31.583.
GROGGY. (1926.) Bronze. 14¼ high. 31.82.
MAN WITH WHEELBARROW. 1915. Bronze. 15¼ long. 31.84.
THE OUESSANTINE SHEPHERDESS. (1926–27.) Bronze. 9½ long. 31.83.

Yunkers, Adja. b. 1900.
TARRASA, XIII. 1958. Pastel. 69 x 48. Gift of Theodore R. Racoosin. 58.31. (p. 222.)

Zerbe, Karl. b. 1903.
HARLEQUIN. 1943. Encaustic on canvas. 44 x 34. Purchase. 45.8. (p. 123.)
STUDY FOR "GOOD ANGEL TENANTED." 1957–58. Tempera on paper mounted on composition board. 47 x 26. Purchase. 58.28.

Zirinsky, Julius. b. 1898.
LOUIS M. EILSHEMIUS. 1937. Crayon. 15⅞ x 12⅞. Gift of the artist. 47.4.
LOUIS M. EILSHEMIUS. 1941. Crayon. 21 x 14½. Gift of the artist. 47.5.

Zorach, Marguerite. b. 1887.
MAINE SHERIFF. (1930.) Oil on canvas. 20 x 30. Purchase. 31.386.

Zorach, William. b. 1887.
THE ARTIST'S DAUGHTER. (1946.) Replica of damaged original done in 1930. Georgia marble. 25½ high. Purchase. 46.19. (p. 61.)
BROOKLYN BRIDGE. (1928.) Watercolor. 14⅝ x 21⅝. Purchase. 31.590.
BUNNY. (1930.) Stone. 9 long. 31.86.
DRAPED FIGURE. 1927. Bronze. 13½ high. 31.87.
THE FUTURE GENERATION. 1942–47. Botticini marble. 40 high. Purchase (and exchange). 51.32. (p. 134.)
MAINE LANDSCAPE. (1930.) Watercolor. 14⅜ x 21¼. Purchase. 31.591.
NEVADA FALLS, YOSEMITE VALLEY. 1920. Pencil. 18¾ x 11⅞. Anonymous gift. 59.40.
PEGASUS. 1925. Wood. 15 high. Gift of Mrs. Juliana Force. 31.88.
PORTRAIT OF HUNT DIEDERICH. 1920. Pencil. 13¾ x 9¾. 31.584.

Zuckerman, Jack. b. 1920.
ONE IS HIGHER THAN THE OTHER. (1950.) Casein and crayon. 13½ x 16⅜. Purchase. 52.23.

index by mediums

The majority of works in the Museum's collection are paintings.
Artists represented by work in other mediums are indexed below.

Takal, Peter
Webster, Tom
Wheeler, George Bernard
White, Charles
Wilde, John
Wood, Grant
Wood-Thomas, Alan
Young, Mahonri M.
Zirinsky, Julius
Zorach, William

SCULPTURE

Albert, Calvin
Amino, Leo
Archipenko, Alexander
Baizerman, Saul
Barthe, Richmond
Baskin, Leonard
Bilotti, S. F.
Bourgeois, Louise
Bowes, Julian
Brown, Sonia Gordon
Browne, Byron
Burroughs, Betty
Caesar, Doris
Calder, Alexander
Caparn, Rhys
Clews, Henry
Cook, Robert
Cornell, Joseph
Davidson, Jo
Davis, Emma Lu
de Creeft, José
de Rivera, José
Der Harootian, Koren
Diederich, Hunt
Duble, Lu
Eberle, Abastenia St. Leger
Esherick, Wharton
Faggi, Alfeo
Ferber, Herbert
Ferguson, Duncan
Fiene, Paul
Flannagan, John B.
Fuller, Sue
Gabo, Naum
Gershoy, Eugenie
Gordin, Sidney
Greenbaum, Dorothea
Grippe, Peter
Gross, Chaim
Hague, Raoul
Hardy, Tom
Hare, David
Harkavy, Minna
Harwood, Stuart
Haseltine, Herbert
Hebald, Milton

House, James, Jr.
Howard, Cecil
Hunt, Richard
Jenks, Jo
Kaz, Nathaniel
Kearns, James
Kent, Adaline
Kohn, Gabriel
Konzal, Joseph
Kreis, Henry
Lachaise, Gaston
Lassaw, Ibram
Laurent, Robert
Lee, Arthur
Lipchitz, Jacques
Lipman-Wulf, Peter
Lipton, Seymour
Lucius, Florence
Maldarelli, Oronzio
Margoulies, Berta
Martinelli, Ezio
Midener, Walter
Moir, Robert
Moore, Bruce
Moselsio, Simon
Nakian, Reuben
Nevelson, Louise
Nivola, Constantino
Noguchi, Isamu
Phillips, Blanche
Polasek, Albin
Prophet, N. Elizabeth
Quinn, Edmond Thomas
Reder, Bernard
Reynal, Jeanne
Robus, Hugo
Rocklin, Raymond
Rosati, James
Roszak, Theodore
Rothschild, Lincoln
Rumsey, Charles Cary
Sardeau, Hélène
Scaravaglione, Concetta
Schnabel, Day
Simkhovitch, Helena
Smith, David
Squier, Jack
Stankiewicz, Richard
Steppat, Leo
Sterne, Maurice
Swarz, Sahl
Talbot, William
Tovish, Harold
Townley, Hugh
Vagis, Polygnotos
Walters, Carl
Wasey, Jane
Weinberg, Elbert
Werner, Nat
Weschler, Anita

Wheelock, Warren
Whitney, Gertrude V.
Wickey, Harry
Wines, James
Young, Mahonri M.
Zorach, William

WATERCOLOR, CASEIN, GOUACHE, AND PASTEL

Bacon, Peggy
Baum, Mark
Baziotes, William
Beal, Gifford
Bell, Cecil C.
Bernstein, Sylvia
Berresford, Virginia
Biddle, George
Bloch, Julius
Bluemner, Oscar
Bohrod, Aaron
Boyd, Fiske
Burchfield, Charles
Calder, Alexander
Callahan, Kenneth
Campbell, Charles
Carter, Clarence Holbrook
Chaiken, William
Coiner, Charles T.
Coleman, Glenn O.
Corbett, Edward
Corbino, Jon
Corcos, Lucille
Curry, John Steuart
Dasburg, Andrew
Davey, Randall
Davis, Stuart
Dehn, Adolf
Demuth, Charles
Dickinson, Preston
Dirk, Nathaniel
Dohanos, Stevan
Donnelly, Thomas
Dove, Arthur G.
Dozier, Otis
Driggs, Elsie
Edie, Stuart
Ernst, Jimmy
Feininger, Lyonel
Fiene, Ernest
Fine, Perle
Frazier, Susan
Free, Karl
Ganso, Emil
Goff, Lloyd Lózes
Gonzalez, Xavier
Gottlieb, Adolph
Gottlieb, Harry
Graham, Ellwood

Graves, Morris
Greitzer, Jack J.
Grosz, George
Harriton, Abraham
Hart, George O. ("Pop")
Hartman, Bertram
Haucke, Frederick
Heidenreich, Charles
Heliker, John
Henry, Everett
Higgins, Eugene
Holzhauer, Emil
Hopper, Edward
Horter, Earl
Johnston, Ynez
Kantor, Morris
Keller, Henry G.
Kent, Rockwell
Kienbusch, William
Kingman, Dong
Kinigstein, Jonah
Kirschenbaum, Jules
Kittredge, Kraemer
Klitgaard, Georgina
Koehler, Florence
Koppe, Richard
Kuniyoshi, Yasuo
Kupferman, Lawrence
Lawrence, Jacob
Levi, Julian

Lockwood, Ward
Luks, George
Mandel, Howard
Mangravite, Peppino
Margules, De Hirsh
Marin, John
Marsh, Reginald
Mecklem, Austin
Miller, Harriette G.
Mitchell, Bruce
Myers, Jerome
Olsen, Earle
Ossorio, Alfonso
Parker, Bill
Parker, Robert Andrew
Parsons, Betty
Perkins, Harley
Perlin, Bernard
Persons, Simmons
Philipp, Robert
Picken, George
Prendergast, Maurice
Prestopino, Gregorio
Ribak, Louis
Robinson, Boardman
Rohland, Caroline S.
Rohland, Paul
Rothko, Mark
Ruggles, Carl
Saalburg, Allen

Salemme, Lucia Autorino
Schanker, Louis
Schnakenberg, Henry
Schrag, Karl
Schreiber, Georges
Sennhauser, John
Shahn, Ben
Sheets, Millard
Shinn, Everett
Siporin, Mitchell
Smith, Pamela Coleman
Stamos, Theodoros
Steiger, Harwood
Stella, Joseph
Stevens, Edward John, Jr.
Taylor, John W.
Thon, William
Tucker, Allen
Turnbull, James B.
Vickrey, Robert
von Wicht, John
Walkowitz, Abraham
Weber, Max
Whorf, John
Wiltz, Arnold
Wyeth, Andrew
Yarrow, William
Yunkers, Adja
Zorach, William
Zuckerman, Jack

exhibitions, 1914-1960

The following is a list of exhibitions held at the Whitney Studio, the Whitney Studio Club, the Whitney Studio Galleries, and the Whitney Museum of American Art. All catalogues for the years 1914–30 are out of print. The one-man exhibitions at the Studio, the Club, and the Galleries were of paintings or sculpture, unless otherwise noted. They were often held for two, three, four, or five artists simultaneously, in separate galleries, and at the Whitney Studio Galleries generally with separate catalogues.

WHITNEY STUDIO

1914   Benefit Exhibition.
       "50-50" Exhibition and Art Sale.

1915   Benefit Competition in Painting, Sculpture, and
         Architecture.
       A. E. Gallatin Collection.
       Warren Davis.
       Friends of the Young Artists (three competitions:
         June, July, September).
       The Immigrant in America Competition.

1916   Artists of Six Nations.
       John Sloan.
       Gertrude Vanderbilt Whitney.
       "To Whom Shall I Go for My Portrait?"

1917   "To Whom Shall I Go for My Portrait?" (second and
         third exhibitions).
       Friends of the Young Artists Competition.
       Introspective Art: Claude Buck, Abraham Harriton,
         Benjamin D. Kopman, Jennings Tofel, who called
         themselves the Introspective Painters; and the fol-
         lowing guests: Jacques R. Chesno, Robert Laurent,
         Van D. Perrine, Felix Russmann.
       Landscapes by Young American Painters.

1918   Indigenous Exhibition.
       Chinese "Modernists."
       Indigenous Sculpture.
       Ernest Lawson; Guy Pène du Bois.
       Allen Tucker.

1919   Randall Davey; Gifford Beal.
       Malvina Hoffman; Arthur Crisp.
       Florence Lucius; Grace Mott Johnson.
       Gertrude Vanderbilt Whitney.

1920   Russian Posters.

1921   Overseas Exhibition (an exhibition of American
         paintings organized and financed by Mrs. Whitney;
         sent to the International Art Exhibition, Venice,
         1920; to London, Sheffield, and Paris, 1921; ex-
         hibited at the Whitney Studio on its return).

1923   Recent Paintings by Pablo Picasso and Negro Sculp-
         ture, arranged by Marius de Zayas.

1924   Group exhibition: Charles Demuth, Walt Kuhn,
         Henry Schnakenberg, Charles Sheeler, Eugene
         Speicher, Allen Tucker, Nan Watson.
       French and American Lithographs and Etchings, ar-
         ranged by Marius de Zayas.
       Henri Rousseau; Aristide Maillol.
       Charles Sheeler (paintings and photographs).

1925   Cecil Howard.
       Greek Art.
       Self-Portraits by Contemporary Artists.

1926   Florence Lucius; Jeanne Poupelet (drawings).
       John Duncan Ferguson.

1927   Paintings by Children of the King-Coit School.

WHITNEY STUDIO CLUB

Annual exhibitions of paintings and sculpture by members were held in December, 1918, and in the spring from 1919 through 1928. The 1928 annual exhibition was in two parts, one for painting and one for sculpture. Traveling exhibitions of members' works were sent out in 1924, 1926, and 1927, and in 1928 the last and largest went to the Minneapolis Institute of Arts; the California Palace of the Legion of Honor, San Francisco; the Denver Art Museum; the Arts and Crafts Club, New Orleans; the Fogg Museum of Art; and the Art Students League, New York.

1918   Works by Members.
    Abbott H. Thayer and Gerald H. Thayer—Camouflage Pictures.
    Works from Mrs. Whitney's Collection.

1919   Works by Salvatore A. Guarino, William G. Watt, Charles T. Rising, Miriam A. Gerstle.
    Art by Children of the Greenwich House School.
    Nan Watson; Mahonri M. Young (drawings); Herm M. son Linding (watercolors and wood carvings).

1920   Edward Hopper; Kenneth Hayes Miller (drawings and etchings).
    Photographs of American Indians by E. L. Curtis.
    Drawings by Italian Masters.
    Work by Girls of Greenwich House School.

1921   Karoly Fulop; William Grimm.
    Olaf Olesen; John Sloan (etchings); Randall Davey (etchings).
    Stuart Davis; Torres Garcia.
    Joseph Stella; Henry Schnakenberg.
    Lydia Bush-Brown (textiles); S. F. Bilotti; Gerome Brush; Harold Erskine.
    Etchings and Drawings by Charles F. W. Mielatz and Donald Corley.
    Paintings and Drawings by Members.

1922   William J. Glackens; Max Kuehne.
    Paintings by Members.
    Boardman Robinson (drawings).
    Edward Hopper (Paris watercolor caricatures).

1923   Adelaide J. Lawson; John Dos Passos; Reuben Nakian.
    Alexander Altenburg; L. William Quanchi; Katherine Schmidt.
    Drawings and Watercolors by Arthur Faber, Thomas Hunt, George Picken.
    Kimon Nicolaides; Roy V. A. Sheldon.
    Watercolors by Thomas Donnelly, Richard Lahey, Richard Marwede, Mary F. Wesselhoeft.

1924   Paintings and Drawings by Contemporary American Artists, selected by W. E. Hill.
    Early American Art, selected by Henry Schnakenberg.

Work by Pablo Picasso, Marcel Duchamp, Marius de Zayas, Georges Braque, selected by Charles Sheeler.
    E. L. Henry.
    Portraits and Religious Works, selected by Yasuo Kuniyoshi.
    Eloisa Schwab; Sandor Bernath (watercolors), Lydia Bush-Brown (silk murals).
    Reginald Marsh; Joseph Pollet.
    Molly Luce; David Morrison.
    Konrad Cramer; Lucile Blanch; Reeves Brace; Carl Walters (glazed terra cottas).

1925   Henry Mattson; Gerrit Hondius.
    Andrew Dasburg; Katherine Schmidt.
    Exhibition and Sale of Drawings, Lithographs, Etchings and Woodcuts.
    Group exhibition: Blendon Campbell, Max Kuehne, Boardman Robinson, Henry Schnakenberg, Eugene Speicher, Allen Tucker, Nan Watson.
    John B. Flannagan; Léon Hartl; Charles Howard; Dorothea Schwarcz.

1926   Watercolors by Members.
    Harry Hering; Frank London; Jan Matulka; Dorothy Varian.
    Glenn O. Coleman; Henri Burkhard.
    Works by Members.
    Robert W. Chanler (portraits); Reuben Nakian.
    Flower Paintings.
    Stuart Davis (retrospective).

1927   Léon Hartl; Tennessee Mitchell Anderson.
    Paintings and Drawings of Women by Men.
    Georgina Klitgaard; Arthur Conrad Le Duc.
    Works by Members.
    Glenn O. Coleman.
    Gertrude Tiemer; Caroline Speare Rohland; Georgina Klitgaard.

1928   Contemporary Portraits.
    Watercolors by Edith Dimock Glackens and Beulah Stevenson.

WHITNEY STUDIO GALLERIES

1928   Glenn O. Coleman (lithographs); Ernest Fiene (gouaches).
    Kenneth Frazier; Reginald Marsh (lithographs); Isabel Whitney.
    Christmas Sale Exhibition.

1929   Henri Burkhard; Joseph Pollet; Max Kuehne; Karl Free.
    Blendon Campbell (monotypes); Emil Ganso; Paul Rohland; Harry Gottlieb; John B. Flannagan.
    Hermon More; Charles Rosen; Dorothy Varian; Henry Schnakenberg (watercolors).
    Nan Watson; Arthur E. Cederquist.
    The Circus in Paint.
    Oscar Bluemner.
    Watercolors by Richard Lahey, Paul Rohland, Stuart Davis, Mark Baum.
    Gerard Cochet.

1930 Lucile Blanch; Ward Lockwood; Herbert Morgan.
John Steuart Curry; James d'Agostino (watercolors); Jacques Loutchansky.
Rosella Hartman (drawings); Dujam Penic; Caroline Speare Rohland (pastels).
Four Sunday Painters: Arthur E. Cederquist, Beauford Delaney, Prosper Invernizzi, Kalman Oswald.
Flower Exhibition.

WHITNEY MUSEUM OF AMERICAN ART

Every year the permanent collection was shown, and frequently recent acquisitions. Catalogues of the collection were published in 1931,* 1937, 1954,* 1958, and 1961. Catalogues out of print are marked *. Exhibitions with no catalogue are marked =.

1931 The permanent collection was shown in a series of exhibitions.

1932 American Society of Painters, Sculptors, and Gravers.*
Glenn O. Coleman Memorial Exhibition.*
First Biennial Exhibition of Contemporary American Painting.*
The Arts of Life in America: A Series of Murals by Thomas Hart Benton.

1933 Paintings and Prints by Chicago Artists.
Nineteenth-Century Paintings from the Addison Gallery of American Art.*
Artist Fellows of the John Simon Guggenheim Memorial Foundation.*
Twentieth-Century New York in Paintings and Prints.=
First Biennial Exhibition of Contemporary American Sculpture, Watercolors, Prints.*

1934 Self-Portraits by Living American Artists.=
Maurice Prendergast Memorial Exhibition.*
Paintings and Prints by Philadelphia Artists.*
Paintings by Adolphe Borie.*
Second Biennial Exhibition of Contemporary American Painting.

1935 Textiles and Sculpture by Arthur B. Davies; Paintings by Robert Loftin Newman.*
Abstract Painting in America.*
American Genre: The Social Scene in Paintings and Prints.*
Shaker Handicrafts.

1936 Second Biennial Exhibition. Part One: Sculpture, Drawings, Prints. Part Two: Watercolors, Pastels.*
A Hundred Etchings by John Sloan from the Permanent Collection.*
Paintings by David G. Blythe and Drawings by Joseph Boggs Beale.*
Treasury Department Art Projects: Sculpture and Paintings for Federal Buildings.*

Third Biennial Exhibition of Contemporary American Painting.*
Winslow Homer Centenary Exhibition.*

1937 New York Realists, 1900–1914.*
Paintings and Prints by Cleveland Artists.*
Drawings and Small Sculptures by Gaston Lachaise.=
Contemporary American Ceramics.*
Annual Exhibition of Contemporary American Painting.
Charles Demuth Memorial Exhibition.*

1938 A Century of American Landscape Painting, 1800–1900.*
Annual Exhibition of Contemporary American Sculpture, Watercolors, Drawings, Prints.*
Paintings by Frank Duveneck.*
Paintings by Artists West of the Mississippi.*
Annual Exhibition of Contemporary American Painting.
William J. Glackens Memorial Exhibition.*

1939 Annual Exhibition of Contemporary American Sculpture, Drawings, Prints.*
Annual Exhibition of Contemporary American Watercolors.
Twentieth-Century Artists.*
Allen Tucker Memorial Exhibition.

1940 Annual Exhibition of Contemporary American Art: Sculpture, Paintings, Watercolors, Drawings, Prints.*
Mural Designs for Federal Buildings from the Section of Fine Arts, Washington, D.C.*
National Sculpture Society.*
National Society of Mural Painters.*
Annual Exhibition of Contemporary American Painting.*

1941 Annual Exhibition of Sculpture, Watercolors, Drawings, Prints.
This Is Our City.
Jerome Myers Memorial Exhibition.*
Two Hundred American Watercolors Selected by the Section of Fine Arts, Washington, D.C.*
"Growing Art" by Pupils of The Children's Art Classes.*
Annual Exhibition of Paintings [devoted this year to work] by Artists Under Forty.
Oils and Watercolors by Emil Ganso.*

1942 A History of American Watercolor Painting.*
Between Two Wars: Prints by American Artists, 1914–1941.
Contemporary American Sculpture and Sculptors' Drawings.=
Power of America in Buildings: Drawings by Hugh Ferris.=
Artists for Victory Sculpture Competition.=
American Provincial Paintings from the Collection of J. Stuart Halladay and Herrel George Thomas.

1942 (continued) Annual Exhibition of Contemporary American Art: Sculpture, Paintings, Watercolors, Drawings, Prints.

1943 Gertrude Vanderbilt Whitney Memorial Exhibition.
University of Arizona Collection (held at the Metropolitan Museum).*
Annual Exhibition of Contemporary American Art: Sculpture, Paintings, Watercolors, Drawings.*

1944 Oils and Watercolors by Winslow Homer.=
Annual Exhibition of Contemporary American Painting.*

1945 Annual Exhibition of Contemporary American Sculpture, Watercolors, Drawings.
European Artists in America.*
The Hudson River School and the Early American Landscape Tradition (organized by The Art Institute of Chicago).*
Ralph Earl.
Annual Exhibition of Contemporary American Painting.*

1946 Annual Exhibition of American Sculpture, Watercolors, Drawings.
Pioneers of Modern Art in America.*
Metropolitan and Whitney Museum Accessions, 1943–1946.=
Robert Feke.
William Rimmer.
Annual Exhibition of Contemporary American Painting.*

1947 Painting in France, 1939–1946.*
Annual Exhibition of Contemporary American Sculpture, Watercolors, Drawings.*
Ralph Albert Blakelock Centenary Exhibition.
Albert P. Ryder Centenary Exhibition.*
Annual Exhibition of Contemporary American Painting.

1948 Annual Exhibition of Contemporary American Sculpture, Watercolors, Drawings.*
Yasuo Kuniyoshi Retrospective Exhibition.*
The State Department Collection of Paintings.=
Annual Exhibition of Contemporary American Painting.*

1949 Thomas Cole (organized by the Wadsworth Atheneum, Hartford).*
Max Weber Retrospective Exhibition.*
Annual Exhibition of Contemporary American Sculpture, Watercolors, Drawings.
Juliana Force and American Art.
A. H. Maurer (organized by the Walker Art Center, Minneapolis).
Annual Exhibition of Contemporary American Painting.

1950 Edward Hopper Retrospective Exhibition.*
Annual Exhibition of Contemporary American Sculpture, Watercolors, Drawings.

Index of American Design: 100 Original Renderings.=
Annual Exhibition of Contemporary American Painting.*

1951 Arshile Gorky Memorial Exhibition.*
Annual Exhibition of Contemporary American Sculpture, Watercolors, Drawings.
New York Artists Equity Association Building Fund Exhibition.*
Mark Tobey Retrospective Exhibition.*
Annual Exhibition of Contemporary American Painting.*

1952 John Sloan.*
Annual Exhibition of Contemporary American Sculpture, Watercolors, Drawings.*
Edith and Milton Lowenthal Collection.*
Annual Exhibition of Contemporary American Painting.*

1953 Loren MacIver; I. Rice Pereira.
Annual Exhibition of Contemporary American Sculpture, Watercolors, Drawings.
Annual Exhibition of Contemporary American Painting.*

1954 George Grosz.
Annual Exhibition of Contemporary American Sculpture, Watercolors, Drawings.
American Painting in the Nineteenth Century (organized by the American Federation of Arts).
Roy and Marie Neuberger Collection.*

1955 Annual Exhibition of Paintings, Sculpture, Watercolors, Drawings.*
Hyman Bloom (organized by The Institute of Contemporary Art, Boston).
Jack Levine (organized by The Institute of Contemporary Art, Boston).
The New Decade: 35 American Painters and Sculptors.*
Reginald Marsh.*
The National Council for U.S. Art, Inc., Mural Sketches and Sculpture Models: Competition for the Decoration of the United Nations Headquarters Buildings.=
Annual Exhibition of Contemporary American Painting.

1956 Charles Burchfield.*
Morris Graves (organized by the Art Galleries of the University of California, Los Angeles).*
Annual Exhibition of Contemporary American Sculpture, Watercolors, Drawings.
John Marin Memorial Exhibition (organized by the Art Galleries of the University of California, Los Angeles).
Theodore Roszak (in collaboration with the Walker Art Center, Minneapolis).
Annual Exhibition of Sculpture, Paintings, Watercolors, Drawings.

1957 American Paintings, 1815–1865 . . . from the M. and M. Karolik Collection in the Museum of Fine Arts, Boston (organized by the Museum of Fine Arts).
Young America 1957.*
Hans Hofmann Retrospective Exhibition (in collaboration with the Art Galleries of the University of California, Los Angeles).*
Bradley Walker Tomlin (in collaboration with the Art Galleries of the University of California, Los Angeles).
Stuart Davis (organized by the Walker Art Center, Minneapolis).
Annual Exhibition of Sculpture, Paintings, Watercolors.

1958 Nature in Abstraction.*
Robert Edmond Jones: Designs for the Theatre.
Twentieth-Century Highlights of American Painting (organized by the United States Information Agency).
The Museum and Its Friends: Twentieth-Century American Art from Collections of the Friends of the Whitney Museum of American Art.

1958 Fulbright Painters (organized by The Smithsonian Institution in cooperation with the Institute of International Education).
Arthur G. Dove (organized by the Art Galleries of the University of California, Los Angeles).
Annual Exhibition of Sculpture, Paintings, Watercolors, Drawings.

1959 Four American Expressionists: Doris Caesar, Chaim Gross, Karl Knaths, Abraham Rattner.

The Museum and Its Friends: Eighteen Living American Artists Selected by the Friends of the Whitney Museum of American Art.
Attilio Salemme (organized by the Institute of Contemporary Art, Boston).
The Collection of the Sara Roby Foundation.
Project I: Longview Foundation Purchases in Modern American Painting and Sculpture for the Union Sanatorium Association of the International Ladies' Garment Workers' Union.
American Prints Today (organized by the Print Council of America).
William Zorach.
Paintings and Sculpture from the American National Exhibition in Moscow.
Annual Exhibition of Contemporary American Painting.

1960 Milton Avery (organized by The American Federation of Arts, New York).
Lee Gatch (organized by The American Federation of Arts, New York).
Business Buys American Art: Third Loan Exhibition by the Friends of the Whitney Museum of American Art.
Philip Evergood.
José de Creeft (organized by The American Federation of Arts, New York).
Hugo Robus (organized by The American Federation of Arts, New York).
Young America 1960.
Annual Exhibition of Contemporary Sculpture and Drawings.

books published by the
Whitney Museum of American Art

Books marked (*) are out of print.

George Bellows by George W. Eggers, 1931.*

Alexander Brook by Edward Alden Jewell, 1931.*

Charles Burchfield by John I. H. Baur, 1956.

Mary Cassatt by Forbes Watson, 1931.*

Glenn O. Coleman by C. Adolph Glassgold, 1931.*

A Critical Introduction to American Painting by Virgil Barker, 1931.

Arthur B. Davies by Royal Cortissoz, 1931.*

Charles Demuth by William Murrell, 1931.*

Guy Pène du Bois by Royal Cortissoz, 1931.

Thomas Eakins: His Life and Work by Lloyd Goodrich, 1933.*

Philip Evergood by John I. H. Baur, 1960.

Four American Expressionists: Doris Caesar, Chaim Gross, Karl Knaths, Abraham Rattner by Lloyd Goodrich and John I. H. Baur, 1959.

William Glackens by Guy Pène du Bois, 1931.*

Arshile Gorky by Ethel K. Schwabacher, 1957.

George Grosz by John I. H. Baur, 1954.

Robert Henri by Helen Appleton Read, 1931.*

A History of American Graphic Humor by William Murrell, Vol. I (1747–1865), 1933.

A History of American Graphic Humor by William Murrell, Vol. II (1865–1938), 1938.*

Winslow Homer by Lloyd Goodrich, 1944.*

Edward Hopper by Guy Pène du Bois, 1931.*

Bernard Karfiol by Jean Paul Slusser, 1931.

Yasuo Kuniyoshi by Lloyd Goodrich, 1948.*

Ernest Lawson by Guy Pène du Bois, 1931.

George Luks by Elisabeth Luther Cary, 1931.*

Henry Lee McFee by Virgil Barker, 1931.

Loren MacIver; I. Rice Pereira by John I. H. Baur, 1953.

Kenneth Hayes Miller by Alan Burroughs, 1931.

Nature in Abstraction by John I. H. Baur, 1959.

The New Decade: 35 American Painters and Sculptors ed. by John I. H. Baur, 1955.*

Maurice Prendergast by Margaret Breuning, 1931.*

H. E. Schnakenberg by Lloyd Goodrich, 1931.

John Sloan by Guy Pène du Bois, 1931.*

John Sloan by Lloyd Goodrich, 1952.

Eugene Speicher by Frank Jewett Mather, Jr., 1931.*

Bradley Walker Tomlin by John I. H. Baur, 1957.

Allen Tucker by Forbes Watson, 1931.

John H. Twachtman by Allen Tucker, 1931.

Max Weber by Lloyd Goodrich, 1949.*

Young America 1960 by Lloyd Goodrich and John I. H. Baur, 1960.

William Zorach by John I. H. Baur, 1959.

Friends of the Whitney Museum of American Art, 1956-1960

Mr. and Mrs. Harry N. Abrams
Mr. and Mrs. Arthur G. Altschul
Mrs. Allan E. Anderson
Jean Appel & Co., Inc.
Mr. and Mrs. Hans Arnhold
Mr. and Mrs. Simon Askin
Mr. Lee A. Ault
Mr. and Mrs. Louis Cecil Baker
Mrs. Herman Baron
Mr. Charles B. Benenson
Senator and Mrs. William Benton
Mr. and Mrs. Philip I. Berman
Mr. Herbert C. Bernard
Mr. and Mrs. Edward L. Bernays
Mr. Alexander M. Bing
Mrs. Leo S. Bing
Mr. and Mrs. Donald M. Blinken
Mr. and Mrs. Lawrence H. Bloedel
Dr. and Mrs. Melvin Boigon
Mr. and Mrs. William Braden
Mr. and Mrs. Harry Lynde Bradley
Mrs. Grace Borgenicht Brandt
Mr. Jerome Brody
Mr. and Mrs. W. Douglas Burden
The Honorable and Mrs. William A. M. Burden
Mr. and Mrs. Selig S. Burrows
Mr. and Mrs. Harry I. Caesar
Mr. and Mrs. Cass Canfield
Miss Sylvia Carewe
Mr. and Mrs. Edward Tinsley Chase
The Chase Manhattan Bank
Mr. and Mrs. Walter P. Chrysler, Jr.
Mr. Arthur Cinader
Mr. John Clancy
Mr. and Mrs. Fred Clark
Mr. and Mrs. Wilfred P. Cohen
Mr. and Mrs. Sidney Elliott Cohn
Mr. and Mrs. Ralph F. Colin
Dr. and Mrs. John Alfred Cook

Mr. and Mrs. Peter Cookson
Mr. and Mrs. Thomas R. Coward
Mr. and Mrs. Gardner Cowles
Mr. and Mrs. William L. Cullen
Mr. and Mrs. Willard W. Cummings
Mr. and Mrs. Stephen R. Currier
Mme. Lilly Daché
Mr. and Mrs. George T. Delacorte
Mr. and Mrs. Richard Deutsch
Mrs. Theresa K. Dintenfass
Mr. and Mrs. Selvin Donneson
Mr. and Mrs. Albert Dorne
Mr. and Mrs. Walter G. Dunnington
Mr. and Mrs. Allan D. Emil
Mr. and Mrs. Richard C. Ernst
Mr. Armand G. Erpf
Mr. and Mrs. Lawrence A. Fleischman
Mr. and Mrs. Malcolm K. Fleschner
Mrs. Edsel Ford
Mr. Daniel Fraad, Jr.
Mrs. Muriel Francis
Mr. and Mrs. Ulrich Franzen
Mr. and Mrs. B. H. Friedman
Mr. and Mrs. Frederick Gash
Mr. and Mrs. Otto M. Gerson
Mr. and Mrs. Charles G. Goldsmith
Mr. Morton R. Goldsmith
Mr. and Mrs. Herbert A. Goldstone
Mr. and Mrs. Milton A. Gordon
Mr. and Mrs. Robert C. Graham
Mrs. James B. Greason, Jr.
Mr. and Mrs. Albert M. Greenfield
Mr. and Mrs. Alvin M. Greenstein
Mr. Joseph T. Grippi
Mr. Walter K. Gutman
Mr. Joyce C. Hall
Mrs. Edith Gregor Halpert
The Halpert Foundation
Mr. and Mrs. Robert Halsband

Mrs. Louis S. Hardin
Mr. Huntington Hartford
Mr. and Mrs. Ira Haupt
Mr. and Mrs. Crane Haussamen
Mr. and Mrs. George William Headley, 3rd
Mr. and Mrs. Ben Heller
Mr. and Mrs. Benjamin Hertzberg
Mr. and Mrs. Frederick W. Hilles
Mr. and Mrs. John S. Hilson
Mrs. Hannah Scharps Hirschhorn
Mr. Joseph H. Hirshhorn
Mr. and Mrs. Walter Hochschild
Mr. and Mrs. Arthur A. Houghton, Jr.
Miss Elisabeth Houghton
Mrs. Howell H. Howard
Mr. William Inge
Mr. and Mrs. Michael H. Irving
Mr. O'Donnell Iselin
Mrs. Justin B. Israel
Mr. and Mrs. Alfred Jaretzki, Jr.
Mrs. Marian Willard Johnson
Mr. and Mrs. Allen Kander
Georges Kaplan
Mr. and Mrs. Jacob M. Kaplan
Mr. Maxim Karolik
Mr. and Mrs. Jack J. Katz
Mr. Steven N. Kaufmann
Mr. and Mrs. Nicholas Kelley
Mr. Donald P. Kircher
Dr. and Mrs. Milton Lurie Kramer
Mr. Alvin S. Lane
Mr. William H. Lane
Mrs. Albert D. Lasker
Mr. Jack Lawrence
Mr. and Mrs. Alexander Lerner
Mr. and Mrs. Fernand Leval
Mr. and Mrs. Irving Levick
Dr. and Mrs. David M. Levy
Mr. and Mrs. Michael H. Levy
Mr. and Mrs. Howard Lipman
Mr. and Mrs. Albert A. List
Mrs. Alfred L. Loomis
Mr. and Mrs. Joe Lowe
Mr. and Mrs. Milton Lowenthal
Mrs. Cyrus McCormick
Mr. and Mrs. James Edgar Marcuse
Mr. and Mrs. Arnold H. Maremont
Mr. and Mrs. John C. Marin, Jr.
Mr. William A. Marsteller
Mr. Joseph B. Martinson
Miss Patricia V. Marx
Mr. Gunnar Maske
Maymar Corporation
Mr. and Mrs. Paul Mellon
Miss Doris Meltzer
Mr. and Mrs. Matthew A. Meyer
Mr. Ronald Miglionico
Mr. and Mrs. G. Macculloch Miller
Mr. and Mrs. Jan Mitchell

Mr. Leon A. Mnuchin
Mrs. Paul Moore
Mr. and Mrs. Arthur Murray
Mrs. Harry Nessler
Mr. and Mrs. Roy R. Neuberger
Mr. John S. Newberry
Mr. lee Nordness
Miss Katharine Ordway
Mr. and Mrs. Charles Shipman Payson
Mr. Henry Pearlman
Mr. and Mrs. Myles Perrin
Mr. and Mrs. C. Leonard Pfeiffer
Mr. and Mrs. Seymour J. Phillips
Mr. and Mrs. E. G. Poindexter
Mr. and Mrs. Jack I. Poses
Mrs. Margarita Delacorte Potoma
Mr. and Mrs. David A. Prager
Mrs. Ethel L. Reiner
Mr. and Mrs. Jules Reiner
Mr. and Mrs. Charles H. Renthal
Mrs. S. M. Barnes Roby
Mr. and Mrs. David Rockefeller
Mrs. John D. Rockefeller, 3rd
Mr. and Mrs. Laurance S. Rockefeller
The Honorable and Mrs. Nelson A. Rockefeller
Mrs. Mary G. Roebling
Mrs. Faith Robinson Rose
Mr. and Mrs. Saul Rosen
Mr. and Mrs. Morton M. Rosenfeld
Judge and Mrs. Samuel I. Rosenman
Mr. and Mrs. Edward J. Ross
Mr. Walter Ross
Mr. and Mrs. Herbert M. Rothschild
Mr. and Mrs. Peter A. Rübel
Mr. and Mrs. Harry Rubin
Mrs. Henry Potter Russell
Mrs. John Barry Ryan
Mr. and Mrs. Howard J. Sachs
Mr. and Mrs. Richard Salomon
Mr. and Mrs. Alexander E. Salzman
Mr. and Mrs. Herbert Salzman
Mr. and Mrs. James H. Scheuer
Mr. and Mrs. Norman M. Schneider
Mr. and Mrs. M. Lincoln Schuster
Mrs. Ethel K. Schwabacher
Mr. and Mrs. Robert C. Scull
Mr. Stanley Seeger, Jr.
Mr. and Mrs. Carl L. Selden
Mr. and Mrs. Irvine J. Shubert
Mr. and Mrs. Jerome A. Siegel
Mr. and Mrs. Philip Sills
Mr. Charles Simon
Mrs. Leo Simon
Mr. and Mrs. Sidney Simon
Mr. Allen D. Sirotto
Mr. and Mrs. Joseph Slifka
Mr. and Mrs. Howard Sloan
Mrs. John Sloan
Mr. Marvin Small